THE ART OF WRITING GREAT LYRICS

THE ART OF WRITING
GREAT LYRICS

Pamela Phillips Oland

ALLWORTH PRESS
NEW YORK

To Mum, Who Gave Me the Words

≡

To Dad, Who Gave Me the Music

≡

To Bobby, Who Gave Me the Love

05   04   03   02   01   00   5   4   3   2   1

Published by Allworth Press
An imprint of Allworth Communications
10 East 23rd Street, New York, NY 10010

Cover design by Douglas Design Associates, New York, NY
Back-cover author photo by Christine Loss
Page composition/typography by SR Desktop Services, Ridge, NY

Library of Congress Cataloging-in-Publication Data
Oland, Pamela Phillips, 1947–
    The art of writing great lyrics / by Pamela Phillips Oland.—Rev. and expanded ed.
        p.   cm.
    Rev. version of the author's: You can write great lyrics, 1989.
    Includes bibliographical references (p.   ) and index.
    ISBN 1-58115-093-8
    1. Lyric writing (Popular music).   I. Oland, Pamela Phillips, 1947–   .
You can write great lyrics.   II. Title.
MT67.O4   2001
782.42164'0268—dc21   2001022261

A revised and expanded edition of the book formerly titled You Can Write Great Lyrics.

Printed in Canada

Contents

The Difference Between Poetry and Lyrics • Using the Three Basic Tools
• Painting Better Pictures • New Thoughts • Building a Better Vocabulary
• Song Words • Before You Can Become a Great Lyricist, Become a
Good Writer • A Word on Grammar

Seeing the World Visually • Knowing It When You Hear It • Setting Up
the Writing Environment • Is There a Moon Out Tonight? • Writing Lyrics
on a Schedule • Self-Confidence Can Speed Up Your Thinking Process
• Open the Doors of Perception • Going Dry • Real Songwriters
Never Say Die (Except in a Lyric!) • Word Association • Visualization
• The Writing Process

Popular Music is a Conversational Art • What Are You Trying to Say?
• Developing Characters • Universal Ideas • Mind Versus Heart

The Elements of a Song • Song Formulas Are the Tools of the Trade
• Exceptions to the Rules • If You Don't Have a Title, Why Are You Writing
This Song? • Dummy Melodies • The First Line • Laundry Lists
• Lyric-Crafting Exercises • Let's Write a Song

Help Wanted: *Collaborator* • Yours, Mine, and Ours • Styles in Which to
Collaborate • Intuitive Choices in Collaboration • Fear of Collaboration

ACKNOWLEDGMENTS

I want to acknowledge everyone who has ever inspired me with a casual comment that I've transformed into a lyric; I want to acknowledge all the pairs of lovers who have crossed my path and left behind a hint of their romance, the scent of an idea.

I take this opportunity to acknowledge a host of wonderful and talented collaborators whose imagination and inspiration has led me to explore my own potential. Thank you, each of you, for the fun of it, the joy of it, the great uplifting feeling of creating a work of art together.

I must acknowledge my incredible friends—in and out of the industry—whose affection and nurturing has uplifted my spirit while keeping my feet planted on terra firma.

Personal thanks to my publishing administrator, Dean Kay, who wrote the amazing "That's Life!"—a more honorable person never breathed. And I want to thank the never-to-be-forgotten Mr. Frank Sinatra for giving me my first big break, leading me to think I must be doing something right!

Many thanks to all of the many artists and producers who have chosen to interpret and record my songs over the years, for the incomparable delight of hearing my work take on a life of its own.

And, finally, a note to my publisher, Tad Crawford, who wanted to see this book back in print: Thanks for believing in my personal method for writing great lyrics, and giving it this terrific new forum and home with Allworth Press.

FOREWORD TO THIS REVISED EDITION

This book was first published in 1989. When Allworth Press invited me to create a twenty-first century edition of this work, I found that my "voice" had changed somewhat, and so went about revising and simplifying my original manuscript. What you'll find here is a tried-and-true songwriting method that is hopefully even easier to understand and make your own.

It also seemed reasonable to change the title as long as the book was being updated. While *You Can Write Great Lyrics* is a mantra that applies to any writer who applies him- or herself to the process, that title doesn't address the fact that writing great lyrics is an art, every bit as much as painting, sculpting, photography, or ballet. Lyric writing at its heart is a personal expression of your very unique talent. You have a perspective on life, love, and the world that no one else on earth has. In these pages, secrets will unfold that will help you make a good idea a great idea, turn a moving poem into a wonderful song lyric, develop a thought that you've never really fleshed out, and watch it become a recordable song.

I wish you many happy hours developing your art as a lyricist, and great success as your reward; and I remind you that the one song you will definitely never get recorded is the one you never write!

PAMELA PHILLIPS OLAND
Los Angeles, California, April 1, 2001

Introduction: If You Can't Write a Lyric, You Haven't Got a Song!

"It's a terrific melody, but the words need work . . . "

"I'd publish that song in a second if you could just tighten up that lyrical concept . . . "

"Wow! That's a hot groove, but the lyrics don't quite make it for me . . . "

"Great title! I love the hook! But the verses don't go anywhere . . . "

"I'd love to record it—I mean, the melody kills me—but I just don't relate to the lyrics. Can you rewrite them?"

Well, can you?

This book is for you if you are:

1. A composer who wants to write the *whole song* and have the lyrics come out as inspired as the music.

2. A lyricist who has fragments of good ideas but wants your work to be consistently excellent from the first to last line.

3. A songwriter who spends triple the amount of time trying to craft lyrics as you do pouring out melody ideas.

4. A lyricist who writes *good* songs but wants to write *great* songs.

5. Someone who writes marvelous poetry and has always wanted to master the art of songwriting.

6. A composer, singer, music publisher, A&R person, artist's manager—in fact, any user of music who wants a better yardstick by which to judge the lyrics that come into your hands.

7. A member of the music industry who needs to be able to make well-directed critiques and insightful evaluations that will make it easier for lyricists to better judge and, when required, rewrite their lyrics.

From my experience talking to hundreds of songwriters, I would say that *writing lyrics* is the area of songwriting that gives people the most problems. Many gifted songwriters can write a fantastic melody, program an amazing track, play half a dozen instruments, sing their heads off, arrange, produce, and score for days, but when it's time for lyrics, the words just don't come.

Yet when you look at the problem realistically, it does make sense: Musical talent, no matter how profound, has no connection to the ability to manipulate language. Notes are one thing, and words are entirely another.

Then there are those of you who are stronger with words than music. But your terrific ideas and pieces of songs are bursts of inspiration that never quite hang together properly as viable commercial lyrics. You become very frustrated when a few industry professionals—to whom you happen to show your lyrics—agree that something is wrong in the way they're written, but unfortunately they can't actually *verbalize* what it is they don't like. You then blindly struggle to rewrite your lyrics to please a particular publisher/producer/artist/manager/A&R person. But when you don't know what's wrong in the first place, how are you supposed to fix it?

Many composers simply leave the lyrics to people who specialize in lyric writing, while other songwriters *like* to come up with the title, or the title and concept, leaving the actual writing of lyrics to a collaborator they trust. There are a lot of composers, however, who don't have much experience or skill in the art of lyric writing, but are scared of trusting their melody to someone else. So they grapple with the unfamiliar and uncomfortable world of words and syntax, when they would much rather be composing music!

Thousands of poets dabble as amateur lyricists and find great joy in the avocation. However, success eludes them, and they can't understand what they're doing wrong. I hope we can clear up the mysteries.

In this book, I am sharing with you what I've learned in over twenty years of working and growing in the music industry. My personal lyric-writing method, which has resulted in more than three hundred recorded songs, is a series of thought processes and considerations that always enable me to come up with the goods, whether I have two weeks or two hours to complete my lyric-writing assignment!

Certain basic understandings must become second nature to you before taking your first step on the path to success as a lyricist. Before you plunge in and find yourself way out of your depth—unable to figure out what it is about a line you've written that makes it great or how to write another one to follow it up—you must do your homework.

Learning by trial and error has been long, grueling, fascinating, and occasionally disheartening. I have built my theories on lessons learned from umpteen *rejections*. I have analyzed ways to relax, ways to develop intuition, and the impact of the work environment. I have considered the lyricist's tools, the substance of inspiration, what makes collaborations successful, and how to better use language. I have examined who to write songs about, who's singing, who's listening, who cares, what's the art, what's the craft, how to make a demo, how to keep your integrity, how to keep your heart from breaking at rejections, how to work, how to analyze your work, and even how to think. I have spent hours in philosophical discussions on the process of lyric writing with other professionals in the field. My conclusions are all in this book.

My "secrets" go beyond the obvious song formulas and rhyme patterns, because there is a whole lot more to writing powerful lyrics than learning "rules," which can be broken anyway. There is a certain individual philosophy and style that you must develop. As I began writing this book, I discovered dozens and dozens of the conscious and unconscious processes that I use to write unique but dependably commercial and interesting lyrics. My reputation depends on always being able to come up with the right lyrics, day or night. I rarely have the luxury of catering to the encroachments of personal matters, mood swings, so-called "mental blocks," or my preference to be lying under a palm tree on Bora Bora at the time of the assignment.

This book will take you on a comfortable, leisurely trip through the mental, emotional, and professional steps in the quest for your own secrets to writing great lyrics. You will find that it's not just a matter of picking up pen and paper and knocking out a few lines that rhyme; but is a very holistic process that incorporates your lyric writing as an integral part of your life. Much of what you will learn involves using your knowledge of yourself as the basis for your lyric writing: who and what you are; what you like, love, and hate; what makes you laugh and cry and tick; what you have observed and can recall; and the special color of glasses you look through to see the world go by. We will look at how you can take control of your creativity, environment, work habits, style, point of view, and desire for success.

This is not a book about how to bake a cake, however. It is rather about creating your own recipe for success. In all the arts, it is the differences in individual approaches and talents that make each artist's work stand out from the rest. This book—while covering the mechanics and formulas found to be effective for the process of lyric writing—recognizes that you are unique. It is therefore designed to motivate you, bolster your faith in your talent, and help you explore and discover how to maximize your potential to be great in your own way.

So let's go!

1

SONGWRITING IS A LOVE AFFAIR WITH WORDS

W e are songwriters: hence, words are the tools of our trade. Our songs are only as good as our ability to manipulate language. Unless we know the capabilities of the language, we sell ourselves short. Imagine a Mexican cook who'd never tasted cilantro, a carpenter who'd never used an electric saw, a secretary who'd never learned to type, a record producer who'd never used delay, a clothes designer who'd never experienced wearing silk. We are more limited by *what we don't know* than by what we do know. As a lyricist, you cannot know what interesting words are available if you've never bothered to study the language.

But let's get one thing straight from the start: There is no such thing as writing *badly*. There are *clichés* or outlandish streams of consciousness. There is writing naïvely, and there is writing without sophistication. There is also writing inappropriately for the intended market, and even writing "original" things that have been written dozens of times before. But "good" and "bad" are personal value judgments; I don't think anybody is qualified to characterize anyone else's creative outpourings so categorically and simplistically. How can self-expression through the arts be called "bad"? On the contrary, seeds become flowers; an embryo grows into a person. And you must begin writing . . . at the beginning!

THE DIFFERENCE BETWEEN POETRY AND LYRICS

Clearly, lyrics can be poetic, *but poetry is not lyrics, and lyrics are not poetry.* They are two different art forms.

My first few hundred "songs" were actually poems put to music, which is fine. We all start that way—we have to start somewhere, and poetry is the starting point for lyric writing. I'm sure a great many of you reading this book are poets of long standing. For some of you, there has been an intensely per-

Lyrics can be poetic, but poetry is not lyrics, and lyrics are not poetry. They are two different art forms.

sonal relationship between you and your feelings, recorded in secret diaries, or doodled on the corners of odd pages. The more gregarious of you may have started writing poems in grade school to your friends and teachers, or maybe you wrote clever poems to co-workers on their birthday cards. Some of you may even have published poetry in local or national papers and magazines. One thing's certain: You know when you've written a poem. You knew it before you started writing and, during the writing process, you felt the poetic flow. When you read it later, you were confident in the knowledge that it was a poem.

Why doesn't this absolute assurance occur when you're attempting to write *lyrics?* You intend what you're writing to be a lyric, but somehow you don't have that same confidence. Even as you're setting down the words, you're not sure whether they qualify as lyrics. What's the difference?

There are at least nine telltale signs that what you've written is a poem and not a lyric.

We're speaking of rhyming poetry here, not "free verse," which has no strict formulas, generally has obscure rhyme patterns (or no rhyme patterns at all), and pretty much rambles until it gets to the point. *Rhyming* poetry is what gives aspiring lyricists problems, because its form is so similar to that of lyrics.

This is embarrassing, but I'll illustrate my point with the first song I ever wrote. I can safely say that this "song" embodies everything you should never do when writing a lyric!

REFLECTING

Affection real and shared I've little known
Its warmth and peace of mind to call my own

Companionship in earnest I have sought
But friendship is a gift that can't be bought

Idyllic is the dream I can't express:
Its shadow I pursue with tenderness

Indifference does rebuff the joy I seek
By way of callous words I hear you speak.

Each word and touch I cherish fervently
For every one is very dear to me

'Tis happiness embodies everything
Without it there's no song for me to sing

My words cannot define my *inner* truth.
And wisdom shuns the frailty of my youth.

Let's look at some general clues that say this is a poem and not a lyric:

1. *The setup of the song has not followed a prescribed formula* (as described on pages 84–92 of this book). Is there a definite structure, such as first verse followed by the chorus, second verse followed by a repeat of the chorus? No. Do several verses follow each other, all in the same pattern, but without anything repeating? Yes. *The rule of thumb:* If you have *more than two* sections in a row that follow the same structure, it is a poem.

2. *There is no apparent title!* The title I've used here, "Reflecting," relates to the state of mind I was in while writing the "song" but has no relationship to the message. *The rule of thumb:* If you have to search through what you have just written to come up with something that might sound like a title, it is a poem.

3. *There is no "hook," refrain, repeating word, phrase, or sentence.* (This will be discussed in more detail in chapter 4.) The essence of a good song is that the listener walks away singing the "hook." Yet in this song, I have not written one memorable or repeating idea. *The rule of thumb:* If you aren't trying to leave the listener with a memorable idea, ask yourself whether it's worth writing the song at all. If it's something you *must* say just for you, it's fine as a poem.

4. *The language is not conversational.* The words are in reverse order. Nobody would ever say something like, "Companionship in earnest I have sought." They probably wouldn't say "I have sought companionship in earnest" either, but at least those words fall in the order of normal speech. The same goes for "Each word and touch I cherish fervently," which in a conversational sentence would read, "I fervently cherish each word and touch." I'll break it down into parts of speech: The sentence should start with the pronoun *I,* followed by the adverb *fervently* describing the verb *cherish,* then the adjective *each* describing the noun *word,* followed by the conjunction *and,* ending with the noun *touch.* The sentence is still hopelessly old-fashioned, but at least it's conversational usage. *The rule of thumb:* If you twist your words around just to get a rhyme, you've immediately turned your song into a poem. Rewrite the sentence so it sounds more the way people really talk, and come up with a rhyme for the new end word.

If you twist your words around just to get a rhyme, you've immediately turned your song into a poem.

5. *The lyric uses archaic words and phrases.* The likes of "Indifference does rebuff . . . " and " 'Tis happiness . . . " might belong in an English madrigal, but they have no place in popular songwriting. *The rule of thumb:* If you wouldn't say it, don't write it in a song.

6. *The lyric uses words you can't sing!* Words and phrases such as "idyllic" and "wisdom shuns the frailty" are not words that you would comfortably sing. They are acceptable in a poetic form, but have no place in a popular song. *The rule of thumb:* If they don't sound like song words to you, they won't sound like song words to anyone else either.

7. *The story doesn't go anywhere.* My "song" just repeats the same old thing seven different ways. All that it establishes is that I feel lonely, and "you" have acted coldly toward me. Then it says I feel lonely and don't know what to do about it. *The rule of thumb:* A song must have a story with a beginning, a middle, and an end.

8. *The message is a real downer.* This song-poem is written from the place of a loser. The mentality is strictly depressed. Now, that's okay if I want to sing it to myself in the privacy of my bedroom, but who else is going to want to hear it—let alone record it! *The rule of thumb:* If the story is so downbeat that it only relates to *your angst* at the moment you wrote it, it's a poem.

9. *It's too introspective.* In reading this song-poem, I am thoroughly embarrassed. *It's so personal!* Every one of you knows how deeply I was hurting that day. I'll bet you would want to look the other way if I were standing in front of you! You'd see me blushing for having shared such an intimate moment with you, and you wouldn't know where to put your own face. *The rule of thumb:* If it's so personal that it's embarrassing, it's a sure sign that it's poetry, not lyrics.

Any time you want to evaluate one of your lyrics to make sure it isn't a poem, try looking for these "clues" in your work. If the whole lyric fits into one or several of these categories, it's probably irretrievable as a song. Since it's virtually impossible to change a poem into a lyric, you'd be better off collecting your poetry separately and enjoying it for what it is. Personally, I have written hundreds of poems apart from my songwriting over the years, for quite different reasons and motives.

In any event, rest assured that the more often you evaluate your *lyrics* by the foregoing nine points of poetry, the faster you will train yourself to disqualify the poetic idea before it even reaches the paper. You will be able to spot the poetry in the work of other lyricists, and you will have the ability to separate and thoroughly enjoy both art forms.

USING THE THREE BASIC TOOLS

Becoming the best writer one can be is obviously no accident! The unique and sometimes inexplicable talent that is your gift from the Powers That Be is only half the equation. The other half? Learning your *craft*. It isn't enough to think in images—we must have the words to express them. So I suggest that the larger your working vocabulary is, the more of a word-bank resource you will have at your command to make lyrical concepts and images more interesting.

As a songwriter, three basic tools will be your best friends in time of need! They are the *dictionary,* the *thesaurus,* and the *rhyming dictionary.* Get good copies of each, hardbound with clear typefaces, and treasure them as you would your musical instruments, your personal computer, or your grandfather's gold-nibbed fountain pen. They are as important to the creation of a song as your imagination.

The Dictionary

Every office has a dictionary, but you'd be surprised at how infrequently they are used. Oh, we might go digging around for the dictionary when we're trying to figure out the difference in meaning or spelling between "stationery" and "stationary" or whether "canceled" has one *l* or two. But by and large, this great old book stands forgotten on a shelf, gathering dust. My advice: Take another look! It could be the key to separating you from the ordinary lyricists and propelling you into the ranks of the greats.

You should consult your dictionary each and every time a word is used in reading, writing, or conversation whose meaning you do not fully understand. And when I say fully, I mean *fully*. Every day we hear someone using a familiar word in a brand-new context. We also hear words we've heard a thousand times and never really figured out quite what they meant except from context. (*Context*—now there's a good word we've heard many, many times. But most of us have never bothered to look up the definition!) So often, we use words casually in conversation without bothering to make sure we're using them correctly. And what fools we look to the rest of the world when we use a word improperly while trying to make an impression. A friend of mine often uses the word "supposably." I used to grin to myself, thinking she meant to say "supposedly." Then one day I stopped and asked myself, "What if it really is a correct usage? Maybe I've been wrong all these years." I looked in the dictionary and to my amazement, there it was: *supposable*—an adjective meaning "that can be supposed." I called my local library and asked the research librarian to look it up in the unabridged dictionary, which, of course, contains far more definitions than my own book, to see if "supposably" was listed. She said that, indeed, this is a correct usage and adding the "ly" simply makes it an adverb. So there you go, I looked it up and found an unexpected answer.

Every time we pick up a newspaper or magazine, we find unfamiliar, interesting words relating to history, politics, cooking, fashion, science, psychology, travel, dance, music, sports, gardening, real estate, law, medicine, and on and on. Each subject has its own formal vocabulary, its own words to express its realities. Some technical or medical words have come into popular usage. I'll never forget the first time I heard a couple of snot-nosed kids utter the phrases "Don't be so paranoid!" and "I'm tryin' to psych you out!" These were such sophisticated usages but, unfortunately, the kids only understood the street usage and not the intrinsic meanings.

> Some words are borrowed from other languages and have been adopt-
> ed into English by common use (e.g., in music, adagio, à capella; in dance,
> jeté, plié; in food, hors d'oeuvres, crêpe; in psychology, weltschmerz,
> angst; in architecture, façade; in drama, denouement; in food service,
> maître d'(hotel), à la carte, and so on). Don't be afraid to try them out,
> learn them, and use them.

Obviously, a major rule in writing of any sort is to be thoroughly versed in the vocabulary of the subject about which you are writing. It is a prostitute's business to have a clear understanding of a phrase such as "a short time" just as much as it is a diplomat's business to know what is meant by "détente."

Each style of songwriting has its own vocabulary, too, and it's important to understand the parameters of words that are acceptable in each style. Arguably, R & B, Country, and Heavy Metal would each approach language and vocabulary from a different angle. What Heavy Metal might find outrageous and titillating, Country might find crass, and R & B might find irrelevant. And so forth.

As a writer, you are responsible for knowing if the particular word you have used connotes the exact shade of meaning you are trying to express. You have a duty—not only to the artist who is singing your song, but to the audience as well—to write a lyric that is both literate and meaningful.

A song lyric can often be taken in two ways by the listener. One way is the way you intended it, and the other is an entirely different personal interpretation. Any time you can write a *double entendre* lyric, you're ahead of the game. Why? Because you are not only pleasing the artist by giving her something meaningful to sing about, but you are also pleasing her *listeners* by inadvertently capturing a thought that evokes something special for them.

For instance, in my title "They Don't Make Love Like That Any More," I am defining *Love* as an overall relationship. However, the term *Make Love* is, of course, a sexual reference that, for many listeners, recalls a passionate encounter. Lyricists should be able to manipulate words in this way.

You cannot know too much about the use of words. You cannot sprinkle your vocabulary too heavily with the interesting, rich colors that thoughtful use of the language provides. Keep depositing new words and phrases in your word bank. (See page 13, Building a Better Vocabulary.) It is much harder to try to create expansive ideas from a limited vocabulary than it is to write simple thoughts with knowledge of *what* you're leaving out and *why*.

If you don't have time to look up a word the moment you hear it or see it written, write it down to look up later. (The only problem with that solution is that by the time you look up the meaning of the word, you've usually forgotten who said it and in what context!) If you can, jot down its context—a sentence or phrase—on some scratch paper. When you're reading, have a handy little pack of colored sticky labels—strips or 3-M Post-Its–to mark for future reference the place in the book where an unfamiliar word appears.

OTHER STANDARD USES FOR YOUR DICTIONARY

If you have the slightest doubt about how something is spelled, look it up. If you don't know what you don't know, you'll probably think you're an accurate speller. And that can prove to be a terrible embarrassment as you submit your songs throughout the industry.

Finally, use the dictionary to check which syllables are emphasized or accented. Mis-emphasis is common and happens when lyricists try to fit a lyric to a melody that won't accommodate their thought. So instead of working to come up with a thought that *will* fit the melody correctly, they stick in a word that incorrectly accents the syllables. Such as in the word "fantasy," where the emphasis is on the "sy." Though it's been done in successful songs, this is totally against the craft of songwriting.

The Thesaurus

If the only word we were taught as children to describe a large object was "big," then we would use big for big girl, big train, big bug, big universe. And maybe they all *are* big, but not the same kind of big. By using the thesaurus, I came up with the following replacement words: *blowsy* woman, *colossal* train, *enormous* bug, *infinite* universe. Now we get a more precise mental picture of the concept we are trying to describe. We have shaded the meaning of each noun by using an adjective that more particularly describes it.

Using words is more than just writing the first thing that comes into your head. You must ask yourself, "How does that sound? Is it *precisely* the right word for the job?"

Since it isn't always easy to come up with every likely word contained in the language, let alone

> Using words is more than just writing the first thing that comes into your head. You must ask yourself, "How does that sound? Is it precisely the right word for the job?"

remember its exact meaning, the thesaurus is a writer's best friend. My personal favorite has always been the *Roget's Thesaurus* with index. What I do *not* recommend is a pocket paperback thesaurus, although even this has its use when you're on the run and need to stick it in a pocket or purse. I am far more enamored of the indexed volume; it allows me to look up the word I think sounds most like what I'm seeking and then check the variations under it.

The thesaurus is an incredible tool for expansion of vocabulary. When looking at the list of available synonyms, I'm reminded of words I'd forgotten about, and introduced to new ones. As I look over the choices, sometimes just glancing at a word will trigger an idea.

The key is to keep your dictionary side by side with the thesaurus, so that you can look up the precise definitions of words you believe to be closest to the meaning you want. Then you pick the best one. Each time, you will be building your vocabulary with several new words whose dictionary definitions you have actually studied. As a little bonus to this process, you'll be surprised and often mortified to learn that a word you've been using for years to mean one thing actually means something quite different!

One thing's for sure: You will know which words *aren't* appropriate for your thought. This will be an important step in learning to eliminate useless or inappropriate ideas from your songwriting. As you scan a list of synonyms in the thesaurus, your mind will automatically reject the ones that you don't want. This is a very similar process to one we will discuss later regarding rejecting inappropriate ideas and concepts at first thought, before they ruin your song.

One final point regarding the thesaurus: If you find that none of the words listed under a category fits the bill, your problem is that the word you looked up in the first place was not close enough in meaning to the concept you want to express. Keep following other leads—sooner or later you'll find the exact word you're looking for.

The Rhyming Dictionary

My Aunt Ethel was horrified when she heard Stephen Sondheim admit in a TV interview that he uses a rhyming dictionary. "You don't use one, do you?" she inquired confidently. I had to laugh when I dispelled her romantic notion of lyricists having every possible rhyme float into their minds like magic. "Of course I do!" I told her. "It's not knowing what the rhymes *are* that makes a good songwriter; it's knowing what to do with them!"

Rhyming dictionaries by various authors are available in technical, college, and used bookstores. I have a very old one by Clement Wood, printed in 1936, which, unfortunately, contains hundreds of archaic and useless words. Some of the modern ones

> *"It's not knowing what the rhymes are that makes a good songwriter; it's knowing what to do with them!"*

are directed specifically at the needs of popular songwriters and cut through to the realistic words you can use for songs. Check them all out, new and used, to find the rhyming source that is most likely to suit your needs. Using a rhyming dictionary is simply permitting yourself to see the possible rhymes for any given word. There are very few perfect rhymes for *love,* for instance, so given the choice of *above, glove, shove,* and *turtle dove,* it's no wonder that most songwriters don't use *love* at the end of a line! With the exception of *above* (and that's been used more times than the turnstile at Grand Central Station), none of the other words are particularly easy to slip into casual conversation! "You fit me like a glove," "Our hearts gave us a shove," "You sing like a dove!" Well, it's not an easy choice. Why waste hours searching for a better perfect rhyme than these? In the rhyming dictionary, all the possible words in the English language that rhyme with *love* (or any word) are listed in a neat row. *If it's not on the list, it doesn't exist!*

There is one other reference guide I haven't included among my "three reference works," and that is a dictionary of antonyms. An antonym is a word that is opposite in meaning to another; *good* is the antonym of *bad, high* is the antonym of *low, fast* is the antonym of *slow,* and so on. Sometimes you will need an opposite word and will strain to think of what it could possibly be. You could call your local library and have them look it up for you, or you could acquire one of the following two books: *A Basic Dictionary of Synonyms and Antonyms,* by Laurence Urdang (New York: Elsevier Nelson Books, 1978); or *Funk & Wagnall's Standard Handbook of Synonyms, Antonyms, and Prepositions* (Funk & Wagnall's, 1947).

I carry my rhyming dictionary and thesaurus with me wherever I go to write. I keep a spare in my office, and I always make sure I have a dictionary on hand at any location in which I am working. Don't make the mistake of thinking these reference books are simply burdensome to carry around and a nuisance to consult. You could be shortchanging your career by not taking advantage of what they can offer you. While the art of songwriting very much comes from the heart, the craft entails research and hard work.

PAINTING BETTER PICTURES

For five thousand years or more, human beings have been writing down their ideas through the use of graphic symbols in the hope of communicating these ideas to others, and thus being better understood. Before there ever were alphabets, the scribes of the times had to express their thoughts using pictographs of events and ideas that set them down in a totally literal fashion.

That meant every one of the thousands of words in a language had a specific picture that accompanied it when written.

So, in the olden days, if you wanted to communicate, you had to have a clear understanding of what those pictographs represented and how to draw them, or you might accidentally convey the wrong idea. In the same way, we who are the communicators of today really need a clearer understanding of how to use our language, not only in order to be grammatically correct and paint better word pictures, but also to be better understood.

One of your most powerful tools is the "Descriptive Quad": nouns, verbs, adjectives, and adverbs. Just like the pictographs and hieroglyphics of ancient civilizations, most words in our language have pictures inherent within them. Yet the picture for that word standing alone varies for every person who hears the word. Ask two people what "dog" (a noun) means to them, and one will describe an Irish setter, the other a Chihuahua. One person's interpretation of "run" (a verb) might be a sprint, fully dressed, to catch a bus, while another's might conjure up a marathon. If you had qualified "good-sized red-haired dog" or "tiny Mexican dog," if you'd said "run to catch a bus" or "run the Boston Marathon," those you'd asked would have related with visuals much closer to your own mental pictures.

To use more colorful speech, it is essential to qualify what you are talking about by describing it in the most interesting and precise way possible. A noun can be *simple:* "dog," or *descriptive:* "Chihuahua." Similarly, a verb can be plain: *run,* or picturesque: *sprint.* Thus, expressing concepts and ideas in lyrics so that listeners will widely recognize and connect with the mental pictures you paint turns on using interesting nouns and verbs.

The words that best tap your listener's imagination to conjure up mental images, however, are adjectives, so using adjectives properly is a vital skill you must develop.

Adjectives

Your choice of adjectives (words that describe) can turn an ordinary song into a fascinating song, a mediocre idea into a heart-stopper.

Let's consider an example: "I met him on a _____ night." The type of night it was will convey the mood of the meeting. The listener will immediately create a setting in his or her mind, visualizing all the personal images he or she associates with the adjective you've chosen to describe the night. A *rainy* night; a *stormy* night; a *winter's* night; a *chilly* night. Any of these words will convey a miserable night. But a *starry* night; a *moonlit* night; a *heavenly* night—these will convey a pretty, romantic night. Want to express a sexy night? How about a *hot* or *sultry* or *steamy* or *passionate* night? But then again, what about coming up with an original kind of night that creates a picture that hasn't been so overused? Perhaps a *golden* night, a *star-kissed* night, a *hearth-fire* night, a *crackers-in-bed* night, a *champagne-and-roses* night, an *only-in-the-movies* night, a *Sugarland* night, and so on.

The question is, why use an ordinary adjective when you can find a more colorful, original one? What will set you apart as a special lyricist is your ability to conjure up interesting word pictures for your listeners. The more evocative adjectives you can come up with, the more vivid the picture you will paint for your listeners.

In lyric writing, this can create a dichotomy because, while you want to project clear mental images, you also want listeners to be able to fill in their own blanks. For instance, if you're writing a song about a blue-eyed blonde, your listener may not be able to relate if his girlfriend has dark hair and brown eyes. If you feel this could be a problem, consider using adjectives that are universal, such as "sensual," "beautiful," or "dynamite."

Remember that as you are selecting your adjective you will instantly be creating the visual presentation of the thought you wish to convey. So choosing the wrong adjective will create a picture that could be uneasy, uncomfortable, vague, or inexact.

A common problem that arises when a songwriter first attempts to insert "clever" adjectives is that they come out sounding far-fetched. They are too clever, and the listener can easily hear that the writer strained to "say something interesting." Usually, if it sounds wrong to you, it will sound wrong to everyone else. If you're not comfortable with what you've written, it's probably a good bet that it will come across as awkward.

Finding the right adjective is part of developing your intuition as a lyricist. Believe it or not, you'll know it when it's right. You'll say the word, in context, and it will give you just a little chill of satisfaction, and you won't have to think about it twice. Choosing adjectives is a very good way to begin your process of developing intuition. (We'll discuss other ways to develop intuition in chapter 2.)

As an example, let's look at a sentence using plain adjectives to modify the nouns, followed by two identical sentences that use more interesting adjectives. (They are obviously exaggerated to make the point.)

Plain: Dan was a *nice young man* who lived in a house at the center of town with Maria, his *new wife*, his *big* dog, and his *attractive* mother-in-law.

Interesting: *Dashing* Dan was a *wildcat of a* man who lived in *the crumbling ruins of a Victorian* house at *the mean, broken heart of the squalid* center of *an itchy-footed* town with *vapid little* Maria, his *boring new child-wife*, his *great, snarling, mangy mutt of a* dog, and *his fascinatingly seductive* mother-in-law.

Interesting: *Brother* Dan was a *well-loved* clergyman who lived in a *tired, old boarding* house at the *once-great* center of a *broken-down memory of a* town with *ever-beautiful* Maria, *his faithful, long-time companion and new* wife, his *enormous, gangly, floppy-eared brown* dog with *white paws and a tan splotch around its right eye*, and his *shriveled old shrew* of a mother-in-law.

Obviously, Dan is anybody I want to make him. Just by a choice of adjectives, he can be wild or mild, powerful or reedy, magical or dull as dust. I am the puppeteer who decides which string to pull and what happens in the show. But the power I have in my pen is only useful to the degree that I know how to use it. I cannot be a great lyricist without being a great storyteller, and I cannot be a great storyteller if I am not a master of the adjective.

Adverbs

The fourth partner in your Descriptive Quad is the adverb. When you want to tell how something happened, you have to come up with an interesting adverb. For instance, if you were to say, "He entered the room _____," you might want to add *hastily, quietly, silently, proudly, laughingly.* To be even more interesting, use *demandingly, disgracefully, ferociously, impetuously.* Or you could use an *adverbial clause,* such as *on cold feet, in a shotgun mood, like an earthquake, laughing in my face,* and so on. Those "hows" can be so very interesting if you deliberate on them.

In literature, one of the most famous "hows" that comes to mind is the one that says that "the fog comes on little cat feet." How simple it would have been to just say the fog rolled in. Period. But Carl Sandburg was inventive and tried to give the fog life. A lyric is like that: It can't just sit on the paper; it must have a life of its own.

Adverbial clauses help with the "whens" and "wheres": *at the midnight hour; after the loving; in my hour of need; somewhere over the rainbow; at the end of my prayers; on the street where you live.* Adverbs and adverbial clauses also relate to how much: *with all my heart, inseparably, incredibly, overpoweringly,* etc.

NEW THOUGHTS

Every now and then I'll write something down that sounds absolutely preposterous. And my mind will say, "You can't write that! It's never been written like that before!" And then I say, "Dummy! That's why it's good!" You can't be afraid to try something original.

New words and phrases come into the language periodically, when people make them up. For instance, my old friend Walter "Clyde" Orange of the Commodores wrote a song called "Bump the La La!" Clyde had coined this interesting phrase to mean "cut the bull." In this case, *Bump* obviously has a basic interpretation that we're all familiar with; and *La La* is traditionally either the sixth note on a tonic scale or a nonsense word to sing when you forget the lyrics to a melody! But together, *Bump the La La* takes on a whole new meaning. I'm convinced that if this song ever becomes a hit radio song, "Bump the La La" will become a household phrase, interchangeable with any phrases that mean the same thing, as it has a very hip sound. The only difference from its synonyms is that it's clean!

When an original phrase creeps into your mind, that's all part of the inspiration and reward of being a songwriter. It's often just a hunch, but it's important to learn to go with your hunches, as they are the true essence of your genius. The hard part of songwriting is coming up with the lines leading to and from the lines of genius and inspiration. But when those lines hit you, boy, it's smack between the eyes. You know they're something special. You recognize them in other writers' songs, too. You hear a line such as, "Ev'ry mother's nightmare, ev'ry schoolgirl's dream" in Loverboy's "Notorious," and all you wish is that you'd written it!

Now, mind you, a line doesn't have to be a "cute" twist of phrase by any means. It can also be a simple, touching, emotional line that hasn't been said quite that way before. I am always moved when I hear Dan Hill sing, "And sometimes when we touch, the *honesty's* too much" (emphasis supplied). In this emotional Barry Mann–Dan Hill ballad, the singer is expressing what I like to call a "new thought"—meaning I've never thought a thought quite like that before. The use of the word *honesty* is both special and unusual. We talk of the "warmth" of a touch, the "feeling" of a touch, the "heat" of a touch, the "emotion" of a touch. But *honesty*—it made me immediately flash on the honesty of the touch I share with the one I love. I think about all the touches in past relationships, which came in a package deal with verbal promises, heavy half-lidded sultry eyes, provocative facial expressions, neurotic passion, and all the rest. But *honesty* makes me think of something fresh and unsullied, pure and open and, best of all, real. So, in effect, listening to that line helped me understand and actually define what was going on in my own relationship! Those songwriters have chosen a phrase that has forever altered my perception of what love can and should be for me.

The point of all this is that we must learn to reach beyond obvious word choices to those that paint more precise and interesting pictures. We can only do this by expanding our vocabularies and by enhancing our knowledge of the points of view of those with whom we share the world. We cannot write in a vacuum. Our opinions and views on relationships and life are limited by our own experiences. We obviously cannot actually have all the experiences in the world; therefore, we must try to experience them vicariously through reading, listening, and *watching*.

In the following section, we'll explore ways to make your work more worldly, more universally interesting, more current, and more to the point—simply by expanding your vocabulary.

BUILDING A BETTER VOCABULARY

Since our songs are, in fact, only as good as the words we can muster to put in them, we need to constantly be expanding our vocabularies to include, as they used to say, "two dollar words" (big words), as well as street lingo and current vernacular. It is important not only to know a word, but to feel comfortable using it. The first time you use a new word in conversation, it might feel awkward on your tongue. But in time, it will become part of your ability to communicate.

Many years ago, someone gave me a book called *Thirty Days to a More Powerful Vocabulary* (now, unfortunately, out of print). It was a series of exercises that first explained a group of unrelated words and then called on the student to learn to use them in a sentence. The student was then quizzed on comprehension. Believe it or not, that paperback home course taught me dozens of new words that remain with me to this day. I imagine some copies must have survived on the bookshelves of your local thrift shops and used paperback stores. Another terrific ongoing source for improving your vocabulary is Reader's Digest Online. Go to *readersdigest.com* on the Internet and click on "Word Power." Each issue provides marvelous word games that help you to brush up on your understanding of twenty less-than-frequently used words with four multiple-choice definitions. At the end of each game, you can browse the definitions at leisure. Finally, you might want to check occasionally with your local bookstore or a mail-order publishing house as to new publications on increasing vocabulary.

Our vocabularies increase and change every day, just as a matter of course, because language is like that. New words find their way into conversation, and people draw these words into common usage; old but unfamiliar words jump out at us from the headlines of the news or the marquee of a movie house. For most of us, however, the changes in vocabulary stay minimal. So as writers, we need to work at keeping our points of view from stagnating. The resources for increasing our word banks and world views are limitless. All we have to do is increase our awareness and remember the old biblical adage, "Seek and ye shall find." The following list will help get you started.

1. *Always question any new words that you hear in conversation.* Don't be embarrassed to ask the speaker, "What does *that* mean?" I always ask, and I think people respect that I didn't just let a word go by, nodding as if I understood it when I didn't. I used to do that in high school a lot. The teacher would say something about, for instance, geometry or the parts of speech, and I didn't have a clue what she was talking about. But I was so intimidated by the teacher and the class that I would bravely pretend I knew what had been discussed, even to the point of repeating in a rote fashion what was written about the subject. But remembering a description was a far cry from comprehending meaning, and I was more the fool for it; when test time came around, I certainly proved my ignorance. So now, if I

don't understand something, I either ask right then and there what it means, or I jot it down and look it up later. Frankly, it's probably a good idea to look it up anyway, as people are often apt to use words incorrectly, so the "definition" they might give you could lead you to start using it incorrectly, too! Also, put "on the spot" to define the word they used, the chances are they might, to their great discomfort, be unable to come up with a clear definition.

2. *Spend every spare moment reading everything you can get your hands on.* The vocabulary of any given subject changes over time, so although you may feel thoroughly versed on an issue, you could still be out of step with reality in what you have to say. Thus it's important to keep a variety of magazines in the bathroom, the bedroom, and at your office. Subscribe to a local newspaper, keep a current book on your bedside table, and keep reading matter in your car. Stay in touch with world affairs, domestic policies, problems affecting society, the arts, pop psychology, and today's vital issues.

Also start reading the great classic fiction and nonfiction of the last several hundred years, from Shakespeare to the Brontës, Melville to Hemingway. Studying their writings will increase your vocabulary one hundredfold, not to mention nurturing your romantic soul. Read anything and everything to do with relationships and points of view on life. Then when you write songs, you will have a literate and interesting gift to give your listeners.

Though you may never find the need to use many of the words you will learn in your pursuit of a wider vocabulary, you will have acquired a much broader point of view and will have a better handle on the attitude of what you are about to write.

The most basic grasp on language a songwriter must have is a clear picture of how women and men *think, react,* and *speak.*

Since the beginning of time, men have had trouble understanding women. Let's face it, women are different! (And even if you're a woman, that doesn't guarantee that you'll understand broader points of view than your own private ones on women's issues.)

Since women represent half the population, it is important for male writers to understand how a woman perceives life—especially love—and what her needs are. Reading women's magazines may help in that quest to figure out the elusive thought process known as the "feminine mystique." If a man is planning to write songs from a woman's point of view, he certainly had better know what a woman's point of view is! Otherwise, the words come out sounding like something a man wishes a woman would say! Or even worse, they sound really strange and unbelievable. Men: Do your homework!

(continued)

Conversely, if a woman intends to write a lyric for a man to sing, she had better stay away from rainbows and fairy tales and try to get a grip on the masculine point of view. Magazines such as *GQ* and *Playboy* cater to the intellect of the "average" male, with highly paid editorial staffs taking on pleasures and issues of the day.

Keep in mind that if you have neither the time nor the desire to do your homework on an issue that you are writing about, or to really try to understand the point of view of the narrator of your song, you are in the wrong business!

3. *Tune in to radio talk shows.* It has been my experience that in listening to talk radio, say, in the car or while doing chores, one becomes privy to hundreds of slices of life and conversations that we would never otherwise have the opportunity to hear. Listening to radio shrinks is like having a telephone "party line," where you can listen in as a secret voyeur to all the most private conversations, admissions, and confessions of your neighbors and friends. The dialogues you hear on talk radio will help you develop points of view on great and small issues of the day. Some hosts interview politicians and heads of state; others interview authors and lecturers on every subject imaginable. You can hear stars of every magnitude as well as citizens-at-large who reflect points of view with arguments from the sublime to the ridiculous. And from the pop psychologists such as Dr. Laura Schlessinger, we get to hear two-minute efforts at solving the most desperate and devastating personal problems that confront the population. Believe me, there is never a dull moment. For those of us who are wishy-washy on political and social issues, radio talk shows give us an opportunity to privately consider all sides of an argument as presented by the most well-versed and thorough minds. Later, when we tackle these issues in songs or special material (novelty songs) for musical shows, we'll be much more confident in our writing, knowing that we won't have written something that will rebound like egg on our faces.

4. *Go to the movies and watch TV.* Films and television provide perhaps the best source of conversational vocabulary available to us today. Just think of it: These film and TV writers are paid astronomical sums to come up with interesting dialogue and new ways of saying things. You'll pick up interesting turns of phrase in almost every movie or TV show. Since *titles and concepts are not subject to copyright* (unless they are specifically registered as *trademarks*) I believe that snatching a wonderful, wise, or colorful line here and there from a show you've seen can only enhance your chances of coming up with a hit song. I can't tell you how many lyrics I have been pre-

sented by students using a title stolen from Clint Eastwood's most infamous on-screen remark, "Make my day!" That's an obvious one, of course, but there are hundreds more that slip by every time you turn on the tube or plunk down eight bucks to see a film. Carry a pad and jot down any line that sounds interesting. You'll be amazed at how many song titles and song lines you can collect from just one show! Some of these will not be in final form—you may have to bend the words a little, slightly alter their use—but sometimes a good concept is all you need.

5. *Learn the fine art of conversation.* Engaging in stimulating conversations with your elders, your betters, and your peers, is a marvelous source of titles for any songwriter. Sometimes the great lines actually come out of your own mouth! Profoundly enough, it takes the stimulation of another's input into your thinking to prompt you to come up with a line or idea that is the making of a brilliant song. Train your friends and loved ones to say, "Hey, that's a title!" But the real key here is to *become a great listener.* We so often think that, as the writer in the group, we are the ones called on to say clever and witty and profound things all the time. Sometimes we forget that listening is important, too. If we go through life simply regurgitating the same points of view over and over again to anyone who cares to listen, how will we grow? How will we ever have anything more interesting to say? The truth is, we become greater speakers and writers when we are better listeners.

I am reminded of a time when my mother quizzed me on how a date had gone. I repeated to her all the clever and witty things I'd said all evening, all the stories I'd told him about myself, all my commentaries on life. She responded, "It sounds like the poor fellow didn't get a word in edgewise!" I had to stop and think about that. "The best conversationalist," she informed me, "is someone who is a good listener. Let him talk about himself all evening, and he'll go home and tell his friends what a wonderful evening he had and what a brilliant conversationalist you are!" I never forgot her advice.

SONG WORDS

"*Song words*" *are words that sing well.* We've spent a lot of time so far considering the idea that you should use the whole vocabulary when writing songs. It may frustrate some of you when, having grasped the idea of using the entire language, I throw a wrench in the works by saying that many words do not "sing." It's very important to learn not to use "interesting" or big words just for the sake of being different. For instance, you would never use the word "phlegm" in a song! Perhaps that's taking it to

We don't have to turn in a song until we think it's finished. Nobody else needs to be privy to the details of our quest for the perfect lyrics, until we play the finished song.

extremes, but you must consider the sound of a word and decide whether it works well in a song or whether it sounds ugly when sung.

Some words work well in the middle but not at the end of a line. Other words are great at the end of a line but sound awkward in the middle. You will find that this has a lot to do with the word in question and how the melody goes.

Most medical words—other than *die, died, sick, stung, bitten,* or references to pains in the heart—are unacceptable in songs, even if you think you've found a clever title. "I Asphyxiated on Love," is, in any event, not as commercial as "I'll Die for Love." I'd also stay away from most surgical and psychiatric terms.

Technical words and scientific, heavy-sounding words, such as *presumption* or *frenetic,* are usually unsuitable for lyrics. Ditto for words that are difficult to enunciate such as *capricious* or *prestidigitation,* words with more than four syllables (*interest* is good, *interesting* is not as good, *interestingly* is unacceptable), and words that tie the mouth into knots, such as *segue* and *quickly.* There are always exceptions. *Imagination,* which has four syllables, is an acceptable song word.

A songwriter must be aware of whether open vowel sounds are being correctly placed. Open vowel sounds are *a* as in "paint," "land," "heart"; *e* as in "yes" and "her"; *i* as in "high"; *o* as in "know" and "now"; *u* as in "under." Less open vowel sounds are *e* as in "here"; *i* as in "him" and *u* as in either "you" or "pull." Sing all these words for yourself and feel how your throat constricts over some sounds and not others. Let your own experimentation with sounds be your guide on these choices. Remember that open vowels are only important in places where the musical note supporting the word needs to be sung out in an open fashion.

Also, if you're a singer, be aware that you should be emphasizing the vowel sound and not the consonant. (If you're singing the word *sing,* emphasize the "i" in sing, not the *ng* sound at the end.)

Words in songs should flow naturally and not be contrived. Sometimes we want to show off our vocabularies by using important-sounding words and phrases, but what these actually do is cut the songs off from their potential audience. While it's okay to tastefully introduce intelligent and even sometimes obscure usages, they must be used with care. Too much heavy verbiage weighs a song down.

That doesn't mean it's not okay to experiment with words. I'm just saying that once you've looked at the finished lines, go back and reevaluate whether they work; if they don't, you must be ready to cut back and rewrite.

So here's a good plan: Regardless of whether you consider yourself a singer, sing the lines yourself into a tape recorder. Listen critically to the tape, and see if any words jar your ears. If they do, it's a good bet they'll bother other listeners, too.

The thing about songwriting that's so great is that we don't have to turn in a song until *we* think it's finished. Nobody else needs to be privy to the details of our quest for the perfect lyrics until we play the finished song. So fool be he who doesn't take advantage of the opportunity to review and correct improper word usages before someone else does.

If we go through life simply regurgitating the same points of view over and over again to anyone who cares to listen, how will we grow? How will we ever have anything more interesting to say? The truth is, we become greater speakers and writers when we are better listeners.

BEFORE YOU CAN BECOME A GREAT LYRICIST, BECOME A GOOD WRITER

Have you ever written a lyric and thought to yourself, "If only I had about six more verses to tell this story; I hate leaving out all these good ideas"?

This should be a clue that your delight in writing extends beyond lyrics only. I heartily encourage you to write in as many forms as possible. Write long letters to family and friends, and go into detail about things that interest you. Keep a loose-leaf pad beside your bed, and write observations about your life or love, the world, the day's events. Personally, I go back and forth between writing free verse poetry and letters to God. I find both very cathartic, as I get out an immense host of feelings and expressions. I don't like "diaries" per se, as they limit you to writing only a few lines in a limited space. One thing you never want to do when you're writing is inhibit yourself by the framework of space (with the exception of assignments for magazines that require a specific number of words).

Have you ever considered writing a play or a screenplay? Perhaps you've never looked at it this way, but lyric writing for the popular market actually amounts to conversations between two people or one-sided conversations. In learning the craft of songwriting, chances are you've become quite adept at dialogue writing without even realizing it. Try your hand at writing a dialogue outside the framework of a song. You'll get the feel of expressing more than can be said in the confines of two verses and a chorus. The more fluent you become in using language, the easier lyric writing will become.

You might try writing a short story or even a novel. All you need to start with is a subject. Then you need to think up characters to populate the story. I find it helpful to write a paragraph or two on each of the characters, describing their nationality, appearance, upbringing, job, and preferences. That way, when I write their dialogue, I know where they're coming from.

As an exercise, start by coming up with an idea for a conversation that two people might have regarding something you find of interest. Don't worry about sets and stage directions. Don't worry about lighting and props. Just write the conversation the way you think it would really happen. You will find this a fascinating experience, as you will see some of yourself in each of the characters in whose mouths you are putting words. And who knows? You may come up with a concept for a song.

Once you have your story idea and your characters, you are well advised to write an outline of the story from beginning to end, so you know what happens. This could be done as a list or synopsis or both. The biggest cause of unfinished manuscripts is that the writers don't know where the story is going.

Writing a script or novel can be a helpful exercise in discipline and a way of developing a comfortable and friendly relationship with the language in which you are writing. If you read it back and discover you haven't written *Gone With the Wind,* don't worry about it!

Yet another way to exercise your writing chops—and earn money to boot—is to write publicity releases. In fact, my largest source of cash-in-the-pocket during the years of learning my craft as a songwriter was writing press releases. In every town there are many small businesses that cannot afford the services of a full-time public relations or advertising agency. They are happy to find the modest-priced services of a freelance person who can send out releases about what they're doing to all the local papers. Perhaps there is a manufacturer or sales business in your neighborhood that needs short articles sent to their trade magazines. These articles are easy to research, quick to write, and bring in $50–150 per article, depending on length.

Another idea is writing brochures and promotional copy for fliers. *Every* kind of business, from a dental clinic to a pizza parlor, could use well-written fliers and brochures. Get to know a local printer, work out the details, and you're in business.

The point is, keep those writing juices flowing at all times. Keep pen and paper with you everywhere you go. Keep separate pads for each project—one for lyrics, one for poetry, one for short stories, one for a play, and one for the PR. It's somewhat unnerving to have all things in one pad, as you can never find what you want in it—and when you do, the chances are good that you have written something unrelated on the next page, which psychologically stops you from ever completing either project. In fact, my own favorite pads are 8½-by-11-inch college-ruled pads with wire binding down the left side. I prefer these to legal-style pads because with legal pads, you can only use one side of the paper, unless you tear it out (and then you mislay it, and there goes your ability to keep track of anything). With the side-bound pads, you can write the body of your work on the right-hand page and use the left-hand page to make notes and corrections. Then you can look at both the body of work and the corrections to the left.

Anything you can do to stretch your writing skills, to be daring and adventurous with words, to exercise your vocabulary and become familiar with rarely used words, is a gift to yourself. Before you can write well, you must be comfortable with language, and the only way to become comfortable with language is to *write!* and *write!* and *write!*

A WORD ON GRAMMAR

I'm not an English teacher, and it's beyond the scope of this book to provide a course on grammar. Nevertheless, I think it would be of great value to you as a songwriter to look back and get a good handle on elementary grammar, such as how a sentence is structured and the parts of speech. Pick up a basic grammar book in a used book shop, or consult the "Grammar" section in the appendix of an encyclopedia-style dictionary. It's a bit of a plod to get through this material but, as a result of your efforts, you will be able to better examine your lyrics for awkward and mistaken usages of words, phrases, and sentences. *And* you'll know how to fix them. Does this grammar research sound dreary? Perhaps. But remember: Knowledge is power. The more you know about language, the better writer you will become.

GOING BEYOND THE ORDINARY

Current street slang is all very well, but it changes more frequently than Madonna's hemlines, and becomes outdated just as fast. It simply doesn't have staying power. Clearly, if we want to write songs that will have long-term royalty-earning power, we need more than current street slang at our disposal.

We have already discussed colorful adverbs and adjectives, interesting nouns, original uses of verbs. We also have to invent *metaphors* and *similes.*

According to my *Webster's New World Dictionary,* a metaphor is "a figure of speech in which one thing is likened to another, different thing, *by being spoken of as if it were that other;* implied comparison in which a word or phrase ordinarily used of one thing is applied to another." Examples:

"Time is a thief"
"Love is a rose"
"You are the sunshine of my life"
"I am the wind"
"Night is a hunter"
"Wrong is right"

(continued)

> *Webster's* defines a *simile* as "a figure of speech in which one thing is likened to another, dissimilar thing by the use of *like, as,* etc." Some of my favorite similes appear in lyrics I've written over the years, including the following excerpts:
>
> > *Love is stealthy as a thief*
> > You turn around your heart is gone
> > Love makes you forget to breathe
> > Oh what a strange phenomenon
> > *From "After the Dance Is Through," Lyrics/Pamela Phillips Oland, Music/William Zimmerman and Wilmer Ragland, Jr.*
>
> > I love a man who understands
> > *Love is rare as the midnight sun*
> > He's always sweet, he'd never cheat
> > Cause he knows that I'd come undone
> > *From "He's On the One," Lyrics/Pamela Phillips Oland, Music/Wardell Potts, Jr. & Joey Gallo*
>
> > I awake on Christmas Day
> > To the laughter of children's play
> > *Window panes like Jack Frost's eyes*
> > Hiding blue skies
> > *From "Love So Rare," Lyrics/Pamela Phillips Oland, Music/Ron Ramin*
>
> > *Your touch is like a whisper*
> > As it brushes past my senses
> > Telling dreams that hid inside me to awaken
>
> > *You are as tempting as an apple tree in Eden*
> > Your lips are so ripe and sweet
> > *From "Mesmerized," Lyrics/Pamela Phillips Oland, Music/Wardell Potts, Jr. & Joey Gallo*

Practice making up unique metaphors and similes. It could even be a great game if done in groups with friends, collaborators, or family. For instance, instead of the simile "Good as *gold* . . . " or instead of the metaphor "Life is a *cabaret* . . . ," finish those with your own endings. They don't even have to make sense—just stretch your brain: "Good as a *garden snake*"; "Life is a *cartwheel down the beach.*" Think! Not just, "You are pretty as a *picture,*" but "You are pretty as a *china doll.*" Get the idea? Inventive thinking is what will make your work unique.

Ultimately, what makes for a good simile or metaphor is that it is believable in the lyric, and it conveys a clear and striking image that's simple to relate to. While far-fetched works as an exercise for developing this skill, it obviously doesn't work in the middle of a song. It's my belief, however, that you must at first think broadly with no restrictions stifling your creativity. Your good judgment will keep your ideas in line when writing similes and metaphors for your songs.

2

THE GREAT AHA!

ood ideas are everywhere. Like where? Like on TV, in movies, novels, books, magazine articles, newspaper stories, people's conversations, and even in business reports. Sometimes you can steal an idea from an advertising campaign, movie title, photo caption, or even another song. (I said steal an *idea,* not a line from another song!) Don't sweat it, as there are no original stories, only original ways of presenting them. Every now and then I think I've come up with an idea the world's been waiting for, only to turn on a 1938 black and white movie on cable TV with my exact idea! Well, ideas are up for grabs and *titles cannot be copyrighted!* There are dozens and dozens of songs written every day with titles that have been used before. In 1985, two songs named "Jump" were hits at precisely the same time, one recorded by Van Halen and one by the Pointer Sisters. A few years before that, two songs were out simultaneously with the name, "I'm Easy." BMI informed me that they catalogued and serviced no fewer than thirty-five songs titled "Shakedown," including my own! And doesn't it always happen that we've just completed our masterpiece with the unusual title, and someone has to spoil our day by saying, "Hey, did you know there's a new hit song on the radio with that exact title?" Of course, the song is always a big smash and dashes our hopes of ever seeing our own gem recorded. But hang on to it for a while. After the furor dies down, there may yet be room for another song of that title to be recorded. I must inject a note of caution here: Even though titles are not subject to copyright, I don't recommend writing another song called "Eleanor Rigby" or "Stagger Lee." Specific names or household words that are created by such titles may, in fact, be subject to copyright protection. Use common sense.

SEEING THE WORLD VISUALLY

Your eyes are your camera. You must frame everything you see as a picture, and describe it in your mind. You will constantly find ideas in the world around you, stories suggested by people you see or meet. You will never run short of new and interesting topics if you become visually adept.

KNOWING IT WHEN YOU HEAR IT

While good ideas are around us all the time, great ideas are as rare as cactus flowers.

How do I explain the euphoric feeling I get when a great idea suddenly floats unbidden into my mind? It's a physical as well as a mental sensation, a flushing of the face, a sudden lightheaded giddiness, a dilation of the pupils, a tingling of the cheeks. I've never analyzed it before, but when I think about it, there's sort of an explosion of white light in my mind as I recognize it. Perhaps that's why cartoonists have always depicted the great idea with a lit electric light bulb. I call it *The Great Aha!*

There's nothing quite as special in all the world of writing as The Great Aha. We've all felt it, and I truly believe it's part of why we continue to pursue writing careers. It's such an extraordinarily pleasurable experience that it is singularly fulfilling.

The Great Aha is a mysterious gift from the cosmos. It's the payoff for the investment of your time, energy, and talents, and it's as short-lived as it is powerful. Like all pleasurable sensations, its enjoyment cannot be prolonged. It's a momentary and magical release of anxiety and tension.

So whenever you get a great idea—and baby you *know* when it's a great idea—*Write It Down!* Keep pens and paper everywhere—in the car, beside the bed, on the coffee table—I'm not even above writin' on the Charmin'! When those ideas attack, scribble them down exactly as you thought of them, since they may never come again. How many times have you heard somebody say something interesting and thought, "Gee, that sounds like a title for a song! I'll have to remember that." Remember what? By the next day, you can't even remember who said it, let alone what they said. So you try to backtrack and reconstruct the sequence of events and the conversation that led up to the line, and always, but *always,* you say to yourself, "I should've written that down."

Maintain a file of ideas. You never know when an idea you had months ago may come in handy for a song you need to write today.

I carry around a small digital voice recorder, a "Voice-It." It records short ideas instantaneously and in my own voice. I've also found that shorthand is a very useful tool. If you can jot down your ideas in shorthand, you can catch them before they run away because it's amazing how transient ideas are. You get the whiff of them, start to write them down, and then find you can't quite grab hold of the exact turn of phrase. Was it "I'm Over You Being Over Me"? Or was it "Can't Get Over You Being Over Me"? Or maybe "Can't Get Over Getting Over You and Me"—Oh, drat! When the idea first came through, the concept may have been very clear, but by the time it was written down, your brain may have paraphrased it.

So what do you do with the Great Aha once you've duly recorded it on paper? Do you sit down and write a hit song right then and there? Certainly, if the spirit moves you. But if you're in the dentist's chair, or cooking dinner, or sitting in a dark movie theater, you may not have time right then. And when you're through with what you're doing, you may not be in the mood to write. So the only thing to do is maintain a file of ideas. You never know when an idea you had months ago may come in handy for a song you need to write today.

You will have to find the most comfortable style of filing for your own personal needs. Those of you who are very organized will be able to separate all the scraps of paper with ideas on them and categorize them in files according to subheadings such as "One-syllable titles," "Two-syllable titles," "Love titles," "Brotherhood titles," "Statements on life," and so on.

Oddly enough, I've found that when I type my ideas into long lists— usually two columns to a page—I never look at them. The titles all seem to blur into one. Maybe it's a personal quirk, but there's something about having them scribbled on that original piece of paper that seems to help me better focus my eyes and mind.

Writing on the Run

You should also scribble down fragments of lyrics when they occur to you. Although I say elsewhere that it is ideal to finish a song in one sitting, sometimes time just doesn't permit. So we often say, "Well, I'll just have to get to it later." But later often doesn't come, and we abandon the idea altogether, or else we can't remember what we intended to deal with it. So I can't recommend strongly enough to you: Write It Down *Now!* Whether it's just one line, or a whole verse, or the first verse and chorus—whatever part of the song has spontaneously occurred to you—get it on paper while it's fresh. You may not pick it up and finish it for hours, weeks, or even years, but some day you may be thankful for the inspiration that you didn't throw away.

Let me sum it up this way: If someone gave you a diamond ring, would you throw it away? Of course not. Well, when the Powers That Be in the universe gift you with Great Ideas . . . you get the picture.

Great Ahas don't always pick perfect times and places to occur to you, but you'll now have your notes to pull out later. And when "later" comes, you want your working environment to be appealing, so that all you have to do is get to work.

> *Write It Down* Now! *Whether it's just one line, or a whole verse, or the first verse and chorus—whatever part of the song has spontaneously occurred to you—get it on paper while it's fresh.*

SETTING UP THE WRITING ENVIRONMENT

Can you write a better song because you're sitting in a softer chair? Maybe. Believe it or not, the when, where, and how of writing can make a great difference in how the final product turns out.

It's been my experience that I write better in some environments than in others. These work environments, which I shall call "creative spaces," have changed locations through the years, but one fact remains the same: I feel less stressed and more creative in some areas than others. I believe that writers are terribly sensitive to our environments. We need very much to have a desirable workspace in order to let our creativity unfold. Painters and sculptors have long been associated with painstakingly selecting studios that have the lighting and windows "just so." As a child, I remember my musician father shutting himself in the back bedroom with his violin, clarinet, and alto sax, all muted, and standing with the music stand silhouetted against the garden window, practicing his playing for seven or eight hours at a time. Why did he always go to that particular spot? It just felt right, and judging by the results when he would come out and serenade us later, it was a very creative space for him.

Although I feel quite certain now that there is an emotional relationship between my work environment and the quality of my songwriting, in a pinch I have written in cars, trains, ships, planes, airports, kitchens, offices, studios, and in many collaborators' homes. In some of these places, I have found spots to write that were immediately satisfying. For instance, I remember Richard Carpenter calling me to come to A&M Studios at around 9:00 one evening to write a lyric he needed to record for his album. It was an extremely special song, a tribute to Karen, and he had taken months to come up with just the right melody and was finally satisfied with it. He seemed anxious to record it, and I had the impression immediately wouldn't be too soon. He gave me the title "When Time Was All We Had," and I said I'd go and find a place to work. I walked down the hall and came to the coffee lounge and looked around. It was rather warm and well-used and had an intimate feeling. I looked for a place to sit and was instinctively drawn to one corner of the sofa. I made some coffee, curled up, and wrote the song in about forty-five minutes, seemingly impelled to write it, without any hesitation or loss for words. It fairly flew out of me, line after line. And it was recorded without a single change.

Perhaps that was a lesson that said, "You have to *make* a place the right work environment if you don't have a choice." I always try to make the best of whatever environment I find myself in. All in all, however, my work is generally the best when I have a sense of true oneness with my creative space.

Find Your Own Creative Space

First, explore your home for the right room, the one that just feels the most cozy and creative to you. It may be the bedroom, or perhaps the den, if you have one. Some of you may like to write at the kitchen table; others have actual studios where you do your writing. If all the rooms in the house are occupied and noisy, perhaps you could adapt some part of the garage as a makeshift office, with a cozy, old armchair, maybe a bridge lamp and a small table. It should be fairly quiet there. Some people in crowded houses like to sit outside on the patio or even resort to curling up in the backseat of the car. Others are most creative outdoors—in a park or at the beach.

Never lose sight of the fact that music and words are totally different media, and the energy with which you approach melody and/or tracks is entirely different from the energy that brings out the best in you verbally.

Those of you who are primarily musicians and do most of your songwriting in your studio may find that the quality of your lyrics will increase dramatically if you get out of your music space into a living space for the lyric-writing process. Never lose sight of the fact that music and words are totally different media, and the energy with which you approach melody and/or tracks is entirely different from the energy that brings out the best in you verbally.

Most likely, you become part of your instruments and they move you when the musical ideas flow through you. Lyrics work in the same way; they must be allowed to subtly influence you. They are about life and people and, very often, about love. To reflect on these subjects, you need to be sitting somewhere conducive to these thoughts. A hard-backed chair at a piano or a stool facing a rack of synthesizers is not exactly conducive to thoughts of tenderness and affection.

Writing on a Computer—Breakthrough or Hindrance?

Some highly respected and famous lyricists have told me they have no trouble at all and, in fact, prefer working directly on a computer screen. Obviously, I can't argue with success. However, my own opinion as to the advisability of this particular method of songwriting is that it leaves a whole lot to be desired.

Yes, it's a lot of fun to be able to write one's thoughts up on the screen and be able to erase and correct, move lines, bold print, center, auto indent, and play with all the rest of the gizmos that make a computer such a distracting and absorbing device. Those of you who are happy and content with the results of your direct-to-computer writing, go for it! However, for those of you who are either considering buying a computer to provide you with a screen to work on, or who are less than delighted with the results you've been achieving writing on a computer, let's examine the drawbacks.

Without a doubt, the major disadvantage is the inability to retain prior drafts. Now I'm not talking about completed drafts here, as obviously these can be printed out and saved. What I'm talking about is the accumulated work in progress.

> *Until it is in its complete and final form, a lyric is in a constant state of evolution. What we first write may be a sketch of the idea, a series of lines that stimulate the thought process to get to what it is we mean to say.*

Until it is in its complete and final form, a lyric is in a constant state of evolution. What we first write may be a sketch of the idea, a series of lines that stimulate the thought process to get to what it is we mean to say. For me, the scribbling process on a pad is akin to the sand in the oyster that creates the stimulus to induce the production of a pearl. (In this case, a pearl of wisdom, one hopes!) So sometimes, along the way to discovering the perfect line, phrase, word, or stanza, we discard some wonderful ideas that, for a brief moment, seemed "right." We discard them because somehow they don't fit the concept we're going for.

However, once we get rolling on the song and the ideas start falling into place, the concept often breaks free of its original bounds. We find we go back and rewrite the beginning so that it will fit better into the altered (and hopefully improved) concept. If we are using pen and paper, we have all our first ideas still available to us for a second look. In my own experience, I often find that a word or part of a phrase I'd come up with at an early stage of the songwriting process can now be reconsidered, slightly rewritten, and made into the ideal image for another spot in the song.

Working on a computer, however, the discarded thoughts and ideas are literally as well as figuratively discarded. Usually, the exact turns of phrase we had jotted down and then rejected are lost forever, unless we happen to have photographic memories for strings of ideas and lines. The computer has only saved the final ideas we have come up with. Even if we have not erased the series of sketched ideas from computer memory but have them stored, it's very distracting and time-consuming to go back and retrieve the information, set it out correctly on the screen, and make heads or tails of the printout. And that detracts from creativity. Let's face it: It becomes *work*. If anything, what we actually need to do in songwriting is *simplify* the process, not make things more complicated. While I can, with great alacrity, compose powerful letters, draft contracts, and write this book on my computer, I find myself severely limited in the creative process when it comes to dialogue— either in lyrics or plays. Perhaps another reason is simply that, due to screen size, only a certain amount of what I'm writing appears at any given time. I always like to have in front of me the overview of my work, including all notes and corrections, alterations and rewrites. That way, I know instantly if I've already used a word in a verse that I'm about to use again in the chorus. I know instantly if the scan of verse two matches the scan of verse one; I know instantly if I've used the same rhyme scheme in an earlier verse or if it conflicts with the chorus. I can constantly resubmerge myself in the concept and particulars of the project.

It's probably easier to write prose on a computer than by hand because there are fewer limitations on getting straight to the point than there are in the dialogue or lyrics formats. In a letter, you have unlimited space to say, "I love you because . . . " In a lyric, you have maybe two verses and a chorus. Every word counts; therefore, we need to see the whole, including any prewritten notes we may have made to ourselves, analyzing the concept and annotating the artist's or producer's input.

> *When you don't exercise for two months, it's pretty slow going on your muscles until you get in shape again. Songwriting is like that, too: The more you do it, the easier it gets.*

In sum, I feel that while it's highly desirable to use a computer to print out an attractive presentation of my finished lyrics; the writing process is more convenient and satisfying if I have the entire lyric—with all possible lines, changes, amendments, and notes—right in front of my face.

IS THERE A MOON OUT TONIGHT?

Are you one of those writers who talks about writing all the time? Or are you one who actually writes? Can you always find a marvelous excuse not to write? You have to make a phone call; a traveling salesman interrupts your train of thought; your favorite soap star's long-lost daughter is about to make a dramatic reappearance and you can't miss the episode; you're Not in the Mood. That's the *real* reason, isn't it? You're Not in the Mood, are not likely to Get in the Mood, and don't know how to Work With Your Mood.

As a professional lyricist, I can't afford the luxury of waiting for a full moon to put me in the mood. If I have a song that needs to be written, I have to sit down and write. Any number of people talk to me about how they write songs, but when we get down to the nitty gritty, I discover that all they do is talk. "When was the last song you wrote?" I ask them. "About a month or two ago," they say blithely. Or even, "Last year!" *Last year,* I tell you! Unless it's January 1, I cannot find it in my heart to take these people seriously! Who are they kidding, saying they're songwriters! Dilettantes perhaps, but where's the dedication? Hate to break it to you, but writers *write.* How do you ever expect to get good at what you do if you wait for a full moon? When you don't exercise for two months, it's pretty slow going on your muscles until you get in shape again. Songwriting is like that, too: The more you do it, the easier it gets. The more times you use all the tools and devices, the formulas and turns of phrase; the more trial and error, the more reaching and stretching—well, the better your lyrics will be! One day you'll suddenly realize how thoroughly familiar and comfortable you are with your own lyric-writing process. Though not all great ideas turn into great songs, the more you see your ideas developed on paper, the more you will recognize your strengths and weaknesses and will grow and evolve as a lyricist.

What's certain is that the hardest part of writing is *beginning*. So you have to start making a conscious effort to create the time and space necessary for the process. Writing lyrics may not be the top priority of your life, but unless you make and keep your dates with yourself to put forth your best efforts at songwriting, you'll be shortchanging yourself from ever finding out how good a lyricist you really might be.

WRITING LYRICS ON A SCHEDULE

A constant lament among songwriters who don't have the luxury of writing full time is, "I just can't find enough time to write!" Sound familiar? The truth is, even people who write songs full time often can't find the time. We get caught up in business—meetings, lunches, dinners, recording sessions, e-mailing, and phone calls (my greatest time robber). And, like everybody else, we get caught up in general matters of life, love, family, and friends.

And the bad part about it is that it never gets better. There always seems to be "one more thing" to take care of before you sit down to write a song.

So what's the answer? Since you can't *find* time, you're gonna have to *make* time. Something else is going to have to wait instead.

If you want to write songs, you'll just have to learn to work around motherhood, fatherhood, your other job, sports, hobbies, TV, gardening, sewing, being there for friends, cooking, and home repairs. And, of course, that harmless-looking but insidious device, the telephone.

What's the Best Time to Write?

The point is that, just as there is never a good time to catch the flu or run out of money, for most aspiring writers there is never a good time to sit down and write. We can make time for almost everything else, but our art seems to be the first thing we put off if there has to be a choice.

So the best time to write is whatever time you can make available, pure and simple. Make a schedule for yourself, however arbitrary and subject to change. Explain to those who share your life that you need encouragement and support in your effort to become a successful lyricist, and maybe even get them to suggest times when it would be good for you to work.

While simply telling your family that you need time alone is enough for some of you, for others, it just doesn't work. Someone in the house will always come to you with a request: Can you referee an argument? Can you prepare a meal? Can you help with homework? Can you come to the phone? My theory is that if you let them be a part of your need to write,

Assuming there are no dire emergencies, make a habit of keeping appointments to collaborate. It will help instill in you a sense of professionalism and will teach those you live and work with that you're serious about songwriting and determined to pursue it.

they will shield you from the intrusions. Take some time to share honestly with those around you the great joy you get from writing. Express to them how much more fulfilled you can be if they will help you find the time to write. Then perhaps your wife will tell a caller, "Sorry, John's busy right now, can he call you back?" One kid will say, "I'm gonna tell Mom on you!" and the other will respond, "No you won't! She's writing!" Bring them in on it. You need them to be protective of your need to express yourself in your work, not resentful of the idea that you are taking time away from them. So let them be collaborators in your decision to pursue songwriting.

How do you set up a schedule for writing? One scheduling idea is to make a collaboration appointment at somebody else's home or office. Or invite a collaborator to your home, and inform your family in advance that no one is to disturb you while you're together working. (While families often do not respect our private time, they are less apt to intrude when there's a visitor.) Assuming there are no dire emergencies, make a habit of keeping appointments to collaborate. It will help instill in you a sense of professionalism and will teach those you live and work with that you're serious about songwriting and determined to pursue it. The more often you keep your writing appointments, the more apparent it will become to those who are demanding of your time that they must respect and support your effort. It's all very well to say, "I'm a songwriter," but it's very hard for anybody to take you seriously if all you do is talk about it and never act on it.

If you are working at home, it's up to you to decide that "after dinner on Tuesday, no matter what's on television," you will go to a private place and work until you're ready for bed. And another tip: Look for ways to make more time. For instance, instead of being the martyr who has to do all the chores, delegate jobs to other members of the household.

If you live alone and are used to spending several hours each evening on the phone, get voice mail and leave a pleasant outgoing message that says, "Hi! I'd love to talk to you, but I'm in the middle of writing a song and don't want to lose my train of thought. Please leave a message and I'll get back to you tomorrow!" Then unplug the phone and leave the answering machine on zero volume so you can't be distracted by incoming messages.

Keep a pad with you at work, and write during coffee breaks and those times when your work is caught up and your supervisors are out of the office. Take a pad with you out to lunch, and write at the table; if you brown bag it, find a secluded spot and write through your lunch break.

Make use of "waiting" times. If you have to take a child to a dance class or baseball practice, or if you have to take someone to the doctor for a checkup, take a writing pad with you and find as comfortable a space as possible to do some writing.

If you commute by bus, write on the bus. If you commute by car, use a portable recorder to keep track of your ideas.

If you have a late starting time for work, schedule an hour's writing when you first get up. If you have an early starting time, don't go straight home afterward—give yourself an hour or so to write in a nearby library or park. Because you know the minute you get home, you'll be cooking, answering phone calls, opening mail, cleaning house, and it'll be one more evening of no time to write.

Finally, no matter what your *responsibilities* are in life, you deserve to have at least one day or half a day to yourself every weekend. Make a regular appointment with yourself to write lyrics in that time, and don't let anybody wheedle you out of it.

Once You've Made the Time

Since time is so precious, you can't afford to be temperamental and waste any of the precious moments you've put aside to write. It takes strength of will and character to simply sit down and crank out a lyric, but that is exactly what you must learn to do. After a while, it will become second nature.

My suggestion: Sit down in the space you've made and acclimate yourself. Shut your eyes and do some deep breathing and relaxation exercises. Sigh, if necessary; let go of all your weariness and problems. Have a cup of coffee or tea or your favorite soft drink poured and sitting on a table close by. I don't know why, but drinking a hot cup of English-style tea, strong, with milk, is the most comforting thing in the world to me when I'm about to write! Maybe it's just the feeling of the warm liquid going down my throat, but it settles me down instantly.

Remember that it's easier to talk than to do. Quit putting your creativity and dreams last, because believe me you will always have responsibilities to work around: They're simply a fact of life. Being a successful lyricist means taking responsibility for allocating your time. You may have a Grammy-winning song in you—but you'll never know if you don't *make* time to write it!

Learn to Handle Distractions

Sometimes you can actually make distractions work *for* you. Instead of getting upset by the telephone ringing, the doorbell chiming, or a family member asking a question or favor while you're in the middle of a "great thought," remember this: It's all part of life. And life is what you're writing about! Frequently, there will be something in the interchange between you and the one who interrupts you, that will actually trigger a new idea for the lyric you need. I don't know why that happens, but it often does. So try to incorporate all the distractions as part of life, and when the interruption has been handled, simply go back to what you were doing. And this is

> *It takes strength of will and character to simply sit down and crank out a lyric, but that is exactly what you must learn to do. After a while, it will become second nature.*

important: Don't let the interruption ruffle you! Just let go of it and get back to your work. Don't blame the caller or the family member for ruining the song. If you get back to your chair and your notepad, soon the great idea, or another even better one, will present itself to you. Have faith!

Distractions can be very taxing and sometimes make you want to just give up. But unless you charter a rocket to the moon and sit in a crater up there, you will not be able to prevent the intrusions of life on your art. Take a deep breath, stamp your feet, scream—whatever makes you feel better—and know that you have to find the will and the stamina to prevail over the distractions if you're ever going to go all the way with your songwriting.

SELF-CONFIDENCE CAN SPEED UP YOUR THINKING PROCESS

Back in the days of Silverspoon Productions, Leon Sylvers would drop off a tape of six music tracks on Friday afternoon and pick up the finished lyrics on Tuesday. I felt like a dry-cleaning service! My composer associates at that time used to make jokes about how fast I worked. Leon affectionately called me "Mrs. Lyrics" because he got a kick out of how quickly I'd finish his assignments.

Before I started writing for that organization, however, my average lyric-writing time was anywhere from a week to a couple of months. Oh sure, once in a while I would knock something out in a day or in a couple of writing sessions, but the results were hit or miss.

So what turned me into the human dynamo lyricist? Why am I able to sit down and write a complete, intelligent, recordable lyric in fewer than four hours? *Confidence!* It took Leon's confidence in my abilities to instill the self-confidence I needed to do the work.

I find it an interesting phenomenon that I work better—faster and with greater assurance—with people who trust my judgment and believe that I know what I'm doing. "If they think so, it must be so" is probably the way my brain interprets this confidence.

> Once in a while I get stuck in a collaboration effort that leaves me cold. I could work on a song for four years, let alone four hours, and wouldn't be able to finish it to anybody's satisfaction. I have learned to stay away from noncreative associations. They slow down my thinking process and steal my self-confidence.

Not everybody's lucky enough to have a Leon Sylvers around just when he needs to have the greatest confidence instilled in him. There may be dozens of music publishers and record producers out there who are just dying to have a chance to discover you and express that confidence verbally, but they're not going to knock on your door. You must seek them out. So you need to make a real effort to connect with someone *in the industry* who can be a stepping-stone for your career; someone to whom you can always send material, someone who will advise, critique, and perhaps send out your songs when they're good enough. *Songwriter's Market* lists many names of publishers, managers, A&R professionals, record producers, and the like. Start by calling and making contact in person, and then stay in touch—without becoming a pest, which will surely alienate the very people you want to get on your side.

Unfortunately, there are no guarantees that we'll immediately find mentors to give us the strength and support that'll back us up as we pursue our careers. So remember that strength and support have to start within yourself. I can tell you with absolute certainty that once you start to approach the task of writing a lyric with an attitude of healthy confidence that says you're good at what you're doing, your writing speed will increase immeasurably.

Does Speed Mean Sacrificing Quality?

My former publisher, Lance Freed, president of Rondor Music, once sat me down and said, "Pamela, you don't have to write so many songs. Write less and think them through carefully. Spend longer on each one." I took his advice: I write less than I used to. I do prefer to allot more of my time and energy to each song, rather than cramming a lot of work in and not having time for rewrites. In taking on fewer assignments, my temperament is calmer, and I feel more serene when I am working.

But I still write quickly! I think that if it takes you two weeks to write a lyric, it's because you're not sure what you want to write about. If the idea and the concept are absolutely clear to you, then you should be able draft a complete lyric in one-half to one full workday.

I repeatedly asked the students in my classes at UCLA and elsewhere, "Have you ever had a song that you just *couldn't* finish, no matter how many times you sat down to try?" *All* hands would always go up. I pursued it further: "Is it always a song you're really anxious to finish?" Again, all hands go up. My answer is no mystery. When you can't finish a song, it is invariably because you haven't any clarity on elements such as the characters, what the song's about, the direction the story should take, and the resolution of the plot. You probably have a great title idea and just start writing lines that seem to relate to it, but never map it out.

> *When you can't finish a song, it is invariably because you haven't any clarity on elements such as the characters, direction, and resolution of the plot.*

Here's my advice on songs like these: If you can find a direction or replan the story line, you may be able to finish the song. Frankly, you're probably bored to tears with looking at it by now, and if it were mine, I'd just scrap it and start over with a new song. If there are any great lines in the song, jot them down and save them for another song later on. The moment will come—days, weeks, months, or even years later—when you'll be searching for just the right line, and there it will be.

Don't get stuck on an idea that goes nowhere. Just start new songs as often as necessary, even if that means having hundreds of unfinished starts. Don't finish a lyric that you don't believe in, just for the exercise. Only finish the ones you feel driven to write. The main lesson here is this: You will be able to complete a good lyric if you have a good foundation for writing it.

> There is no rule anywhere that says you have to finish every song you start to write! You will have hundreds of false starts before you're through, so don't waste any time getting annoyed and frustrated with yourself for not being able to finish a lyric with a particularly good start. A good start doesn't always guarantee a great song. It only means you had a good opening concept. It doesn't necessarily mean you have a great point to deliver.

Eventually, there will be fewer and fewer false starts. Once you start gaining the right amount of self-confidence in your ideas and start relying more heavily on your intuition, you will find that you reject inappropriate ideas, words, lines, and concepts before they ever reach the paper. Your brain will scan the sequence of words with a basic understanding of which words have the desirable flair, style, meaning, message, attitude, meter, and rhyme, as well as recognizing clever turns of phrase and fresh, interesting use of language.

And when you succeed, indulge yourself in the thrill of how good something you've written is. I mean, that's as good as it gets as far as the process goes. Songwriting should be a positive, not a tortured, experience. Permit yourself the pleasure of enjoying confidence in your talent.

OPEN THE DOORS OF PERCEPTION

Remember that your thinking process, and thus your writing process, depends very much on your ability to call up stored information at a moment's notice. So you have to start training your eyes to tell your brain to store every tiny thing you notice as you go about your life.

Start listening to conversations on two levels. First, what people want you to hear, and second, what you perceive to really be going on in their minds. Most people shield their true selves with some sort of a veneer—happy, bright, joking, self-confident. The idea is not to call them on what you see, as that would be very embarrassing and unpleasant for both of you, but to make a mental note of the vulnerability you have perceived.

> *Sometimes you will call on observations you've stored away in the depths of your memory that will surprise and amaze you. Each of us has assembled, stored, and catalogued a wealth of information that is virtually on tap, just waiting to be rediscovered.*

Notice familiar objects with a new eye. See the frayed armchair in all its charm instead of its tatters. Look at the old porch swing that no one sits on, and imagine a romantic setting for a song. Notice the one you love and for the first time rhapsodize on his freckles or her elegant toes.

I am of the firm opinion that we hardly perceive anything of what we look at. We see only what we expect to see, and very little else. Once my mother discovered an earring missing while at a large dinner party at my home. We scoured the house and the grounds, even went through the icky job of taking the garbage apart. All of us had seen her wearing this pair of her favorite earrings and assured her that it must be around somewhere, as she hadn't left the property all evening. The next morning, she found the missing earring in her jewelry case in the guest room. She had been wearing only one earring all evening, yet we had all perceived her to be wearing both of them!

Develop your memory—it's a gold mine! Sometimes you will call on observations you've stored away in the depths of your memory that will surprise and amaze you. Each of us has assembled, stored, and catalogued a wealth of information that is virtually on tap waiting to be rediscovered.

Recollection seems to be very much tied to stimulus. For instance, I know hundreds of good jokes. But ask me to tell you a joke and I can't think of a single one. Yet somebody can make a comment, or tell a story about a certain subject, and suddenly half a dozen jokes dealing with the same premise will pop into my mind, fully remembered.

In the same way, when I start to write a lyric about a certain aspect of life or love, thoughts and ideas come flooding into my mind that deal with that particular subject. My memory is acutely selective and somehow knows exactly what piece of trivia to dig up seemingly out of nowhere. If I'm writing about star-crossed love, for instance, I may remember a certain doomed couple I met five years ago; if I'm writing about first love, I may recall a long-buried encounter at a high school dance or the embarrassment of my first teenage "make-out" party. They are all the colors of the threads of my life that have been woven into a rich tapestry of memories—mine to take out and examine in intricate detail as often as I care to.

Every memory you've ever stored in your life, back to the earliest ones, can one day be called up as an important part of something you want to write.

The police have proven many times that people see more than they think they saw. Victims or witnesses of crimes often recall small details such as eye and hair color, license plate numbers, and so forth, which they don't consciously remember seeing. Under induced hypnosis, minute details and intricate conversations are easily recalled. I have been hypnotized on occasion, and have found that my mind could perform amazing feats. I was able to produce similar results with self-hypnosis.

So I ask you, isn't the semi-trance that lyricists go into when they allow ideas to float in from the subconscious akin to some sort of self-induced hypnotic state? We are, in fact, letting ideas and images channel through us. Times beyond recall I have said, in the first flush of coming up with a terrific line, "I wonder where *that* came from!"

Thus, the more we observe, the more attention we pay to what goes on in every corner of our lives—the more information we will store away, waiting for the day we are ready to retrieve it for a lyric. The more vivid the recollections, the more interesting and unique our lyric choices are going to end up being.

Relying on Intuition

When I write lyrics, rather than straining my brain to "come up with a great line," I clear my mind and allow the inspiration to come to me. I know it when I hear it. Sometimes you can "think up" a great line, but usually the really spectacular "Wow!" lines are intuitive and require no effort whatsoever!

I contend that we no longer trust our intuitive ability to recognize our own insights because we have been so spoon-fed by the constant barrage of media. We've been told what to think, what to wear, what to eat, what constitutes fun, what constitutes love, and what constitutes beauty so often that many of us no longer practice thinking for ourselves.

When you as a writer can distinguish the difference between true intuition and an ordinary thought, you are on the road to being among the greats. What's the difference between the two? In simple English, an intuition seems to come "through" you unbidden. It's just there without any conscious effort at all. A thought is something you conjure up while concentrating on a subject.

But intuition isn't "magic." Writing lyrics is more than the intuitive recognition of a clever grouping of words. For instance, when I came up with the title "You're Just a New Name for an Old Feeling," it originally started with my perception that something my collaborator, Jack Conrad, had said was worth a second look.

We were talking about a new professional manager in a publishing company we both knew of. Jack described him as "a new face doing the same old thing." He kept on talking, but I couldn't get past that line. I knew there was something more in it. It seemed to be the *new* something that was repeating a familiar *old* thing. This led me to think about love being the same old thing until you meet that someone rare who makes it all feel new and special. Since we were thinking about Tina Turner as we wrote this lyric, I imagined her looking sardonically at an upstart who was trying to seduce her and telling him, "Honey, I've seen 'em like you before, you've got it all in the right places, but you ain't got nothing new for me!" Jack and I discussed this idea and became excited about it. We knew it was good.

I said, "You're a new face, but the feeling's the same." Then I said, "You're a new face with an old feeling." Then the inspiration came to me: "You're a new name for an old feeling." We both said, "Yeah!" But we still knew something wasn't quite there, and then I blurted out, "You're *just* a new name for an old feeling!" And that was it. That was the line that captured the thought completely.

So, you see, the final title came as the result of setting the thought process in motion. The first ideas I came up with were contrived. The final title was inspired. In time, with practice, you will be able to duplicate the process I have just described, which means learning to distinguish between the lines you think up and the lines that simply come as if "out of nowhere."

Start learning to trust your intuitive process. Now in order to draw forth ideas, you need to start the wheels in motion by writing down whatever lines come into your head. But you know clearly when the line you've come up with is a contrived thought and not an inspiration. Train yourself to recognize the thrill when that old intuition kicks in with the "Wow!" line. I know it when I hear it in my own writing. I know it when I hear it in other people's writing. And, after a little practice, you will, too.

Your ability to take ideas seemingly from thin air and make them work in the context of a song is your own unique gift. Whether the line you write is seemingly intuitive or something you have created by a process of hard work, you'll know that you have achieved the right line when your intuition tells you so.

HOW CAN YOU DEVELOP YOUR INTUITION?

Since developing your intuitive abilities rests largely on trusting yourself to recognize the inner voice of intuition, it will help you to do an exercise to speed up your thinking and writing process.

I suggest that you do the following:

1. Make sure that you have all your necessities with you—notepad, a pen that works, nosh and drink if you need it, rhyming dictionary, thesaurus, and dictionary, a visible clock, etc.
2. Settle down into a comfortable and pleasing work space.
3. Write down the title you have chosen at the top of the page.
4. Note the time at which you are commencing work, and allow yourself four hours to finish the entire draft of the lyric.
5. Begin the process by identifying mentally what you want to talk about in the first verse in order to lead up to the chorus. *(continued)*

6. Don't work too hard at letting first lines flip through your mind. Just toss some out loud, and when you find one you're satisfied with, write it down. Great—you've begun the song.
7. Continue through the song in an orderly fashion—writing the sections in order, from first line to last, without skipping around—until it is finished.

For a second exercise, go through the same process, but limit the time to three hours. For a third exercise, go through the same process, but limit the time to two hours.

It is highly unlikely that you can develop an entire lyric in one hour, though occasionally you will find that you do, so don't feel you have to complete this exercise in a one-hour time frame as well.

When you read what you have written, I believe you will find that it is one of the most cohesive, well-written lyrics you've ever attempted. This is because you haven't allowed yourself enough time for mental machinations as to whether a line is good enough or not, or whether you should change this or that. Also, since you developed the story idea by building from beginning to end, you will find that the concept flows to your satisfaction.

Please note: This does not mean that your lyric will be perfect. The chances are great that you will have to go back through a song and craft and hone the lyric to get it right. You might even flip-flop a couple of the verses to make more sense out of the story. You might shorten or lengthen the chorus or decide there was something better you could say in the bridge. However, all in all, I think you will find that the song has tremendous merit because, given the time limitation, you had to rely more on intuition than struggling to clarify your thoughts.

GOING DRY

Writers often ask me, "Do you ever have 'dry' periods?" When I tell them I don't, they're always surprised. They ask, "Don't you ever worry that you're *going* to go dry?" The truth is, No, I don't. There is a wellspring of ideas in the universe, and all I have to do is open my mind up and let them come in. I never worry about "going dry" and, therefore, I never do.

It's important to differentiate between "dry spells" and simple fatigue or the type of work burnout anybody might have regardless of his or her type of job. We all get tired, need a break, a change of scenery, a vacation, a few days off to putter in the garden or catch up on our reading. A dry spell, which is a very real phenomenon, especially associated with and dreaded by creative people, means the ideas have simply stopped flowing.

I think this "writer's block" is self-perpetuating. It is fathered by the dreaded idea, "What if I never come up with another great (song) (painting) (script) (etc.)?" Having put this thought in motion, the creative person is always waiting for the day it will occur, and occur it will. Once writer's block is perceived as having begun, creative people go into shock, become overwrought with worry, and start to doubt whether they will ever get their talent back. The more they think like this, the longer it will take them to feel they can work again.

Sometimes a tough assignment with insufficient directions can cause a feeling akin to burnout. Especially if you have submitted a couple of drafts and they've all been turned down. Feelings of doubt creep in and, pretty soon, your ego and sense of direction are affected. Your fear of making more missteps stops you from making any attempts at creativity whatsoever. Hence, you believe it's burnout.

So, obviously, the moral to this story is this: Don't think about going dry and you won't. If you don't feel like writing for a short time—a day, a week or two—just acknowledge that you don't feel like writing because you just don't happen to be interested in it right now.

However, you mustn't let too much time pass during these rest periods. You have to discipline yourself or you'll get further and further away from productive work habits. The longer you stay away, the harder it will be to get back to work.

You simply have to make the physical effort to crank up the machinery of songwriting and just get on with it. If you have neglected your songwriting for a couple of weeks in favor of personal activities, simply *make the decision* to write a lyric. Usually, that's a perfect time to make use of your title file to look for a great title you've forgotten about that will jog you into a writing mood. As you go through the file, make a list of several of the titles that seem to jump out at you and say, "Write me," and then choose the one you're most in the mood to write. Don't worry about whether it will be a masterpiece; just start writing something. Do it with a smile. Do it in a new style that is not comparable to or competitive with your regular style, so that you will not have a yardstick by which to judge it. The key here is to *retain control.* Remember that the reason you started writing in the first place was because you loved doing it. Period. Do it because you love doing it again. Anyway, that's the first reason you should be doing it *all the time—not* for fame or fortune, but because it's such an enthralling thing to do. When a writer becomes absorbed in writing just for the pleasurable experience of doing it, anything resembling burnout becomes a thing of the past.

I write songs for the challenge of seeing something develop out of nothing. It's the *real* sorcerer's trick, much more satisfying than seeing a rabbit emerge from an empty hat. It's pulling words, ideas, concepts, clever phrases, and statements out of thin air. When your quest for originality taps into that mysterious and unknown core of your subconscious mind, you discover a way of looking at life and the world around you out of entirely different eyes.

Finally, when you're feeling pressured because of finances, employers' demands, time limits, unclear or impossible assignments, or the like, it's time to stop and look at whether those reasons, those people who are pressuring you, and those particular assignments, are worth the headache that's causing you to feel burned out. Personally, I don't think they are. I can be pushed just so far before I ask myself, "Do I need this aggravation?" The very clear answer is "No." Do your best to fulfill your assignments and

> *There is no greater reward for your diligence and patience, your struggle for artistic expression, than the moment of birth of a great idea!*

writing opportunities. When they start bringing down the quality of your life, your home relationships, and your health, consider giving them a pass. There's always one more contact and one more assignment and one more opportunity around the corner. Giving up something that's making you unhappy is not giving up anything worthwhile at all.

REAL SONGWRITERS NEVER SAY DIE (EXCEPT IN A LYRIC!)

If you walked down the street and stopped ten strangers at random, eight would probably tell you they had at least once written a poem or a song. Many among us have oodles of undeveloped talents and great wellsprings of inspiration and imagination that briefly surface and never again see the light of day. Often, the reason for this is pure and simple frustration. False starts have induced self-criticism; the inability to satisfactorily complete a lyric has led to tears; the lack of a competitive and complete product has prevented professional acceptance; and the would-be songwriter has simply thrown up his or her hands in disgust, dismay, despair.

Not everybody can become a professional wordsmith, but we cannot know our strengths and limitations without exploring them to the fullest possible extent. So if you really believe in your gift as a lyricist, there's only one way to find out just how good you are, and that is to keep writing and honing your craft. Remember always that the purpose for this work is simple: the process itself. Then one day, you'll hear a song of yours performed live somewhere, or on the radio, and you'll be filled with a burst of overwhelming joy, because at that moment you'll know, without a doubt, how good at it you really are!

I repeat the message I gave you in my Foreword: The one song you'll definitely never get recorded is the one you never write! So let all the wonderful thoughts and ideas that you've stored away surface! Enjoy to the fullest extent the pleasure of *The Great Aha* when it strikes, as there is no greater reward for your diligence and patience, your struggle for artistic expression, than the moment of birth of a great idea!

Now that we've explored the process of lyric writing, the next thing to consider is how to go about communicating your ideas, thoughts, and points of view to others in such a way that they understand what you mean and somehow relate to it in their own lives.

WORD ASSOCIATION

You can learn to jog your memory by a little game of association you can play any time, anywhere. Simply concentrate on an object or a face you're looking at, and mentally list all the things it reminds you of. If, for instance, you are relaxing on a beach, in a park, or some other public place, use that experience not only to store away brand-new perceptions in your memory bank, but also relate them and tie them together with old ones. You can even list the associations on paper if you want to.

VISUALIZATION

With the premise in mind that you can work faster and better if you feel good about yourself and your abilities, I'd like to take a moment to share with you a mental exercise I've adapted from an old Hindu practice. Shut your eyes and quiet yourself and imagine a ball of pure white light energy starting deep inside you. Let it slowly radiate outward until it surrounds and envelops you. Push it further out with your hands, still keeping your eyes shut. Draw power from it as you imagine yourself flourishing with success and happiness.

It's no secret among those of us who are drawn to metaphysics that before you can find success you have to imagine yourself already successful. So visualize yourself accepting a Grammy, hearing your song on the radio, signing a publishing contract on your song. You may be early in your career, but the secret is to always visualize the end result.

THE WRITING PROCESS

In subsequent chapters we'll be exploring in detail each of the steps listed in this section. However, I've included this brief outline of the writing process to start you thinking early on about the writing process itself.

Pick up your pad and pen and write down the date in the top righthand corner of the page. If you have a title chosen, write that down at the top in the center. If you haven't chosen a title, go to another page at the back of the notebook, where you store title ideas in progress, and start listing titles. Write down any title that jumps out at you. Write many of them, even twenty-five or fifty. When you find one you feel like working on, you can stop and turn back to the page where you are going to write the lyric.

The next step is to dissect the title and decide on the main idea of the song. When you feel happy that you've got a good idea for what the song is about, follow your instincts and write the song. Begin with the first line and continue through the first verse. When you've finished writing the first verse, analyze what you've written and begin to reshape it only if it makes no sense and doesn't get your point across.

The next thing to tackle, time permitting, is the chorus, assuming you're using one, and where the title fits into it. After you have a working chorus, proceed to the next verse, making sure it leads into the chorus, and then decide whether the song needs a bridge. Should you choose to write a bridge, think carefully as to what else might be said to enhance your story, to make it more touching, more interesting, more whatever you choose.

When you've completed a draft of your song, you'll feel very satisfied at having your idea completely on paper. You can either start rewriting at that time, or put the song away so that you can have time to "live with it" and come back to it later. We cannot know what *doesn't* work until we've written it down, evaluated it, and gotten beyond it.

3

COMMUNICATING
THROUGH SONG

ommunication means getting what's in your mind to jump into the mind of the person with whom you're trying to connect, so that your full intent is heard *and comprehended.* In songwriting, a lack of communication means that you, as a writer, failed to get across to the listener the point that you wanted to express. Thus, even if it was crystal clear to you, if a listener doesn't know what you're talking about and you have to explain it, chances are you didn't communicate your idea. The old adage on this subject is, simply: *If you have to explain why it works, it doesn't.*

A song must also express the *singer's* intent and personality. The art of a good songwriter is to literally put words in the singer's mouth that reflect the singer's own point of view.

POPULAR MUSIC IS A CONVERSATIONAL ART

Today, lyrics are very "street," very down to earth and conversational. That's a fact of life. In the "olden days," meaning the twenties, thirties, forties, and early fifties, songwriters had *carte blanche* to write extremely poetic statements, such as in "My One and Only Love": "The very thought of you makes my heart sing like an April breeze on the wings of spring" (© Lyrics/Robert Mellin, Music/Guy Wood). It's a good bet nobody would ever actually say that to someone in casual conversation, yet it was indeed considered a beautiful line of lyrics. Sadly, such beauty cannot be found in modern songwriting. Lyricists of the past indulged in eloquent flights of metaphor, such as in "The Moon Got in My Eyes": "I thought a kingdom was in sight that I would have the right to claim" (© 1937 John Burke/Arthur Johnston). This very romantic comment on the hopes of attaining someone's affection would hardly be conversational in present-day speech. There are many among us who mourn the passing of such eloquent, romantic songwriting out of the mainstream of popular music.

The modern rule of thumb is this: *If you wouldn't say it, you wouldn't sing it.* Like all rules, this one is broken frequently and brilliantly! However, if you are breaking this particular rule, make sure it is an occurrence that is *infrequent, important, interesting,* and *forgivable* because it adds so much to the content and experience of the song.

I'll briefly illustrate a couple of ways I've successfully broken the rule "If you wouldn't say it, you wouldn't sing it." In my lyrics for the song "Until You," I wrote:

"Until you . . . I was a bird in flight in search of somewhere safe to light
I was a soul the breeze would carry like a drifting kite. . . . "
Lyrics/Pamela Phillips Oland, Music/Joe Curiale

That song was played for quite some time as the love theme on the TV soap opera, *As the World Turns.*

In "Step Right Up," recorded by the R & B group Collage, I wrote:

"You have left a trail of tears . . . shattered hearts like broken glass . . . "
Lyrics/Pamela Phillips Oland, Music/Dana Meyers and William Zimmerman

However, it's important to tell you that the rest of each of these songs was quite conversational.

Finding a Balance

Frank Sinatra once told me that what he liked about my lyrics was that I wrote the way they "used to" but in modern-day terms; that I bridged the gap between the old and the new. I pass this on to you: To be the best lyricist you can be, try to find a way to balance the romantic soul in you with the perceptive, down-to-earth person who's out on the street every day.

There is a certain harshness to reality that is painful, and it's a challenge for lyricists to temper that harshness. Since people often listen to songs with the transference that the lyrics refer to their own lives, they respond to hearing about exactly what they're going through. The only thing is, since most people's lives are fraught with problems, the lyrics they listen to and relate to their own lives have to introduce messages with some beauty and hope. Listeners can then feel just a little bit better about their own lives, their own hopes, their own prospects.

I personally think that romance is one of the great cures for whatever ails the world. When romance is gone from our lives, we feel a sad emptiness. Perhaps that accounts for the incredibly huge market in romantic fiction, especially fanciful, historical romances that take a reader to another time, when beauty and chivalry, pomp and circumstance were held in the utmost regard.

To be the best lyricist you can be, try to find a way to balance the romantic soul within you with the perceptive, down-to-earth person who's out on the street every day.

The secret is to intertwine the romantic with the real. If we have to look at life and see it exactly the way it is; if we have to listen to the way people actually talk to each other, and then reflect what we've seen and heard in our lyrics, then I believe we are also entitled to add a little of our affectionate idealism. I say, *Why shouldn't lyrics to popular songs put a little romance into people's lives?*

But what's the fine line between mushy poetic lyrics and down-to-earth expressions? No typical guy would ever say to his girl, "My dearest darling, the moon glow is flowing, and its radiance is a waterfall cascading down your hair." At best, he might say, "Baby, it's really great the way the moon's reflecting off your hair." But within the context of a song, you can get away with pushing it just a little bit, to say something like, "I love the way the moonlight dances in your hair." It's not far out enough to sound utterly beyond normal speech, yet it captures the romantic spirit just enough that a person who normally wouldn't think to say that, might imagine that he had.

Another example: In normal conversation, a woman wouldn't say, "My heart has grown weary of the weight of the chains of sorrow that have tied me forever to your memory." She might say, "I'm tired of crying when I think of you." In a song, the lyricist might take a little romantic license and say something like, "I'm riding my memories of you down a river of tears."

In both examples, the first choice was overkill and stilted use of language; the second choice was perhaps a little ordinary, though certainly acceptable; and the third choice was a compromise between going out on a limb and being mundane.

Strive to simplify your writing so that there are simple lines that join the colorful and original ones together. The line suggested above, "I'm riding my memories of you down a river of tears," *could* be followed by, "To the looking-glass land where I see my future lies." But that couplet would be too gushing. It needs to lead into a more straightforward line, such as, "I'm riding my memories of you down a river of tears, *to the place where broken hearts go.*"

Obviously, it is learning the balance between cleverness and earthiness that makes a lyricist special. If the whole song is ordinary, the idea never really gets expressed properly; on the other hand, if the whole song is too flowery, it has become poetry and nobody will listen to it. But if you have to choose which side to lean toward—simplicity or romanticism—stick as comfortably to reality as you can, experimenting tastefully with interesting and unique imagery and turns of phrase.

Here's an excellent guideline that you should always remember when it comes to the bottom line: If you read or sing your lyrics back and they strike you as outlandish, overdone, uncomfortable, unclear, preposterous, overly flowery, unintelligible, or romantic to a fault, *you're probably right!* So trust your own judgment!

If you're not 150 percent happy with what you've written on paper, do yourself a big favor and do your own rewrite before somebody else you were eager to please has to confirm to you that indeed the song is not remotely conversational or applicable to life in the real world.

MUSIC IS A REFLECTION OF THE TIMES

If you study the hits on the radio, you'll see that songwriting today has become strictly a straightforward, realistic art, generally lacking (with the exception of Country music) in the witty little turns of phrase and clever plays on words that marked the work of songwriters of the thirties and forties.

What brought about the change? And why is it that a lot of the brilliant, amusing lyrics written by these early greats don't hold up to today's scrutiny? The answer is simple: Different rhymes for different times. In inventive use of language, for instance, Cole Porter had few peers. Consider this verse from his "At Long Last Love":

"Is it an earthquake, or simply a shock
Is it the good turtle soup, or merely the mock
Is it a cocktail, this feeling of joy
Or is what I feel the real McCoy?"

Porter has not only referred to mock turtle soup (an actual type of gourmet soup made to taste like turtle soup) as a synonym for something artificial, but in saying "merely the mock" he has hilariously turned it around so that *mock* is a rhyme for *shock* and also gives us the alliteration of the *m*'s in "merely the mock" to follow the alliterative *s*'s in "simply a shock." This resourceful wordsmith has further given us, in the same verse, the internal rhyme of *feel* and *real*.

In "My Heart Belongs to Daddy," Porter has set himself up with a terribly difficult word to rhyme in *daddy*, but, undaunted, he has written:

"If I invite a boy some night
To dine on my fine finnan haddie
I'd just adore him asking for more
But my heart belongs to Daddy!"

(continued)

Music lovers of the day praised Porter endlessly for his ability to play with words and come up with just such obscure rhymes. His work transcended the theatrical pieces his songs were primarily written for and was popularly recorded by innumerable artists. Today, however, while you might get away with playing with words in the musical theater, as far as popular songwriting goes, the listening public wants plain English, no gimmicks.

Without a doubt, we are living in a far less escapist society today than they were then. The Depression–World War II–Postwar generations went for romantic fantasy as clearly as we today go for stark reality, even shock value. Let's face it: The world's a whole lot different than it was in the thirties and forties and even the fifties. Films and radio programs of those eras clearly show us that there was a greater emphasis on sexual morality, the unity of family, Dad the worker and provider, Mom the homemaker, right towering over wrong, and heroes and heroines who were clean-cut and true blue.

The songs of a culture should accurately reflect the peculiarities and problems of that culture. It's said that films, novels, plays, music—in fact all art forms—are very much mirrors of the times. At any given time, we live in a society with its own set of peculiarities and problems.

In the past four decades, we have lived through rock and roll music; the Beatles (who some people feel changed society forever); hippies; the Vietnam War; peace and love movements; liberation for women, men, gays, African Americans, the elderly (Gray Panthers); and a myriad of religious cults. We have seen a sexual revolution that gave us free love, love-ins, communes, a proliferation of quasi-sexual nudist colonies, and a moral backlash to saving kissing for the second date. We've endured a glut of the "Me Generation" with hundreds of pop psychologists and would-be do-gooders coming up with a truckload of books, theories, and research papers on how to improve the quality of Oneself and One's Life. Women once wore demure taffeta evening dresses and Cuban-heeled shoes to dances, with their hair curled in marcel waves. Today, visit the Rainbow Club on the Sunset Strip and check out the pink-haired young women boldly attired in black lace underwear. And watch how nobody but the tourists pay a whit of attention to this modern-day self-expressionism. Oh yes, our values have changed! And we are the songwriters of the modern era so it's our job to chronicle our times in the language of today.

WHAT ARE YOU TRYING TO SAY?

A common error in the songwriting process is the assumption that the listener will know what you're talking about. But that's asking a lot of the listener. So the rule of thumb is: *Assume the listener knows nothing.*

You have written a lyric that tells a story. But you cannot expect a listener to know what is transpiring in the story and why if you don't make your ideas crystal clear. Furthermore, you can't start a song by simply jumping into the middle of a story and expecting the listener to fill in all the background information.

Most often, this problem occurs when the song is about the results of a falling-out between lovers in the song, without the lyrics ever expressing what went wrong. The writer simply forgets to explain what happened to cause these unfortunate results.

So, in keeping with the unfailing journalistic rules for the lead paragraph of any news story, in most songs you must try to give some clues to the *who, what, when, where,* and *why* of the story. Here are some examples using love songs:

1. The *who* should lead us to understand who is singing and who is the "you" being sung to or about. For instance, in a love song, we need to know how close these two are or were, if this is a new or old relationship, if this was a one-sided love, if they worked hard at staying together, if it was doomed from the start, and so on.

2. The *what* must give us a clear understanding of the situation as it stands right at this moment. Are they together or apart? If they are apart, who left whom, who did what to whom? Is there a problem that took place that led to what exists now? Does the singer want to leave it apart or put it back together? Is everything the way it ought to be? What is the prognosis for the future of the situation? Of the relationship? What has been done to try to make things better? What has been done to pull things apart?

3. The *when* establishes whether this song is about the past, the present, or the future, or whether it is traveling through all three time zones. If it talks about something that went wrong, it should try to place it in near past or far past. If it is about something that's happening at the instant of the singing, we must know that it is presently unfolding, and the lyric must convey the urgency or passivity of the moment. If it is about the future, we need to know whether this is the near future, the far distant future, or the "forever" type of future.

4. The *where* must put us into the intimacy of the situation. Is this taking place at home, long-distance, in their hearts and minds? Is it a confrontation in the car, the park, the bedroom, a parking lot, on the beach, at the movies, at a party, at a dance? The setting of the song can add necessary color and information. It's not enough to say, "We met one night." We have to say we met one night "at a crowded disco" or "on the beach at Ipanema" so that the listener can vicariously go there, too.

5. The *why* must explore the details of the situation as to who is at fault and why, who is right and why, who tried the hardest and why, who is in control and why, who is feeling the loss and why. Why did the situation come

to the point it's at now? Could it have been avoided? Is it intentional? Is it something they have both worked toward? Why is it important enough to sing a song about? Why will other listeners relate to the situation?

Incidentally, if you cannot answer this last question to your own satisfaction, I have a question for you: Why are you writing this song?

Songs on topics other than love would follow pretty much the same rules. They need to tell us who is singing, what is the reason for the song, when and where the song is set. The *why* expresses either what the narrator/singer's part in the story is; what listeners are supposed to learn, think, or believe on hearing the song; or how the situation being sung about has affected the narrator/singer.

Too many lyrics are written without any real purpose. To simply write one more "Hey baby, you're great, I love you" song serves neither the interests of your own career nor the future of the music industry. Unless you have a definite concept or statement to make in your song, don't write it. Vague phrases of love—rambling along for three verses, half a dozen choruses, and a bridge, including rap sections and other sections *ad nauseum*—does not make for a song. There must be a point that you are trying to make. There must be a goal or a resolution. There must be identifiable characters. There must be a strong emotion the listener can relate to. There must be well thought out, articulate use of the language.

Unfolding the Plot by Degrees

Keep in mind that in order to retain the listener's interest right up to the last moment of a song, you must artfully dangle the denouement, the outcome of the story, like a carrot that is almost within reach. In order to be entertaining, you mustn't give the game away.

Imagine going to see a mystery movie in which the sleuth was told the identity of the victim and the murderer at the beginning, and then you had to sit and watch the (painful) unfolding of why and how for an hour and a half. All the fun would be gone from the process. In the same way, a song should be an excellently constructed, three-minute (or however long) movie, which can be visualized and experienced from beginning to end. By the end of the song, of course, the issue at hand should be resolved or explained in a manner satisfactory to the listener. No threads should be left hanging. The entire story should be told, with the outcome quite clear.

In the song, "Show Me What You've Got for Me," I started with a simple story about a girl seeing a man at a dance club and took it through all the stages—from first glance to being locked together in a passionate dance with a promise of the future in their eyes. The song is based on all the thoughts that are going through her head, and we realize that he isn't privy to her thoughts, as we are.

The first verse has her noticing him, then watching him with great interest; the second verse has him dancing with somebody else but staring at her, then coming over to ask her for a dance. The bridge has her asking him scornfully if he's "all dance and no action" or if there's substance behind all those moves. In the final verse, she is so captivated dancing with him that she knows he has won her over and *que sera sera!*

SHOW ME WHAT YOU'VE GOT FOR ME

You got caught in my eye and I couldn't get you out
Captured my imagination with your smile
Wonder what you're all about
I think I'll watch you dance awhile

Chorus: *So don't stop . . . Show me what you've got for me*
No don't stop . . . Show me what you've got for me

You're like something off the silver screen, you're a ladies man
Though you're with some other girl, your eyes are mine
Now you come and take my hand,
And we're moving in slow-motion time

Chorus: *So don't stop . . . Show me what you've got for me*
No don't stop . . . Show me what you've got for me
You've got such a sensuality
You know it's too hot . . . that's what love has got to be

Bridge: *I'm a willful girl and so hard to please*
Are you all dance and no action
Or Baby are you for real?

Now my temperature is rising . . . your lips are much too near
Feels like no one else is even in the room
Body language loud and clear
Dee-jay please play one more tune, and Baby . . .

(Repeat Chorus)

LYRICS/PAMELA PHILLIPS OLAND, MUSIC/RICK NEIGHER (AS RECORDED BY FIVE STAR)

One of the biggest dissatisfactions I encounter in the writer's arts—and I'm including novels, plays, musicals, movies, TV shows, songs, and poetry in this category—is that endings frequently leave me flat.

Here I've listened, read, or watched faithfully for the entire time of the unfolding of the story, only to be left with a mediocre tie-up at the end, which invariably smacks of being a writer's last resort due to his or her inability to come up with anything better. Besides being an insult to me, the consumer, it tells me that the writer never figured out what point he or she wanted to make on starting to write. From my point of view, a disappointingly uninspired ending to what has promised to be excellent writing throughout cancels out all the good work that has come before. It's like the Burlesque joke about the fellow who falls in love with a buxom, blonde, blue-eyed wench, only to take her home to bed and find out that she's wearing falsies, a rubber rear, glue-on eyelashes, colored contact lenses, and a mail-order wig.

At the end of a great novel with a brilliant ending, the reader smiles contentedly, sighs, and perhaps sheds a couple of tears because there's no more story left to read.

A song has fewer lines in which to express its story. So the meat and potatoes of *who, what, when, where,* and *why* have to be unveiled incredibly quickly, and the ending has to take the listener to some conclusion, some point, some irony, some realization.

Being a great writer begins with having a strong point of view. What you have to say simply has to be important enough for others to want to listen to it. Listing a stream of lovely phrases that don't lead anywhere is as unsatisfying as most politicians' speeches.

DEVELOPING CHARACTERS

The people whose points of view you are writing about—both the singer and the person or persons being sung to—need to be well defined in terms of how the listener is to perceive them. The listener must know whether they are good or bad, happy or sad, young or old, experienced or naïve, bold or shy, strong-willed or mushy, desirable or losers. That definition has to come from the attitude of the singer and your choice of words that describe the situation being sung about.

I described earlier the process of arriving at the title "You're Just a New Name for an Old Feeling." Now I'd like to share with you the finished lyrics to illustrate creating well-defined characters in a song. Although we never meet the fellow being sung about, we have a pretty good idea what he's up to, what he looks like, and how successful he's going to be. As for the singer, we hear what she says and enjoy her feisty attitude, but we realize there's a chink in her armor, and she really would love to be loved.

YOU'RE JUST A NEW NAME FOR AN OLD FEELING

What you don't know about love
I've already forgotten
Wanting you's easy enough
But what you've got . . . I've already gotten

What makes you think what you do with those eyes
Is all it takes to make my temp'rature rise?
Who do you think it is you're trying so hard to mesmerize?

Chorus: *You're just a new name for an old feeling*
    It's the same game, but it's all in how you play
    Love's an old word, and I need a new meaning
    Oh but touch me . . . and I won't turn away

Don't get the wrong idea
This ain't about tomorrow
You'll be a souvenir
I'll take out and wear whenever I want to

I won't say no to you, I won't even try
But what we're feeling always leads to goodbye
I've seen those dreams you're selling Baby and I . . . I can't buy

(Repeat Chorus)

Bridge: *You can't lose something that you've never had*
    Don't ask for promises I'll never keep
    Love isn't always fair, but you know that
    So don't go wading where the water's too deep . . .

(Repeat Chorus and Fade)

LYRICS/PAMELA PHILLIPS OLAND, MUSIC/JACK CONRAD

Imaginary Lovers

If I'd had all the lovers I've written about, I'd be dead from exhaustion by now! I've learned to be very inventive and have an active imagination.

It's not a very good idea to write strictly from experience, anyway. When you think about it, *who cares* what you did last night? Who cares who loves you/hates you/called you/dumped you? You, your mother, and your best friend, that's who. But if you foist all that maudlin soul-searching personal stuff on the public, it can be embarrassing. And that means not only embarrassing for you to have the whole world privy to the intimate details of your life, but also embarrassing for them when they have to listen.

> There are no new ideas out there, only new ways to say the old ones. Once, in a song for a musical, I had the young hero, who had never fallen in love before, sing, "And I'll bet this feeling never came to any other guys …" It was a joke, naturally. Love has got to be the most universal of emotions. But the secret is that for each person who feels love, different things occur in his mind and heart. There are a billion different scenarios of love. Many of them are as dull as mud. Others take your breath away and can melt even a heart of steel. But if you describe a breathtaking love affair in mundane words and pictures, the end result will simply be this: Who cares?

So who should you write about? That's easy: *them.*

As good lyricists, we observe everyone around us. We watch the little dramas in the relationships of our friends and relatives. We watch strangers in train stations and airports. We draw inspiration from relationships in novels and magazine stories, in films and on TV. We store all the observations, all this information, away in our little computer called a brain. And then we draw from this vast storehouse, adding and subtracting, mixing and matching, and, yes, even adding some insights and spice drawn from our personal experiences. I want to emphasize my belief that it's a deadly error to write strictly about one's own love affairs. On the occasions when I indeed *have* written from experience, I've usually made the characters and situations in my lyrics composites of several relationships. Very few of them were worthy of sustaining an entire song! Rather, it is the artful blending of all the ideas, whether real, observed, or fictional, that makes for an interesting lyric.

When You Say "I"

The most popular songs are those that appear to be written from the listener's point of view. Since not everybody in this world is good at expressing him- or herself, it becomes the job of writers. Writers—of TV sitcoms, films, short stories, novels, songs, poems, nonfiction or journalism—must express the words that others cannot say, the thoughts that others cannot find a way to get out.

In listening to radio psychologists on occasion, I have repeatedly been moved by the incredible vulnerability of people in our society, caused by their inability to simply say what's on their mind. They wonder, "Does my lover love me? How do I tell my partner I'm angry? How do I explain to my children that I'm not divorcing *them?* How do I tell my mother I'm sorry? How do I say 'I love you?'"

Many people cannot even write letters to express themselves. They are bottled up with tangled emotions—love, hate, frustration, anger, infatuation, jealousy, envy, hero-worship, and the like. But because they cannot express

Since not everybody in this world is good at expressing him- or herself, it becomes the job of writers to express the words that others cannot say, the thoughts that others cannot find a way to get out.

themselves, they draw deeper and deeper within, preferring the privacy of loneliness to the gregarious world of conversation and communication. So we must be ready and willing to take up the slack for them and express their lives in our writings.

Visualization

For listeners to relate to our songs, the characters have to be real. It's not enough just to imagine the characters in a song you're writing—you actually have to *become* the characters. How can you possibly write what the person thinks, feels, and says, when you don't know how he or she thinks? How can you see the character's story from her own unique perspective unless you've been inside her brain?

So you have to learn to visualize, from the inside out, the people who populate your songs. Each has a unique perspective that you must find in order to make every song you write original and interesting. You don't want all your songs to sound like they're about *you*, do you? People want to hear about *themselves*, not you. So you have to envision characters with thoughts, feelings, and personalities that make them easily identifiable to listeners.

Visualization is a miraculous tool that enables you to be anyone at all, anywhere at all, in any conceivable situation. Why be limited by the confines of your own life and experience when there are so many other marvelous possibilities? All you have to do is imagine them!

In a way, all the songs we write are about us (the writers) and contain, however veiled, some personal point of view. If we feel strongly about a moral or social issue, it can be hard to understand the opposite contention. We have to let our imagination take over and lead us to understand the other person's motivation.

If, for instance, the lyric involves a man begging forgiveness of a woman and this never happened in your family, your job is to imagine a scenario where these two people would, in fact, let go of these inhibitions and try doing it this way. In other words, you would actually visualize the people in your life who've taught you, either actually or by example, that this is not correct behavior. Then mentally lead them through an exercise in which they would within their own characters, try a new approach. Knowing these people's facial expressions, body language, and predictable vocabulary, you then mold them into the situation you want them to react to. Since this has nothing to do with reality, you have complete license to make the people in your lyric do and say anything you wish. Perhaps by knowing their frailties and limitations, you can better understand what has to be said in the song.

For instance, you can have the man say, "This is so hard for me to do, I've never said this to a woman before . . . but I love you too much to lose you, and rather than let you walk out that door, I have to tell you that I'm sorry, and I truly hope you'll forgive me." You then have to fathom the woman's response—something like, "I can't believe I'm hearing you say this . . . but you know how much I love you, and the fact that you're telling me how sorry you are really makes the difference . . . and I won't leave you." If the song isn't a duet, then at least you've established the point of view and where it's coming from. Again, I stress that songs cannot be written in a vacuum; there must be a motivation and a scenario.

One rather rude but most effective way to practice visualization is to look at perfect strangers you encounter and try to figure out who they are and what makes them they tick. I often do this for fun in restaurants. I try to imagine how life looks through their eyes, why they dress the way they do, what their line of work is, why they think they're attractive, what would make them dye their hair that unflattering color, what their hang-ups are about themselves. I envision having them interact with other strangers across the room and what their encounters would be like. I *visualize* them in happiness, anger, ecstasy, *everything*. It's great entertainment for the price of a cup of coffee.

Do Your Homework

In order to get your ideas on paper, they must first be properly formed and developed. It can't just be "some guy" talking to "some girl." You must intimately know the cast of characters that make up the song. You must know their race, level of education, appearance, age, social habits, intellectual capacity, sense of humor, prankishness, job level, income and housing level, mood swings, emotionalism or stoicism, degree of openness, lifestyle, and temperament.

Does that seem like a lot of research to do for a song about "you and me" and "I love you baby"? Not if you don't want the characters to sound wooden or unconvincing. If you want them to sound and behave like real people, you have to know who they are! If you've taken a few minutes to create back stories on your characters, you'll have a wealth of information that will give rise to the lines you're having them speak. Otherwise, you might be swinging back and forth between lines a college professor might use and those of a street gang member or beach bum.

If you create a back story describing a rich, young, spoiled, beautiful girl who drives a foreign sports car and wears expensive clothes but whose parents were always too busy traveling to pay attention to her, then you'll have a good idea of how she'd react to a plain, sincere, studious boy's attentions. Partly she would scoff at his attentions and partly shy away from his earnest expressions of tenderness. She's used to having the ones she loves pay no attention to her, and she is armed and ready to prevent him from even trying.

Do you see all the nuances of her reaction I was able to pull out after having fully described her? She wasn't just a pretty girl, but one with true emotions and a past that influences the present. You will find that when you can't finish a song you've started, the only answer is to better explore your characters.

You have to pay attention to the details of the back stories you create about your song characters. And by comparison, aren't all the things you're learning about in this book a back story for your career? Though you may not call on all of them very often, they'll all be there in the back of your mind somewhere, waiting to serve you when you get stuck on an idea.

UNIVERSAL IDEAS

Within the concept of a universal song, there is a common experience that appeals to almost everybody who listens to it. Universal songs cross boundaries of age, sex, race, income, job, marital status, and sexual preference. They can be written in any style.

A universal song can make a lot of money if you manage to get it into the right hands. With proper promotion, universal songs become the ones people sing and sing and sing in every showcase in every nightclub and bar in the country. Universal songs are the ones people hum at work and whistle in elevators.

Diverse songs—such as "I Believe I Can Fly," "Change the World," "We Are the World," "Feelings," "You Light Up My Life," "What the World Needs Now," "Stardust," "Yesterday," "Cabaret," "That's Life," "The Greatest Love of All," and hundreds of others—all qualify as universal songs. They have a wide-ranging appeal and ability to say something that touches a familiar chord in every listener, regardless of who they are or what their background is.

The pitfall with writing universal songs is that it's very easy to become trite, preachy, or maudlin. If it is a "point" song, such as a song opposing war or a song about the celebration of life—themes that have been addressed in songs many times by umpteen writers—chances are lots of interesting approaches to the subject have already been used. Being fresh and original in tackling a popular topic is the challenge, and I suggest not rehashing old issues in a predictable fashion. The key is to find something new to say about a familiar subject. And, in a way, isn't that what becoming a songwriter is all about? It isn't the easiest task in life to write a song that everyone will relate to. But it's the most commercial song you'll ever write, as universal appeal is what makes standards.

Try to make a song universal right from the "get-go," since you have total control of what the lyrics are going to say. I offer you an example of a song I wrote that has been widely received as a universal lyric.

I'LL BE YOUR EYES

You close your eyes . . . the sky falls
I watch you build invisible walls
When you believe that the world has lost its heart
No one can blame you for falling apart
Have faith . . .

Chorus: *I'll be your eyes*
                When you can't see the light
                When your tears blind your sight
                Like a candle, I will show the way

                I'll be your eyes
                When the truth's hard to find
                When your heart cheats your mind
                When the dream dies
                I'll be your eyes

After all, you're flesh and blood
When you fall . . . hold on to love
All of your life you've been strong, you've been proud
A lonely island apart from the crowd
Have faith . . .

(Repeat Chorus)

LYRICS/PAMELA PHILLIPS OLAND, MUSIC/PAUL JANZ
(AS RECORDED BY PAUL JANZ/ALSO ANNE MURRAY)

What made that song so universal? It says things that we can all relate to. We've all needed to lean on somebody at some time in our lives, and this is a song about somebody offering that strong shoulder to lean on.

Some of us who listen to these lyrics think of ourselves as the singer, and we think of those to whom we can offer this kindness. Others relate to the lyrics as the person who needs to hear somebody say this. The lyrics give us something and someone to hope for. They somehow makes us feel less alone.

Actually, the song came about in a rather unusual fashion, and because of the special circumstances that surrounded it, I have always believed it was something important that I was, if you will, "destined" to write.

My co-writer, Paul Janz, gave me the tape of the melody on a trip I made to Vancouver to write with him for his A&M Records album. He said that he was hoping to write the song for his brother, who was feeling kind of down at the time.

I was in my hotel room later that day, and I wrote a list of titles that occurred to me to fill that particular hook spot in the melody. I called him up and read him the list, and he immediately was attracted to "I'll Be Your Eyes."

I suggested a vague story line to him, which he approved of, and I set to work.

I wrote the lyric quite fast, in about two hours, then called him and read it to him. He was delighted and wrote it down immediately. It was to undergo a couple of minor changes in lyrics but stayed essentially the same right up to the recorded version.

Having delivered the song, I stretched out on the sofa in my suite with a novel I'd brought with me, something I had always meant to find time to read. It was the classic *Jane Eyre* by Charlotte Brontë. I opened the book to the page where I'd left off and proceeded to read the next chapter. An hour later, Jane has made the journey back to find Rochester and tell him she can't live without him, only to find the estate has burned in a terrible fire. She takes the buggy to a local inn and inquires about the fire. She's told that Rochester is alive, though blinded in the fire, and he and his servants have gone to stay at the smaller country manor. She rushes there and throws herself into his adoring arms, telling him she wants to be with him always. He responds by telling her that he's blind—how can she want him? And she tells him that . . . yes, she'll be his eyes.

Whereas "I'll Be Your Eyes" was an example of a song that is universal in the sense that it's widely understood, there is a whole category of songs that are universal—quite literally—in that they deal with world issues. This includes songs about war and peace, world unity, brotherly love, the homeless or poor, friendship, social issues of the day, music, dancing, happiness, cars, sailing, the beauty of nature, work, and songs exalting God.

Here's an example of a universal song on a universal theme: home. I wrote it with Cory Lerios for the "Trojan Wars" episode of Hallmark's Crayola Kids Adventures. The universal theme is the feeling that home is never far away as long as you hold it in your heart.

HOME IS IN YOUR HEART
When your home's far away
And all you feel is blue
If you can't fight the tears, let them fall
Dream a dream about a day
Warmth and love surrounded you
And your home won't seem far away at all

Chorus: *Home is in your heart*
Home is in your mind
Home's the one place in this world
You never leave behind

As long as you may live
No matter where you are
Close your eyes and you'll be home
'Cause home is in your heart.

When you yearn to return
And you can't sleep at night
'Cause it hurts to be so sad inside
It's a wond'rous thing to learn
All you need to feel alright
Is to go to your mem'ries and you'll find . . .

Chorus: *Home is in your heart*
Home is in your mind
Home's the one place in this world
You never leave behind

As long as you may live
No matter where you are
Close your eyes and you'll be home
'Cause home is in your heart.

Music/Cory Lerios, Lyrics/Pamela Phillips Oland for *Trojan Wars*

A love song can also be a universal song if the images in it boil down to a very commonly held point of view on love. That means love found or love lost, love sought, or forever love. It may contain details of the relationship, but they must be specific and general at the same time. They must strike all listeners who hear them as a story that could be about themselves.

One final category for universal songs would be simple points of view, or "slices of life," as they're sometimes called. These deal in moments. They are very popular in musical theater, propelling the story forward by explaining the character's thoughts of the moment in song. Examples include "The Impossible Dream" from *Man of La Mancha,* "Old Man River" from *Showboat,* "Whistle a Happy Tune" from *The King and I,* and "Circle of Life" from *The Lion King.*

Love songs may be universal, and so may songs that describe a slice of life. Obviously, the more universal a lyric is, the more fans it will find. So you should always strive to make your work as broadly appealing as possible. Most of the great copyrights (used here to mean "standards") down through the years boast universal lyrics.

> *Love songs are a great gift to give others. Indeed, they are one of the only gifts I can think of that you can give away and still keep.*

Everybody Loves a Love Song

Why does everyone write *love* songs? Why is *love* the single most celebrated subject in popular songwriting?

Early on in every songwriter's career, you develop an intense annoyance at the shallowness of the subject matter of songs. Song after song on the radio provides us with a seemingly endless repertory of lovers' laments, tales of love desired, love achieved, love ended, love mourned. "Who cares?" is the exasperated response. "There's so much more in the world we should be addressing in songs." Well, I can't argue with that; but I have a very practical outlook on the subject.

The fact is, *people love to think about love!* It's *the* universal idea. Just think back a moment to your teenage years, when you were obsessed by the girl or boy sitting next to you in history class, who so totally dominated your thoughts that you kept forgetting to answer when the teacher called on you! Kids always have been and will eternally be fascinated by thoughts of blossoming sexuality. When they listen to songs about young love, they instantly place themselves in the picture. They buy the records and listen to them hundreds of times, fantasizing about their imagined (or sometimes real) love affairs.

The deal is, as songwriters, we are not limited by any constraints at all. We can write as many songs a day, a week, a lifetime, as we can possibly cram in. They can be as diverse as they are numerous. But if they are being written for the popular radio market, they are most likely to get a listen if they are about love. I didn't create the market; I can only report on it.

Someone once said, "Love makes the world go round." And I can think of no better reason to write love songs than the fact that people love to hear them. Furthermore, since love is so important, and so many people are unable to express their own feelings, the songwriter has the opportunity—even the duty—to say what the listener can only think. Love songs are a great gift to give others. Indeed, they are one of the only gifts I can think of that you can give away and still keep.

Types of Love Songs

It's important to differentiate between love songs you write for and about yourself and your private loves (which are wonderfully cathartic as a writing process but not necessarily commercial) and love songs you are creating for the marketplace (for someone else to record). This is not placing a value judgment on whether your song with a very personal story is "good" or "bad." It's simply stating that while your situation may be of earth-shattering importance to you, your song might need a broader outlook to appeal to the mass market.

Since I'm sure you are reading this book because you want to get your songs recognized in the mainstream of the recording industry, we need to focus on the content of commercial lyrics.

Let's consider what types of love songs you can write and which are the most favored:

1. *In first person* to *the loved one.* In this type, you are writing, "*I* love *you*" or, "*you* love *me.*" This is the most successful style of love song, as it is totally personal and likely to be related to by the largest number of listeners. It also has its drawbacks, as lyricists tend to get over-maudlin and sentimental in this style. Just because you are writing a personal love song doesn't mean it needs to send the listener into sugar shock. This style of song can be about successful, positive love ("now that I have you"); about love remembered ("you were the best love of my life"); love unrequited ("why can't you see how I love you?"); love sought ("I'm gonna get you!"); or impossible love ("I can't go on loving you anymore"). The examples are virtually endless, from Ray Charles's hit of D. Gibson's "I Can't Stop Loving You" to Elton John's "Your Song" to Billy Joel's "I Love You Just the Way You Are" to Tom Kelly and Billy Steinberg's composition recorded by Madonna, "Like a Virgin."

2. *In first person* about *loved one.* In this type, you are writing "I love *her* or *him.*" This is not as intimate a style and not as popular as the first person to the loved one. It takes forms such as, "He doesn't know I exist," "Tell her I don't love her anymore," "Where is he now?" and so on. Some successes in this genre include the Beatles' "Norwegian Wood," Jimmy Webb's "By the Time I Get to Phoenix," and Ellie Greenwich and Jeff Barry's "Leader of the Pack."

3. *In first person plural* about *love together.* In this type, you are writing what "we" feel and what "we" have. Examples include Barry Gibb's duet with Barbra Streisand, "Guilty"; Leon Russell's "This Masquerade," a hit by George Benson; and Boz Skaggs's hit recorded by Rita Coolidge, "We're All Alone."

4. *In third person, narrative style.* In this type, you are writing, "He loves her" or "She loves him." It is my experience that songs in the third person—that is, talking about *him, her,* or *them,* songs about other people's love that have no connection with you the narrator or you the listener—are less likely to get recorded and become famous. There are notable exceptions, such as "Jack and Diane," who populated one of John Cougar Mellencamp's biggest hits; the slices of life that fill Stephen Bishop's "On and On"; and Jerry Lieber and Mike Stoller's anthem to trouble, "Poison Ivy," recorded by the Coasters.

To write a successful love song, remember the following tips:

- *Be honest.* Let the song be more meaningful than artsy.
- *Be straightforward.* Get in. Get to the point. Get the story told. Get out.
- *Remember who your characters are.* Be true to their points of view.
- From beginning to end, *make sure they stay in character.*
- *Be original.* Don't rehash tired old ideas.
- *Review your work.* When your song is finished, make sure your ideas come across to the listener.

Get Off the Soapbox

At one time or another, most of us have written songs that warn of the dangers of nuclear war, an obvious universal subject. You'd be amazed at how many songs have been written on that woeful topic, using a thousand unique titles—from the humorous (such as "One Nuclear Bomb Can Ruin Your Whole Day" and "Nuclear War? Not Before I Break the Top Ten!"), to the morose ("Mushroom Cloud" and "No One's Left to Tell the Tale"). Songwriters are a clever bunch—they come up with poignant and moving ways to bring to people's attention subjects such as nuclear waste, energy shortages, child abuse, casual sex, street people, old age, parental love, love of pets, and so on.

But the key to success here is *attitude.* You must present the issue with objectivity—sometimes with irony—and *always* without preaching.

How did you like it when your mother used to tell you how to wear your hair, how to dress, whom to have as friends? Not much. But you see that's exactly how people feel when they listen to your diatribes about how they should become better people, how they should improve the world, and how they should think, feel, and behave.

That's the word that's the big "no-no" here: *should.* It is really a very objectionable way to write, telling people what they *should* and *should not* do. It immediately turns off the listener who doesn't agree. There are always listeners who are going to squirm, knowing that they are guilty of what you have just warned against. Listeners should not be made to feel like they are being lectured.

So how do you handle writing about a cause that is near and dear to you? You write about it from the point of view of *yourself.* This was done brilliantly in the Seidah Garrett and Glen Ballard composition "Man in the Mirror," recorded by Michael Jackson. In this lyric, the singer is expressing what is wrong with the world, what hopelessness and tragedy he sees around him, and he vows to take action to make the world a better place, starting with "the man in the mirror," himself. Instead of saying to the listener, "You should go out and make the world a better place," he is saying, in effect, "I'm starting with me," thus implying that everyone listening can follow suit and start with him- or herself. He doesn't say you *have* to, mind you; he's just saying *he* is going to, which is a whole world of difference in approach.

Preachy lyrics rarely, if ever, get recorded. Nobody likes the guy on the soapbox who appears to think he knows better than everybody else, especially if he hits home with something he says! At best, the writer's preachy lyrics are based on his own experience and opinions. The chances of these being the same as the singer's are slim.

So do yourself a favor: Leave the preaching to the guy on the soapbox at Hyde Park Corner. When you want to give advice, write as if your singer were living an experience and modestly learning the joys and pitfalls of it as the song progresses.

Nobody Loves a Loser

Sadness can be a great concept for a song if it is turned into irony—"Now that you've left me, I can go a week without picking up my clothes"; "I'm only lonely when I'm awake or sleeping"; and so forth.

If you insist on writing a song about being lonely, at the very least make sure that the song's point of view is the *broken heart,* making clear that it is the broken romance that has caused this sadness and this *does not apply to life in general.*

We can all relate to a broken relationship. However, the utter devastation that it can wreak in our lives is something we'd rather not dwell on. Over the long term, we tend to romanticize broken relationships, remembering what was good about them instead of what was hurtful.

Even assuming that you are going through the worst, most pitiful period of your life, don't inflict that mood on *all* your songs, even though it's inevitable that you write it into some of them. It will become boring, like a drone, to those who regularly look at your work. In fact, a blue time could be a perfect opportunity to really exercise your craft muscles and write some stuff based only on observation and instinct, rather than chronicling *My Life in the Pits.*

An artist's image (whether soloist or group) is all he or she has. And while artists can be tender and vulnerable, and occasionally victims of rotten, no-good heartbreakers that make us want to love them more and rush to their rescue, this is the exception and not the rule as far as the material they choose.

It's a good bet that very few singers want to come across with a message that nobody loves them and nobody wants them. Just consider: If you were the artist (assuming, even if you are one, that you are writing a song for someone else to sing), would *you* feel comfortable singing this song of woe and sorrow, this requiem to a dead romance? In other words, would you want to go out of your way to sound like a *loser?*

Not that anything is wrong with writing such songs to get these emotions out of your system. But let them be "living room hits," if you like; play them for friends and family. Just know the difference between personal plaints and commercial songs that you're trying to pitch to recording stars. A song with hope, a song with a happy ending, a song with a promising twist at the end, a song talking about love in a positive fashion—these are your best bets if you're going for the commercial market.

One A&R man who has my total respect explained that a song is like an advertising campaign to sell the product: the singer's image. So remember: Unless the "down" lyrics are so brilliantly poignant that they "stop the heart," most singers will gravitate toward songs that paint positive images of them.

Sarcasm can be an interesting device if used in a humorous, even tongue-in-cheek manner. I'd like to share with you a Country song I wrote with Eric Horner that's filled with sarcasm, but we both think it is a lot of fun. The singer comes across as a charmer and irresistible.

GOOD GIRLS LOVE BAD BOYS

What's a nice girl like you doin' in my face like this?
Don't you know these arms are on your Mama's don't do list?
You can't play at hearts like you used to play with toys
And I'll never understand
Why *Good Girls Love Bad Boys*

Chorus: *Well you're a heart-stoppin', eye-poppin',*
    Breathtakin', crazy-makin' Angel of Desire
    And I'm a heart-breakin', devastatin' Sweet-talkin' devil
    And you're too close to the fire

I oughtta say Go home right now
While you still have the choice;
But you know I won't, Dontcha . . .
Cause *Good Girls Love Bad Boys*

There's a fever in your eyes. Your pulse is running wild.
You love to flirt with Danger . . . and Danger's just my style
You're trying to ignore that tiny little voice
That's telling you I'm trouble . . .
Cause *Good Girls Love Bad Boys*

(Repeat Chorus)

Words and Music/Pamela Phillips Oland and Eric Horner

Anger is also fine in a lyric if it is countered with strength. "You left me for her, and I was all alone; but now she's left you the same way you left me. So you think I'm sitting here waiting with open arms for you to come back, but guess what? I've found someone new who taught me what love *really* means." And so forth.

Conveying an Artist's Image

Obviously, you wouldn't want to write the same kind of song for Michael Jackson that you would for Willie Nelson. You wouldn't pitch a sex-drugs-rock-'n'-roll lyric to Amy Grant. You have to do your homework. Listen to the artist's prior work and get a feeling for what he or she cares about, what he or she thinks is important, how he or she feels about things such as love and relationships. Is the artist cynical, sardonic or sarcastic? Is he or she lucky or tragic in love? For instance, if you study the overall work of successful writer/artist Stevie Nicks (Fleetwood Mac), you'll find that most of her lyrics deal with ill-fated romances. If you study the magnificent lyrics of Billy Joel or Sting, I doubt if you'll find a meaningless, empty, "filler fluff" word or phrase in either's catalogue. And if you're thinking of writing a good R & B funk tune for Stevie Wonder, think again: He is constantly renewing his career with his own marvelous blend of today's pop with old-fashioned gentle ideas that transcend fads or categorization; in other words, he writes and sings standards. By the same token, save the postage money if you're planning to send a Brian McKnight–style tune to a Rap artist.

Once you feel familiar and conversant with an artist's attitude, by all means deal with a current topic or write a fresh perspective on it. But when you get done, ask yourself if that sounds like something the artist would want to sing. And, I repeat: Beware of writing from a depressed point of view. You don't want to convey desperation because it's one subject no artist will want to sing about unless he or she wrote the song!

MIND VERSUS HEART

At opposite ends of the spectrum are lyrics that are *too intellectual* and lyrics that are *too emotional.* Yet the best lyrics have something of both: They are the most delicate balance, the most pleasing combination of sentiment and thoughtfulness. True communication means you've reached your audience both in mind *and* heart.

As a rule of thumb, *intellectual* words, phrases, and concepts are reacted to mentally, with thoughts and evaluations; *emotional* words, phrases, and concepts are designed to impact on a subconscious level first, bringing on tears, laughter, brooding, longing, desire, love, hate, or any other strong feeling. Feelings, though they are purportedly defined in the dictionary, are always new and volatile and can't be confined to mental cubbyholes.

The tendency to be too intellectual often stems from the writer's desire to project an image as intelligent and capable. This is perfectly normal, since each of us wants to appear to have a brain in our head that does more than make our lips flap. So the pursuit of intelligent lyrics often takes the writer into intellectual lyrics. What's the difference? An *intelligent* lyric is one that is carefully thought out and clearly communicates the message or story. An intelligent lyric is readily understandable to the listener and appeals to the listener's values of right and wrong, good and bad, love and hate, happiness and tragedy. An intelligent lyric is thought-provoking and capable of being identified with by any number of listeners.

An *intellectual* lyric, on the other hand, is one that's simply "thinky." It does not impact emotionally, because listeners must spend the majority of their "instant reaction" time trying to figure out what in blazes the singer is talking about! Intellectual lyrics force listeners to devote so much energy to the question, "What does that mean?" that the song is over before the message has ever gotten across, which often takes the lyrics across the border into the realm of poetry.

To complicate matters, there are also what I like to call *clever* lyrics. A clever lyric is one that specializes in playing with language, contorting famous phrases into new variations, conjuring up unexpected pictures, saying things in an unusual and surprising way. Often witty, incorporating intricate rhyme schemes and catchy phrases, clever lyrics show off the writer's talents marvelously but are often sadly lacking in heart. Lyrics that are *too clever* are, except in the case of special material or show music, inappropriate. *Too clever* means a writer is showing off an agility with words, and the lyric has become all show and no substance. But used sparingly, clever lyrics can be a most magical arrow in the songwriter's bow.

Writing what we have called intelligent lyrics does not guarantee that they will have an emotional impact; conversely, not all lyrics need to be vastly intelligent in order to be moving or touching. Lyrics that go for emotional impact touch listeners in a different way than those that are "thinky." They elicit more of a visceral response. Where intellectual lyrics are listened to and digested thoughtfully, emotional lyrics either go straight to the tear ducts or act like a quick kick in the gut.

You'll have done your job as a communicator if your lyrics can move your audience and your listeners neither know nor care how you did it—they just feel a whole emotional/intellectual jumble of responses.

You have a great deal of joy to look forward to when your work gets played and sung on the radio, TV, films, and stage. Through your songs—if you've learned your communication skills well—you will touch the hearts, the minds, and the lives of countless people you've never even met.

THE MOST IMPORTANT SONG YOU'VE EVER WRITTEN

If you're a professional songwriter, people are depending on you for your best work every time. Each collaborator has taken care and pride in his work and expects you to do the same. Thus, my advice is this: *Approach every song you write as if it is the most important song you will ever write.* Don't say, "Oh, this is just for . . . " or, "This isn't a special project." If it isn't an important idea, melody, or project, why on earth should you be wasting your time to write it? Each time a composer asks me to collaborate on a song, I give it everything I've got. If a great line occurs to me, I don't hold it back, saving it for some imagined later, greater project. I choose to make *this* project the great one. There is no tomorrow or next song when you're writing a song. *This one right now* has to carry all your talents, gifts, abilities, aspirations, creativity.

I know it's tempting to hoard good ideas, but the most miraculous thing about ideas is that they never run out. Ideas are like movie heroes: They always come and rescue us just when we need them most! So never worry about putting a great idea squarely into the song you're working on *right now*. Tomorrow's song will take care of itself. Right now concentrate on making *this one* the best you've ever done. Give it all your ammunition, and the rewards you'll see as the results of a job well crafted will exhilarate and delight you.

4

UNDERSTANDING THE CRAFT

t truly amazes me how many people are writing songs. What's even more amazing is that every single one of us writes songs with the absolutely single-minded intention of getting them recorded. In talking to songwriters who live as far apart as Moscow, Helsinki, London, South Dakota, and Phoenix, Arizona, it becomes clear that we all aspire to write songs for the very same projects!

So why are some songwriters successful, regardless of where they live or what else they do with their time, while others write for years and never seem to get anywhere? Successful writers understand the craft and work within the confines of time-proven theories as to what makes a song great.

Great ideas and musical talent are not enough. Winning poetry competitions or talent contests isn't enough. A lyricist must have a genuine affinity for the style and process of songwriting. Language must flow easily for you, and patience and the ability to be self-critical are paramount qualities.

Anybody with a little imagination who has listened to the radio a few thousand times can write what purports to be a lyric. But unless aspiring lyricists understand the process of lyric writing and songwriting overall; unless they have the ability to be self-policing and are willing to rewrite until the lyrics are all but perfect—success will continue to elude them.

In this chapter, we'll explore the mechanics of creating lyrics: song formulas, titles, dummy melodies, and criteria for judging one's own lyrics. We'll talk about the secrets, the pitfalls, the common mistakes. Everyone has unique talents and abilities to think that sets his or her work apart; but the lyricists who make a living writing songs also have a high respect for their craft and the process. To adapt Thomas Edison's famous quote for our purposes, we could say, "Art is 10 percent inspiration; craft is 90 percent perspiration."

THE ELEMENTS OF A SONG

Successful writers understand the craft and work within the confines of time-proven theories as to what makes a song great.

Trying to write songs without knowing the elements of a song is like trying to speak without knowing a language.

I would be lying if I didn't bluntly state that what makes a song fabulous is its unique inspiration, and not how well you stick to the rules of songwriting.

On the other hand, I would also be leading you astray if I didn't emphasize the need to set your beautiful writing into a manageable framework. Compare it with placing a jewel in a setting, or nature's placing of a flower on a stem surrounded by a pattern of leaves. Nobody really pays much attention to the prongs supporting the jewel, just as people pay only passing tribute to the stem and leaves around a blossom. We just accept that they're there to keep the beauty in its place.

First of all, you must understand some of the basic terms used to describe the elements of a song. Understanding each of these elements is *critical*. Trying to write songs without knowing the elements of a song is like trying to speak without knowing a language.

Perhaps this is what has kept *you* from writing commercial songs up to this point: You haven't known how to be consistent. Consistency in songwriting will come when all the elements described below become second nature.

Here's an example of a verse/chorus style song with the parts identified.

Title: **WHEN WE NEED IT BAD**

Verse #1:   You're not tellin' me somethin'
            But eyes don't lie
            You should know by now
            My heart is standing by

Verse #2:   When life feels hard
            And tears fall free
            You've gotta lose that load
            And just lean on me

Build: 'Cause we've got love at last
            We're not alone now anymore

Lead-in: Let me say the words that you're dyin' for

(also known as "walk-up" or "hook")

Chorus: When we need it bad *(hook)*
Baby ain't it nice to know we've got it good overall
And it's understood
That When we need it bad *(hook)*
We can count on one another,
Love will see us through
You've got it good for me, and me for you.

Verse #3:   Draw the shades on the window
And light a fire
I'll kiss you sweet and kindle
Your desire

Verse #4:   Come over here
Turn out the light
I'm gonna make you smile
If it takes all night

Build: 'Cause there'll be other days
When I'm the one who falls apart
"walk-up": And you'll comfort me with your tender heart

(Repeat Chorus)

Bridge: *You taught me love . . .*
Is made of give and take
You used to bend so far
I made you break

But I've changed so much
I've learned that love can touch
With just a word or smile
"walk-up": *So stay awhile, because . . .*

(Repeat Chorus)

LYRICS/PAMELA PHILLIPS OLAND, MUSIC/TAKA TAKAYANAGI AND
PATRICK HENDERSON (AS RECORDED BY PEABO BRYSON)

The Hook

The hook is *the part of the song you walk away humming.* Therefore, if a song is cleverly written, there can be more than one hook in a single song. The main hook of the song almost certainly has to be the title. But the first-line melody can be memorable enough to be thought of as a secondary hook. Certainly, many songs have instrumental solos that are hooks. Also, the use of drum machines and synthesizers as the basis for writing songs has spawned a whole new generation of songs built around drum loops and bass lines, with the melody and lyrics only incidental additions. In the early eighties, Ray Parker Jr.'s catchy "Ghostbusters," relied very heavily on the bass line as a hook and had very little melody at all. Thousands of songs have been written following that style since then. A piano figure that runs through the track and is instantly recognizable can make a terrific hook. The three recorded versions of "Nobody Loves Me Like You Do" have all used the identical piano figure played by Steve Rucker, the pianist Jim Dunne and I hired to play on the demo. In fact, Jermaine Jackson actually brought in Steve to reprise his piano styling on the Whitney Houston/Jermaine version of the song. So remember to write a humdinger of a title hook, but when you're producing that demo, don't forget to add all those secondary hooks. (By the way, please note that, in everyday usage, the word *hook* as it relates to a verse-chorus style song is often used to refer to the entire chorus.)

The Verse

Typically, a verse is the main body of the storytelling. It's the part that contains all the important information about the *who, what, where, when,* and *why* of the situation depicted in the song. As I mentioned earlier, in a journalistic news story this information is all contained in the first paragraph, with the most important, relevant, or juicy information placed at the very earliest point possible to capture the reader's interest. In a song, the goal is the same: Attract the interest of the listener and set up the relevant situation at the earliest possible moment—in the first verse. Advance the story in succeeding verses by expanding the listener's knowledge about the situation, bringing in other information pertinent to what's happening to your song's characters.

The Build

(This is also known as pre-chorus, "B" section, or setup.) This is the section that leads out of the verse and builds dramatically as a release into the chorus. The build is usually two to four lines long and melodically escalates to a dramatic point, usually leading to an unresolved chord that "hangs" there and begs to be resolved by the chorus. Lyrically, the build should lead right into the lead line of the chorus. (For example, if the first line of the chorus began, "Right now . . . ," the lead-in would be something like, "And I'm ready to love you . . . " Thus,

> *Attract the interest of the listener and set up the relevant situation at the earliest possible moment—in the first verse.*

when sung, it would come out, "And I'm ready to love you . . . Right now!" Without a good lead-in to set up the chorus idea, the chorus is disjointed from the story, and comes "out of nowhere."

The Chorus

When a song contains a chorus—and not all songs do—the main function of it is to *hammer home the hook!* The chorus resolves the action, explains why you bothered to write this song, explains the meaning of the hook line, and is designed as the part of the song the listener looks forward to hearing repeated over and over. While there are never more than two chorus sections in a row in the body of a song, at the end of a song with a chorus formula, there is usually a series of repeats of the chorus, known as the "out" or "fade" choruses. In a verse-chorus style song, *the chorus always contains the title of the song.* It is traditional to keep the same lyrics for all choruses, though sometimes a lyric line may be altered in the fade. Just don't change the hook line itself.

Becoming adept at writing a hit chorus is a secret to the art of popular songwriting.

Turnaround

This is a phrase used to explain that the hook line is used not only at the beginning of the chorus, but at the end of the chorus as well, slightly turning around the meaning of the hook line and making a strong payoff for the chorus. Turnarounds are especially popular in Country songs. For example, examine the chorus of my Country lyric "If It Was You":

IF IT WAS YOU
John and I moved in our house today
The moving vans brought all the boxes we'd each stored away
And we began unpacking old memories
Two heartbreaks, two toasters, and two TVs

He played a record that you used to hate
We celebrated with some takeout, on paper plates
He held me as he whispered, "Goodnight, my love"
I felt so guilty for what I was thinking of . . .

Chorus: *You . . . If It Was You*
There'd have been candles and champagne
If It Was You
You would have set the night aflame
And I would have had everything that he'll never do
But I wouldn't have a love that's true
If It Was You

Though his hands are rough, his touch is warm
And they didn't have the finer things where he was born
But all the wonders of heaven are in his eyes
And what I'm leavin' behind with this sunrise . . . is

Chorus: *You . . . If It Was You*
            There'd have been candles and champagne
            If It Was You
            You would have set the night aflame
            And I would have had everything that he'll never do
            But I wouldn't have a love that's true
            If It Was You
            No I wouldn't have a love that's true
            If It Was You

FROM "IF IT WAS YOU," LYRICS/PAMELA PHILLIPS OLAND,
MUSIC/ERIC HORNER

The first use in the chorus has the singer imagining the romantic night she'd have had with the man she is singing to. But in the last line, she reveals that although he doesn't provide the trappings of romance, her new man actually *loves* her.

One of my best uses of a turnaround is at the end of the lyric "End of the Line," a story song of the "American heartland" genre. The title in the song can mean the end of the relationship, the end of the railway ride, the end of the telephone wire, and the end of the line connecting the two lives:

END OF THE LINE
Midnight and the train pulls out
Leavin' him standin' at the railway station
[Spoken]: *He's gonna have a long time to think about her*
Daylight but she still can't sleep
Bein' without him is a strange sensation

Miles and miles are between them now
She'd turn around, but she don't know how

Chorus: *Some days it was just no good*
            Some nights they could make it better
            He said are we out of time?
            She said it's the end of the line.

Meeting on the dark back streets
Mama and Daddy didn't guess her secret
School days are behind them now
Tried to get a job but he just can't keep it

Love flies out the window fast
They're short on cash, how can a first love last?

Chorus: *Those two were the sweetheart pair*
               Those two were the ones most envied
               He said are we out of time?
               She said it's the end of the line.

Bridge: *Together forever . . . the promise is broken*
               What happens to love when it's out in the open
               They took a blood oath and mingled their fingers
               The air hangs heavy with the dream of love that lingers

Mornin' and it starts to rain
Here she comes knockin' at her destination
Watch the phone, that won't make it ring
Given the chance, could they ever change a thing?

Chorus: *Love dies but the heart lives on*
               She cries for the loss of her lover
               He said guess we're out of time
               She said it's the end . . .

               He said where did we go wrong ?
               She said that she'll never recover
               He said guess we're out of time
               She said Let the end of the line . . . Go . . .
               Just let it go.

LYRICS/PAMELA PHILLIPS OLAND, MUSIC/TODD SMALLWOOD

The Vocal Bridge

Many songs seem to cry out for an additional nuance in the story, one additional piece of information that ties everything together, and for this we write a "bridge." A bridge is that part in the middle of the song that gets you to understand the singer's point of view on the subject. It can be an ironic commentary on the occurrences; it can add a vital but heretofore unknown fact to the story; it can add an insight that will change the direction of the song. In any case, it should lead to the concluding portion of the song, be that a final verse or an "out" chorus.

1. In a *verse-chorus (A-B-A-B-C-B)* style song, a bridge or "C" section is generally a "change" device that is used to bring you out of the second chorus and move you into the third verse.

2. In a *verse-bridge (A-A-B-A)* style song, which does not use a chorus, the bridge or, in this case, the "B" section, comes after the first two verses. Its purpose is to link the story to the outcome that happens in the third and last verse.

Break or Breakdown

This is sometimes called *Instrumental Bridge*. Before going into the final section of the song, be it a final verse/"out" chorus, or just a series of "out" choruses, it is sometimes customary to introduce a musical section with no words.

Often, traditionally, this is a sax or guitar solo. Sometimes it's a repeating bass line or an intricate drum pattern. Sometimes this is a substitute for a vocal bridge, and sometimes both a break and a vocal bridge are used. If that is the case, usually the break comes after the second chorus, followed by the bridge, followed by the last verse and the "out" choruses.

Rap

We all know that Rap is a musical art form in which the entire song is chanted in rhythmic speech—with pitch and without melody—to a groove track. Yet, if you're writing Rap, I think it is useful to have an understanding of its historical significance and roots. So I asked my great friend Donald McKayle, a historian of such things, whose lifetime of work includes the brilliant choreography of the musicals *Sophisticated Ladies, Raisin,* and *Ain't Nothin' But the Blues,* to enlighten me. From his rich store of knowledge on this subject, I learned that Rap, or "rhythmic palaver" began its tradition as an oral history of the African American culture. Its roots are in "field hollers" from the days when disenfranchised slaves in the fields communicated by singing from field to field. When the African slaves' drums were taken from them, they started a tradition called "patting juba," meaning a slapping of the body parts—thighs, arms, chest—in body percussion. Along the way, hawkers on the streets co-opted the tradition with "street calls." Railroad conductors famously palavered the long lists of names of upcoming towns, and riverboat captains would use the rhythmic palaver to communicate the safety of their location on the river. In fact, the author Samuel Clements took his pen-name Mark Twain from a riverboat call: "*Mark twine, four fathoms on the starboard line, mark twine . . .*" During the unionist movement, from the thirties through the forties, the "talking blues" were a staple in the Black music community. Country writers such as Johnny Cash picked up that tradition with a kind of "talking country blues." Children's games grew up with a chanting called "ring shouts," which were done while clapping and patting the body. In "hambone," a city version of the "patting juba," kids wore corduroy pants, as the fabric provided a great instrument when rubbed with the fingernails! Today "gangsta Rap" which is an outgrowth of all these "rhythmic palavers," expresses anger and anguish at the injustices of the culture.

In the same tradition, going all the way back to the fifties, a number of hit songs such as Elvis Presley's "Are You Lonesome Tonight?" have featured a spoken section in what would otherwise be the "bridge" of the song. This device enables artists to break down the communication barriers by honestly saying what's on their mind, while the melody just keeps on playin'!

Further, many classic R & B songs feature rap "breakdowns"—breaking into a very rhythmic spoken pattern for eight to sixteen bars before the "out choruses."

My suggestion is that if you feel drawn to writing Rap, make your rhymes extremely clever, be right on the money with the point you want to make, and make sure your "hook" contains a powerful statement.

Meter

A line must always have a measured, patterned arrangement of syllables (known as the "scansion" or "scan"), primarily according to stress and length. This creates a rhythm that can easily be sung, and, of course, it makes the composer's job much easier if you provide a lyric with a well-metered construction. Conversely, any melody you receive to write lyrics to will have a recognizable meter into which you can place your words. When writing a lyric, it should be set up so that it has a pattern you can tap your foot to. Good meter suggests predictable, comfortable rhythm patterns. Each verse in a song must follow the same meter, ditto for each chorus. Keep your meter straight, and whatever else may be wrong with your song, it will be eminently singable!

Remember that you are writing lyrics, not poetry. Know the difference when using sing-songy poetic meters such as: "Iambic pentameter" (literally "five iambs," an iamb being a metric foot of two syllables), which, as a practical matter, reads "I never *thought* - I *had* - a *heart* - to *break;*" and "Trochaic," which is a metrical foot consisting of one long syllable followed by one short one, for instance, "*Now* you – *see* me – *now* you – *miss* me." (Each meter has a different "cadence," which means the rhythm in which the words fall and flow.) It is helpful to look at it this way: Poetry is to lyrics what

Poetry is to lyrics what ballet is to jazz dancing: rigorous attention to form versus free expression within a defined framework.

ballet is to jazz dancing: rigorous attention to form versus free expression within a defined framework.

Rhyme

Within a song, there can be several different rhyme patterns. The verse, chorus, and bridge do not have to have the same rhyme patterns as each other. Each time you write a new song section, be conscious of exactly what rhyme pattern you're going for. The more unusual the rhyme, the more interesting it sounds. Many song writers always fall into the same sort of rhyme scheme in every song they write; if you slip into that habit, it will make your songs boring. Varying rhyme schemes means you'll sometimes rhyme lines that follow each other in order and other times rhyme alternate lines.

If I were to write the following verse with rhymes on the first/third and second/fourth lines:

> The phone is ringing on the wall
> But I pretend I'm not at home
> Don't want to see your face at all
> Why don't you take a hike to Nome

I couldn't follow it with a second verse that rhymed first/second and third/ fourth lines as follows:

> The day you left you took the car
> And you took off to be a star
> You were a flop, and that must sting
> But I can't help that you can't sing

I mentioned there could be several rhyme patterns within a song. Let's look at *internal* rhymes, which are what happens when a word at the end of a line rhymes with a word in the middle of that or the next line, or a word in the middle of a line rhymes with a word in the middle of another line. If you can manage to come up with these *internal* rhymes as well as end-of-line rhymes, you have one more important device going for your song. Here's a simple illustration:

> I love you *so,* I always will
> I don't know *why* we came apart
> I think you *know* I want you still
> I can't *deny* what's in my heart

Internal rhymes also help a lyricist create a more complex verse structure:

Down the river of change we're *sailing*
Bailing out of *here*
I *fear* our lives were *changing* much too *fast*
Without some *rearranging,* our future was in the *past*
The signs were getting *stronger*
Sayin' we'll *pay* if we *stay* here this *way* . . . any *longer.*

There are no hard and fast rules as to which rhyme schemes are the best ones to use, though whenever a lyric of mine is criticized for rhyme, it is more often of the first type, that is, rhyming every other line. Personally, I love to experiment with rhymes, and sometimes even rhyme the first, second, third, and fourth lines of the first verse with the matching lines in the second verse. That means nothing within a verse rhymes, but the two verses rhyme with each other in their entirety. For example:

He blew in like a hurricane
A stranger in this lazy town
His hair was long, his eyes were black
And trouble was his name.

He didn't see her face as plain
And so he never put her down
But people talked behind her back
And called his love a game.

Use rhyme cleverly, trying always to find interesting, new things to say.

Space

Not every moment of a song has to be filled up with words. A song can be wonderful if room is left between the lines, between certain words, to digest what has just been said. For instance, some of my all-time favorite songs that illustrate how to make beautiful use of space are Sting's "Every Breath You Take," which breathes between lines, Billy Joel's "I Love You Just the Way You Are," Simon and Garfunkel's "Sounds of Silence," and Kander and Ebb's "New York, New York."

Fade

At the end of a verse-chorus style song, the chorus can be repeated over and over again and faded out on the control board very slowly until the sound disappears completely. Traditionally, the chorus as first sung is repeated continuously without any variation in lyrics. Let me repeat: Make sure your "out" choruses use *the same hook line;* then, if you like, the lines in between the hook—the descriptive lines of the chorus—may change for variety.

Ending

The last line of a song that does not use the device of a fade must draw the song to a definite conclusion. Frequently, where a song has a definite ending, producers choose to retard the music slightly for effect, and the piano continues with a short solo, echoing the piano pattern that has run through the song. When a lyric ends in this way, it must say something very definitive that ties up the story with a nice little bow. It must leave the listener with the feeling of a completed idea.

Tag

Sometimes in a song with a definite ending, you might want to insert one or two last lines before the very last line that have a lot of impact on making the ending bittersweet or poignant. This might take the form of a "tag," an extra line or two inserted in the final chorus just before the last line.

All the sections above give you some very specific tools you need to structure your songs. Obviously, you will not use *all* these elements in *every* song. However, in popular songwriting, these are the mainstays of practically every song you will hear, and all these terms should be committed to memory and practiced with regularity. Remember that if the elements of a song are not constructed correctly, you are creating roadblocks for yourself before you ever even get a song into a listener's hands. If you insist on being "different" and ignoring these conventions, I'm sure you will find songwriting very entertaining, but it's unlikely you'll achieve much, if any, commercial success or professional standing.

SONG FORMULAS ARE THE TOOLS OF THE TRADE

In this section, we'll fully explore the various formulas that are customarily used as frameworks for lyrical ideas. The word *formula* is used throughout the industry and is an accepted term to describe several styles of songs. I did not make up these formulas; songwriters have used them for most of this century. Why? Because they are effective. When you use an accepted formula to set up your song, this will be one less problem you'll have to worry about when you present it to a potential publisher or artist. They can therefore concentrate on the content instead of worrying about the form.

> *When you use an accepted formula to set up your song, this will be one less problem you'll have to worry about when you present it to a potential publisher or artist.*

I hear some dissenting voices out there: "I don't want my song to sound like everybody else's";

"Formula songs are too predictable—they're boring"; "Formula songs are what's wrong with today's music—they're unoriginal." My answer to these attitudes is to point out that you must rely on *your own unique creativity* to separate your work from the songs of others written in similar formulas. It boils down to what you have to say. You certainly didn't invent the love song, so how can you say "I love you" in a new way? The challenge is to be original within the framework of the accepted commercial song formulas.

Song formulas are very specific. Deviating from them usually results in poetry rather than lyrics. I'll show you some variations of formulas using the song elements described in the previous section, followed by actual examples of songs using these formulas.

There are several variations among the verse-chorus style formulas. Sometimes you'll want one verse before the chorus, sometimes two. Sometimes you'll put a bridge after the second chorus, sometimes not. A bridge is not essential in a verse-chorus style song—if there is nothing to add to enhance the story, then remember the saying, "Less is more." In the rock era of the late fifties through the early sixties, hit songs lasted 2½ minutes, rarely longer. Radio hardly played songs any longer than that, with just a few notable exceptions, such as Marty Robbins's "El Paso," which was closer to 5 minutes. I'm not saying the songs you write should be 2½ minutes long, but I suggest you keep them under 3½ minutes. Although a lot of records last 4 to 4½ minutes with the extended productions, when you are submitting a demo, the listener wants to be able to know by the end of the first chorus whether the song works. If you use all the tools in your arsenal—a *very long musical intro, four verses, two double choruses, a vocal bridge, a musical breakdown, and five fade choruses*—so that your song goes on for 5 or more minutes, it's a good bet the demo will have been turned off long before it ever reaches the fade choruses.

Often, you'll use two verses before the first chorus, and only one verse before the second chorus. This, again, is in the interest of being brief—not dragging the story out beyond what's necessary. The object is not to be wordy and flowery, but to get your story told clearly and concisely. It's easy to fall in love with every word you write. Learn to edit out information that doesn't enhance and further your idea.

Keep in mind that no chorus but the "out chorus" is ever repeated more than twice, and never write more than two verse or chorus sections in a row.

I won't try to illustrate every possible permutation of verse-chorus style songs. As you begin to study songs that become hit records, you'll identify the formulas for yourself. I will, however, show you a few examples within this genre.

> *It's easy to fall in love with every word you write. Learn to edit out information that doesn't enhance and further your idea.*

Specific Verse-Chorus Formulas

1. *Verse-chorus-verse-out choruses.* This is the simplest of all formulas. It sets up the story in the first verse, follows it with the chorus (which explains the purpose of the song), follows that with the verse that wraps up the story, and fades on a simple repetition of the chorus in its entirety.

DON'T LET GO (Theme from the motion picture *Cage*)

Verse: Now is all we have
For all we know
To be together
There's so much I've never said
The words were in my head, yet I was sure
We'd have forever

Chorus: *Don't Let Go*
Just Hold On
I'll be here long after the moment is gone
Don't Let Go
Cause I believe in you . . . how much you'll never know
I'm here . . . Don't Let Go.

Verse: In a perfect world
There are no tears
No dreams are shattered
After all is said and done,
I wonder what we've won if we should lose
What really matters

(Repeat Chorus twice, retard last line for ending.)

WORDS & MUSIC/PAMELA PHILLIPS OLAND AND MARILYN BERGLAS

2. *Verses-build-chorus-verses-build-bridge-out choruses.* It has become very popular in the verse-chorus style of songwriting to include a "build" to lead into the chorus with more impact both melodically and lyrically.

HAVANA

Verses: Rain was pouring down
And it mingled with my tears
As you walked away

In that Cuban town
Where we'd loved a thousand years
One fateful day

Strangers to the dance
We were caught up in the trance
Of the music

Build: And I never will forget. . . .

Chorus: *HAVANA! HAVANA!*
Where the perfume of the breezes
Tempted us so

HAVANA! HAVANA!
You are tangled in my senses
I'll never let you go

Verses: Only in your eyes
Did I ever see myself
So clearly

Love that mystifies
Secrets I will never tell
I hold dearly

Did we understand
We could never meet again
As you held me

Build: Now I'll love you in my dreams

(Repeat Chorus)

BRIDGE: *Silver wings in flight*
Carry me tonight
HAVANA

Far away from you
Fading out of view
HAVANA

(Repeat Chorus)

LYRICS/PAMELA PHILLIPS OLAND, MUSIC/LILO FADIDAS

3. *Verse-double chorus-verse-double chorus-bridge-out choruses.* The difference in this "double chorus" style is that the first half of the double chorus sets up an unfinished thought that's completed by the second half.

MINUTE TO MIDNIGHT

Verse: Daggers of moonlight cut through the dark
           I'm trapped in the silence with all my mem'ries
           Too much time for thinking . . . and only you on my mind
           Did I believe that my touch was all you'd need
           And you could leave his love behind you?

Chorus: *It's a Minute to Midnight*
           I hear the wind at the door
           What am I waiting for?
           Why do I think you'll show?

Payoff: *It's a Minute to Midnight*
           Is it too soon or too late?
           All I can do is wait
           Baby I can't let go.

Verse: Watching for headlights . . . no one stops here
           You promised an answer . . . , tonight you'd tell me
           I'm wond'ring what does he give you
           I'm shadow-boxing my fears

           I won't believe you could walk away so cold
           After you said how much you need me

(Repeat Chorus)

Bridge: *Oh . . . it's me against the night*
           Now at last I fall into my empty bed
           Alone with all the words I never said . . .

(Repeat Chorus)

LYRICS/PAMELA PHILLIPS OLAND, MUSIC/PETER S. BLISS

4. *Verse-verse-double chorus-verse-verse-double chorus-bridge-out choruses.* This formula is useful when there really is a lot of story to tell. In any event, it should be used primarily for up-tempo songs, only occasionally for ballads. A ballad with this much information in it can be utterly interminable

and sometimes a total bore. However, a song in this style that moves along at a good clip, with very few "spaces" in it except for breathing between lines, can be brought in within a reasonable amount of time, assuming that the lines in the verse are short. In any event, this is as long as a song should ever be!

CHILD OF TWO WORLDS

Verse 1:   My heart has walked familiar streets
Feeling my past beneath my feet
Where children play who don't know my face
I'd tell my story but I've lost my place

Verse 2:   Nightlife blares through unknown doors
And voices crash in private wars
The lights are on but it's just not home
My life is crowded but I'm still alone

Chorus: *A child of two worlds is what I must be*
Two sides of a mirror that both look like me
They're present and past
And I'm their common ground

Payoff: *A child of two worlds, and so torn between*
Tugged from both ends till I feel I could scream
I run with the hare and I hunt with the hound.

Verse 3:   I grew up mostly safe and sane
Someone would edit then explain
While life went on in magazines
I learned to love from watching movie screens

Verse 4:   My friends are free and wild and strange
And I'm the one who'd never change
We're living an experience
I bought some dreams with my common sense

(Repeat Chorus)

Bridge: *When I go home the gravity sucks me*
Like a flood from a busted dam
And in a flash, I see who I was
Who I'll be and who I am
I'm a child of two worlds . . .

(Repeat Chorus and Fade on "Child of two worlds")

Lyrics/Pamela Phillips Oland, Music/Jeff Silverman

5. *Verse-build-chorus—verse-build-adapted chorus—half verse used as bridge—out choruses.* In this example, you will notice that the hook is repeated over and over in the chorus, and that the answer lines are different all the way through. This style is used in Black music much more often than pop, which, as I've stated, seems to prefer repetition of the identical chorus line throughout. Another thing to note in this lyric is that where the vocal bridge would normally be located is a *half-verse*. It is preceded in the song by a musical break, playing the first half of the verse as a melody line only.

COVER TO COVER

Verse: Paper dolls they call you from centerfolds
     Sweet dreams for the average guy
     But you don't need to fantasize your love away
     No not another minute
     'Cause it seems to me you don't get the picture
     I am not an airbrushed fantasy
     And satin's not what makes this woman beautiful
Build: To get it all, why don't you read . . .

Chorus: *Cover to Cover*
     And find out what I'm about
     Cover to Cover
     Oh Baby, you'll see you can't put me down

Verse: Sure I know you think it's just physical
     I can read your hungry eyes
     You think I'm just a pretty face and nothing more
     But when you read a book you look past the cover
     'Cause the best part's there between the lines
     So get the inside story, I'm a mystery
Build: Please read me right, and look . . .

Double   *Cover to Cover*
Chorus: *There's more here than meets the eye*
     Cover to Cover
     Oh Baby, I'm a heart soul and mind

     Cover to Cover
     Get to know me from front to back

> *Cover to Cover*
> *The diff'rence between fiction and fact*

(Musical Break)

Half	When you read a book you look past the cover
Verse:	'Cause the best part's there between the lines
	So get the inside story, I'm a mystery
Build:	Please read me right, and look . . .

Out	*Cover to Cover*
Chorus:	*This chapter is just for you*
	Cover to Cover
	Uncover the me no one ever knew
	Cover to Cover
	The picture's not the book
	Take a deeper look
	Cover to Cover
	Oh Baby . . .

(Fade Out)

LYRICS/PAMELA PHILLIPS OLAND, MUSIC/JOEY GALLO AND WARDELL POTTS, JR.

6. *Verse-verse-bridge-verse.* In contemporary songwriting, this is the other popular formula, also colloquially known as "A-A-B-A" style. This type of song does not have a chorus, and thus the hook must appear in some other part of the song, usually in either the first or last line of the "A." Here is an example of this formula using the hook as the payoff at the beginning *and* at the end of the "A." Also in this song, we used a fairly old-fashioned device stolen from the musical theater that I've called an "intro" so as not to confuse it with the other meaning of the word *verse,* which is used in theater to describe this introductory type of section. Finally, this is a song that has a set ending, as opposed to a "fade" ending. It uses a common musical device known as a "reprise," which simply means repeating a portion of the song in a new place. In this case, we used a reprise of the last line of the song, with a slight variation in melody, to resolve the chords, the story, and the song overall.

UNTIL YOU

Intro:	Faces were just faces
	Moonlit scenes just lovely places
	Sweet love songs never made me cry
	But now I see the world through different eyes

Verse: *Until You*
I was a bird in flight in search of somewhere safe to light
I was a soul the breeze would carry like a drifting kite
Never believed I'd find another heart that feels the way I do
Until You

Verse: *Until You*
Love was a word in tunes they always wrote for someone else
Fate is a lady who knows love will come but never tells
I never hoped to recognize my dream the moment it came true
Until You

Bridge: *So I promise to keep your heart in laughter*
To deck our world in wonder and friendship ever after
And I promise we'll always be together
The years will show us how to love as we do now . . .

Verse: *Until You*
I was a hat without a coat, a man without his mate
But I was sure that love was promised to the one who'll wait
So I have waited as romantic schemers
Have been known to do
Until You

Tag: Never before did someone make me want
To share my whole life through
Until You.

LYRICS/PAMELA PHILLIPS OLAND, MUSIC/JOE CURIALE
(A CHARACTER THEME ON *AS THE WORLD TURNS*)

> I hope I've answered the question as to why you would be doing yourself a favor to follow established songwriting formulas. Simply, they work. Formulas not only help you to order your thoughts and make your lyrics concise to create uniform meter, rhyme schemes, and stanza forms, but they make your songs singable and memorable to the ear.

EXCEPTIONS TO THE RULES

For every rule there are excellent exceptions. Songwriters' "rules," as defined in this book and elsewhere, should be considered "rules of thumb."

Nevertheless, my motto here is this: *Know the rules inside out, and if you break them, do it brilliantly.* Know what you're doing, know why you're doing it, and still want to do it because you feel you'll write a stronger song.

It's not enough to know what a song *is;* you also have to know what it *isn't* in order to evaluate it properly. In the same way that you can't define what you need in a lover until you've been through a few lousy relationships and learned what you *don't* want, you can't expect to understand what breaking songwriting rules is about until you've written a good many formula songs.

Any study of songwriting offers various methods from various teachers. There are many differences of opinion as to style and implementation. However, the nuts and bolts—including the study of metrical structure, rhyme, stanza forms, and the like—are a common thread among all the methods. It is perhaps comforting to know that for all songwriters, the basic dilemmas of which rules to keep and which rules to break are the same!

1. *Formula writing.* Once you understand and can implement the basics of formula writing—practically with your eyes closed—you can adjust your song formulas to your own taste. Writing songs with unusual structures is a natural outgrowth of being bored with the basic formulas.

2. *Rhyme schemes.* Only after you have rhymed first and third, second and fourth lines dozens of times, do you have the knowledge of the cadence of rhyme that will allow you to rhyme in a less obvious manner.

   The possibilities for internal rhyme schemes are endless. As I've shown you, rhyming must become a tool rather than an end result. The song must make sense, and the rhymes must be incidental to that goal.

3. *Word emphasis.* Don't sing words in ways you wouldn't say them. Follow natural speech patterns. Even though there are songwriters out there who play fast and free with the English language, remember this saying: "*Don't put the emPHAsis on the wrong sylLAble!*"

4. *Phrasing.* Unorthodox phrasing and unusually shaped verses are part of what keeps popular music interesting. Inventive artists such as Alanis Morissette, Sting, and Cheryl Crowe, for instance, are continually bringing innovative phrasings and rhyme schemes to their work. One of the most skillful examples of a uniquely phrased song is Bernie Taupin and Elton John's "Goodbye Yellow Brick Road." It never ceases to thrill me every time I hear the way that song has created its own unique line lengths and movements, yet moves as smoothly as a needle through silk.

In the following example, written for Disney's "Mousercize," I have used uneven phrasing of the lines in the first verse. Pay attention to the fact that I used the same uneven phrasing in the succeeding verse.

DO YOUR BEST

Verse: What's good for a goose
    Isn't always good for a gander
    Or a panda
    Or an ox or an elephant
    Or a giraffe in Uganda
    And while a ten-foot giant can leap a stream
    A kid can only do it in a dream
    'Cause none of us is quite the same
    As the person inside your name

Chorus: *So Do Your Best*
    Don't try to do like me
    Be your best
    Be the best you can be
    At work or play . . .
    Just Do Your Best all day

    Do Your Best
    In your own special style
    Do Your Best
    Do Your Best and wear a smile
    Show 'em how
    It's time to Do Your Best right now!

Verse: If you've got a friend
    Who can do things better than you can
    Or a toucan
    Or the kid from across the way
    Maybe it's something that few can
    No it really doesn't matter to lose or win
    Don't worry if you finish . . . just begin
    'Cause in your heart you'll be a star
    When you're bein' just who you are

(Repeat Chorus)

Lyrics/Pamela Phillips Oland, Music/Joey Carbone
from Disney's "Mousercize"

5. *Use of language.* It's essential to know the exact dictionary definitions of words before using them in unusual or derivative contexts. In order to bend a definition, you must have a grasp of how it's normally used in a sentence

in accepted conversation. There is no worse (or more generally humiliating) crime for a lyricist to commit, than to misuse a word through ignorance of its true meaning.

6. *Composition.* Schooled musicians often have a problem with playing sounds they were taught are discordant. Songwriters with no musical background continually break the rules of (1) harmony (defined by the Oxford Dictionary as "the combination of simultaneously sounded musical notes to produce chords and chord progressions having a pleasing effect"); and (2) consonance (defined by the Oxford Dictionary as "the combination of notes which are in harmony with each other due to the relationship between their frequencies.")

This may be one exception to my own *"You have to know how to do it right before you can go against the rules"* rule. It's been my experience that the rigidness of classical music training often inhibits or even prevents a composer from being musically adventurous. Unschooled composers are not hampered by the concepts of what is "musically incorrect" or "unfeasible."

7. *Everything else.* Nobody writes alone, in a vacuum. Whether you like it or not, we as songwriters are all influenced—positively or negatively—by what we hear others write. If you as a songwriter disagree with anything or everything I have written in this book, then you still must thank me for one important gift: I have given you a yardstick by which to measure what you think, and I will have helped you to develop clarity as you approach your own creative process.

So go ahead and break the rules. But if you do, you'd better have written something so good, so stirring, so clever, so striking, that it is not only forgivable, but deserves the humble respect of those who *know* that you broke the rules.

IF YOU DON'T HAVE A TITLE, WHY ARE YOU WRITING THIS SONG?

If you tell me you're going to start at the beginning and hope you end up somewhere, all I can say is send me a postcard when you get there. If you're going on a trip, do you just get in the car and hope you'll arrive someplace? Of course not! First you decide where you're going, and then you figure out how you're going to get there.

Songwriting is no different. Though there are those who might debate this point, I firmly believe there is a smart and simple way to approach a song. First, you pick the title. Second, you develop the story around it—deciding what your story is about, who your characters are, and what point you are hoping to make by the end of the song. And third, you don't start writing until you come up with a great first line. Unless you plan ahead, you are likely to end up with a disoriented mish-mash of ideas that never become focused and never really say *anything!*

I admit that I enjoy well-written stream-of-consciousness songs, as defined by the likes of Jimmy Webb ("McArthur Park"), and Don McLean ("American Pie"). Their work and others like it have elevated writing extemporaneously into a high art form. But we're not talking about exceptions here, we're talking about rules to write songs by. Many such writers are artists who primarily perform their own work, though sometimes those songs do get picked up by other artists. They have devoted fan followings who don't care what form they write in. They have sold their unusual songs with the conviction of a writer/artist and do not have to think in terms of "who can I get to record this?" (Who but Dylan, for instance, could have successfully brought the world the marvelous stream-of-consciousness "Subterranean Homesick Blues"?)

Let's define "stream-of-consciousness writing." It's when you get an interesting idea for a first line, then think of a line that sounds interesting after it, and then another, and so on, until you suddenly say, "I wrote a song." Then you look back carefully and try to figure out what the title is.

STREAM-OF-CONSCIOUSNESS TITLES

In the case of Don McLean's "American Pie," which has been a number-one record both for him and for Madonna, it's hard to know how he decided on the title. Although it is a fine title, he could just as well have picked "Bye, Bye, Miss American Pie" or "This'll Be the Day That I Die" or "The Day the Music Died." In Marty Robbins's classic "El Paso," where there is no repeating line or "hook," the name "El Paso" is just the city where the story takes place. The song might also have been named "The Ballad of Selena," the heroine of the song. I cannot speculate as to whether Paul Williams and Barbra Streisand had the title "Evergreen" in mind when they began to write the lyrics to that song, but the word only appears once—as the last word in the song. Which suggests that if they didn't start with the title and build up to it, or work backwards from it, they wrote from stream of consciousness and ended up with the right title, through a combination of perspiration, inspiration, and luck.

While I am not telling you to deny those moments of inspiration when a great first line appears in your mind and you want to take a crack at turning it into a song, I *am* saying that if you are writing for the commercial market, there is a better way to go about writing lyrics.

Start at the Very Beginning

To me it makes complete sense to start with a title. Assuming that this song is being written for no particular reason beyond your feeling like writing a song (i.e., it is not a specific assignment), simply find a title that has a flavor you're in the mood to write a song about, and you're in business. If you're feeling in a good mood, don't pick a depressing title such as "Alone Again." On the other hand, if you just received a Dear John letter in the afternoon mail, it is hardly the time to write "April Love."

Most songwriters I know rely on inspiration and brainstorming and don't often comb through their title files for title ideas. However, if you have a file filled with good titles that you've scribbled down for later inspiration, you definitely should go through it from time to time.

If there is no particular melodic slot you have to fit a title into, one thing you can do is make lists of whatever lines come into your mind that sound like potential titles. Then when you go back through the lists, discard those that are definitely not good contenders. Pick out the best ones, then choose one from among them. (Refer to chapter 2, "The Great Aha!" regarding where to find good ideas)

If what you're working on *is* an assignment—say, for a movie project where you have to use the name of the movie as the title—or if your collaborator has given you a melody with the title already built into it, obviously you have to start the song by considering the context of the title you've been given. Ask yourself what type of song style it is, whether it's earmarked for a male or female singer, and what twist of the story you might be able to come up with based on this title.

If the melody you are given has a melodic hook where the title should be, but no title yet, listen carefully over and over to the melody until you get a firm handle on what the hook sounds like, how many syllables it has, where the emphasis falls, where an open vowel should be, and so forth. Then start running titles to that hook through your head, singing along with the melody to see how they fit. Write them down as you go, so that you don't forget any of them. When you find the one you really like, run it by your composer-collaborator, and if you both agree on it, that's your title.

Let's assume you are in a writing session with a collaborator. The two of you have neither a melody nor a title, but are starting from scratch and don't know where to begin with your song. Here's what you do: Start by either coming up with a melodic hook and then finding an appropriate title, as described above, or by working out an agreeable title first. To accomplish that, you might simply talk about things that interest you, and be on the lookout for a title inherent in your conversation. You might thumb through some magazines and call out interesting lines to each other, or you might just bounce ideas back and forth, trying to refine each other's title ideas until one seems to work for both of you. And again, there's always the old title file to resort to.

Once you have your title, ask yourself, "What does this line/word/phrase *mean?*" For example, say you've chosen the title "Whenever I Think of You." What story lines can that suggest? Let's consider a few of the possibilities:

1. Whenever I think of you: I smile (I fall in love once again)

2. Whenever I think of you: I cry (Wishing you were still here)

3. Whenever I think of you: I think of Paris (that special summer)

4. Whenever I think of you: I want to scream (you made me crazy)

5. Whenever I think of you: I'm so glad I now have *him!*

The question is, which of these stories do you want to write? Let's break that down:

• If you have a melody to work from, which story does this melody suggest best? I have found that every melody has an intrinsic story in it, which becomes very clear on listening to a few times. So ask yourself: Is this melody happy, tragic, amusing, melancholy, a melody that suggests reminiscing?

• What style of song are you writing? Titles 1 and 2 would be R & B/Pop; number 3 would be an MOR/pop song—probably a ballad; title 4 would be a rock idea; and title 5 would be a Country idea. Think of your audience and what they might want to hear, and let that help you gauge what story you ought to write!

The point is, before you put your pen to paper, decide what you are going to write about. Once you know what story to tell, build the song around it so that it has a beginning, a middle, and an end, always paying off with—all thoughts leading to—the title.

Once You Have the Hook, Where Do You Put It?

A hook needs to be placed where it will achieve its best effect. If you're writing to a melody, that melody will suggest where the title goes, but if you are writing lyrics first, you have a decision to make.

Let's take the phrase "I Never Meant to Hurt You," for instance, and consider how best to use it as a title.

If this were the title in an A-A-B-A formula song, it could be used as a payoff at the end of the "A":

> You found the matches in my pocket, with her name inside
> You found the lipstick on my collar that I couldn't hide
> And you put two and two together and came up with goodbye
> But *I never meant to hurt you,* cross my heart and hope to die.

It could alternatively be used as the *first* line of the "A" in the same story.

I Never Meant to Hurt You
Though I know that's what I've done
And I know I should have ended
What I shouldn't have begun . . .

If you were using the line in a verse-chorus formula song, there would be two ways to use it:

1. If it were used at the *beginning* of the chorus, it would need to be made to "pay off" at the end of the chorus, *for example,*

> I Never Meant to Hurt You
> With those foolish things I said
> I Never Meant to Hurt You
> *But that's exactly what I did*

2. If it were used at the end of the chorus, it would be the "payoff" in and of itself, for example:

> I always tried to love you
> But her touch was a wake-up call
> And she's the one I've turned to now . . .
> *Though I Never Meant to Hurt You . . . at all*

What Makes a Title Great?

A title is fantastic if it impacts everyone who hears it. It's memorable, easy to sing, and, at its best, embodies a unique turn of phrase. Remember that your title is the key to your song. If there is no power or impact in the title, it will be hard to come up with any melodic ideas that will drive it home. Consider the following: You want to talk about someone who is walking out on you, so you may consider as title ideas:

1. "I Hope You Won't Leave Me"
2. "Please Don't Say You're Leaving Me"
3. "I Wonder If You're Leaving Me"
4. "I Think You'll Soon Be Leaving Me"
5. "You Say You're Gonna Leave Me"

But all of these ideas are weak as titles. They are dull. Which makes it so surprising that lines like this are used as frequently as they are! Think how much more impact a title on this subject would have if it were phrased in a more interesting fashion:

Don't worry about the next song or the next one after that. Don't hoard good ideas! When you save a good idea "for later," you have to ask yourself, "Why am I writing this song in the first place?"

1. "Don't Leave Me!"

2. "You've Got Leaving in Your Eyes"

3. "Leave Before It's Over"

4. "Leave While the Leavin's Good"

5. "It's the Winter of our Summer Love"

Often, if a title begins with or contains an active verb, it will be very commanding. Some of my titles that I feel accomplish this are "Come On and Break My Heart," "Show Me What You've Got for Me," "Step Right Up," "Stay!" "Don't Break the Rhythm," "Make Me Believe in You," "Leave Me Something to Dream," "Save the Mistletoe for Me," and "Show Me Your Love and I'll Show You Mine!"

Some titles that have used the trick of being decidedly *provocative* have made a huge difference in certain artists' careers. Consider, for example: "Like a Virgin" (Madonna); "Fooled Around and Fell in Love" (Elvin Bishop); "Satisfaction" (Rolling Stones); "Sexy and Seventeen" (Stray Cats); "After the Lovin'" (Englebert Humperdinck); "Slippery When Wet" (Commodores); "I Feel Like Makin' Love" (Roberta Flack); and "Let's Get It On" and "Sexual Healing" (Marvin Gaye).

Many titles over the years have waxed philosophical. In the folk era, titles such as "Both Sides Now" and "Where Have All the Flowers Gone?" were brooding looks at the meaning of life. Universal ideas such as "We Are the World" and "Rhythm of the Night" were songs expressing optimistic points of view.

I was assigned to write lyrics for an end title to a wonderful independent film called *Gideon,* which starred Charlton Heston as a rigid, old, retired teacher and Shirley Jones as the woman he was unable to declare his feelings to. They, along with assorted characters played by Carroll O'Connor, Mike Connors, Harvey Korman, and Barbara Bain, are residents of a retirement home run by a crotchety old woman played by Shelley Winters. Their lives are meaningless and hopeless until a gentle, slightly retarded man named Gideon, memorably played by Christopher Lambert, comes to stay at the retirement home, to everyone's bewilderment. Gideon teaches them the value of enjoying life, and then goes into a decline, as the plot reveals that he has come there to die. Anthony Marinelli and I worked with the film's wonderful director Claudia Hoover to develop an idea for the end title that would capture the universal message of hope delivered by this film. Trying to capture the essence of the film, I thought of the title "All We Have is Now," and it became a very effective end title that reads like this:

ALL WE HAVE IS NOW

One miracle
Could happen any day
So open up your heart
And let it come your way

Time hurries by
To fly the wings of clouds
So stop the clock awhile
'Cause all we have is now

Hearts that never take a chance
Frame the sidelines of the dance
When life's . . . all figured out
Funny, all we have is now

One miracle
Don't let it slip away
The future and the past
Won't matter anyhow
'Cause All we have . . . and All we need . . . is Now.

MUSIC/ANTHONY MARINELLI, LYRICS/PAMELA PHILLIPS OLAND

Over the years, many songwriters have opted to use famous phrases, sayings, proverbs, and movie titles to create song titles that already sound familiar: "Crash and Burn," "Silence is Golden," "Out of Sight, Out of Mind," "A Penny for Your Thoughts," "Thou Shalt Not Steal," "Tonight's the Night," "Too Close for Comfort," "What Kind of Fool Do You Think I Am?" and so on. Another very popular device, especially in Country music, is to take a famous phrase and twist it just slightly, such as "I've Got Friends in *Low* Places," "Total Eclipse of the *Heart*," "Out of Sight and *On My* Mind," "Rhythm & *Booze*." Country writers often create clever titles that sound so catchy they seem to already be familiar sayings, such as "Sleeping Single in a Double Bed," "She Got the Gold Mine and I Got the Shaft," and "Sunday Morning Coming Down."

Catch phrases have found their way into songs over and over again, both as titles and in the body of songs. However, not all catch phrases are appropriate. Make sure that your catch phrase is *current usage* and not passé; make sure that the line won't become immediately dated and make the song *and* its message obsolete; make sure that the language of the phrase is not archaic English or too poetic to be conversational. A catch phrase such as "small world" will never lose its universal meaning, whereas a phrase like "groovy kind of love" becomes anything but groovy.

You have to decide how powerful a title will be in your own song. Remember that since your title is also your main hook, with very few exceptions that title has to be strong enough to grab the listener on first impact. If you have a terrific story with great lines in the verses, but the title is weak, the hook cannot deliver its message properly, and the whole song will probably be the loser.

You have to decide for yourself whether a line is strong enough to be a title. Even after you've written your song, you still have a chance to go back and see if at the other end of your hook you haven't written a stronger line. Frequently, this is the case. You started out with one idea, and it evolved into another, perhaps more intriguing one. Don't get locked into feeling you have to keep your original idea; let yourself follow your creative path so that you can end up with a more powerful song than what you set out to write!

If a line is "borderline," but it's used well, it may work, but know up front that you're taking a risk of not having commercial appeal. If it's borderline and used weakly, the whole song will suffer. You are in total control of what happens in the writing process of your song. The more hooks you can bring into the song, the more commercial it will be. Therefore, don't be afraid to use a precious "title" idea as a line in a song, as it will only strengthen the overall song. In any event, you can always use the phrase again as the title of another song somewhere down the line. But my advice is this: Don't worry about the next song or the next one after that. Don't hoard good ideas! When you save a good idea "for later," you have to ask yourself, "Why am I writing *this* song in the first place?" Make this your mantra: If it's worth doing at all, it's worth doing exceedingly well.

When is a Title Not a Title?

One word of caution here: Not every interesting line you come up with is necessarily a title. Some are simply interesting lines. A title should have a special sort of impact. It must leave the listener with a lasting impression. When the song is listened to, your title should be the phrase that everyone waits to hear, the one you can sing along to and find yourself humming in the shower. It should be a very self-contained idea. It should be a satisfying thing to hold in the mouth, not an awkward combination of syllables or consonants. Also, the open vowel sounds should fit into the melody in the right places, such as when holding a full note.

Not every interesting line you come up with is necessarily a title. Some are simply interesting lines.

The Title Makes the Song

Always remember that the type of musical style in which you are working dictates the type of title you can use. "You Stomped on my Heart and Squashed That Sucker Flat" is not a rock title. "Don't Jive Your Homie" wouldn't be a Country idea. Make sure that:

(1) if the song is for a certain market, the title is fitting; and (2) if the song is for a certain artist, it is something that artist would want to sing about.

There are hundreds of songs in which the title dominates the song. The listener hardly notices any other words in it. Songs such as "Love to Love You Baby," "Wooly Bully," and "Bad," to name only a few, exemplify the important role a title can play in the commercialism of a song. Perhaps you have some songs in your catalogue that you are only half-happy with. Wouldn't it be an interesting exercise to take another look at those songs and see if you can't come up with a better title? Of course, this might lead to a rewrite of either the chorus or the entire song, but wouldn't you rather have a hit title that makes your song sound like a hit song, than "just another song" with a mediocre title?

With precious few exceptions, *the title makes the song!* If you don't have a great title, you probably don't have a great song, regardless of all the work you've put into it. Even if you're working without a melody, just writing a lyric by itself to be given to a composer to write a melody to later, your title still has to be rhythmic, dynamic, and full of impact. One way to accomplish that is to create your title to fit a dummy melody.

DUMMY MELODIES

In order to craft a terrific lyric, there must be form, rhythm, and meter guiding you. In cases where you are creating a lyric without any tune or track to write it to, how do you make sure all the verses and choruses scan the same? How do you make sure that all the lines in subsequent verses are of identical length and meter? Just because you have the same *number* of syllables in two corresponding lines doesn't guarantee that their meter will match. What matters is how those syllables fit the music.

The way to guarantee that each verse is identical stylistically to all the others is to write our lyrics to *dummy melodies.* Clearly, even those of us who cannot write *great* melodies must at the very least teach ourselves to write *dummy* melodies. What *is* a dummy melody? It is a working melody to back up the lyrics we're writing. And here we encounter one of the primary tools that takes us out of poetry writing and into lyric writing.

Poetry is *designed* to be *read,* and works whether it's read silently or out loud. But since lyrics cannot be read or spoken and retain their effectiveness, it stands to reason they must be *sung*—which necessitates those dummy melodies.

Whenever I write a lyric from scratch, that is, one that I am developing for a composer to add a tune to, I *always* have a melody humming through my mind. It is often a very ordinary or simple

Make sure that: (1) if the song is for a certain market, the title is fitting; and (2) if the song is for a certain artist, it is something that artist would want to sing about.

melody, sometimes reminiscent of other tunes I've heard. (As a matter of fact, once I went into a publisher's office with a new song and sang it to him with my melody, and he frowned and scratched his head; then a light went on in his brain and he joined in for the rest of the song: "Hold the pickles, hold the lettuce . . . " I had unwittingly written my lyrics to a Burger King commercial—how mortifying!) It doesn't matter how good or bad your dummy melody is because nobody is ever supposed to hear it. When you hand over the lyrics, you shouldn't sing your dummy melody to the composer, as it might plant a melodic idea in his or her head that's impossible to get away from—and if your melodic idea isn't particularly wonderful, this could be the ruination of your song!

Why Do You Need a Dummy Melody?

1. *In a song, the form of each verse should be identical.* The first line of each verse should have the same number of syllables and the same exact meter, and so on, with the corresponding lines of each subsequent verse. Whatever you write for the first verse ought to be able to fit over the melody for the other two verses. As an example, study the lyrics below and count the meter of each line. Because the lyrics have so clearly defined a form, you will see that you can make up your own melody.

WHAT DO YOU DREAM ABOUT?

Verse:
Last night you and I took a jungle cruise
Down the rivers of Brazil
We met some painted natives
Who were itching for a kill
Build:
They tied me up to a burning stake
And I thought I'd breathed my last

Set-up:
Then you came on with a Bowie knife
You cut me loose and you saved my life
And as you carried me off I heard somebody say
"What a lucky getaway!"

Chorus: *What do you dream about*
         When you go to sleep at night?
         What do you dream about
         When you're turning out the light?

Payoff: *What do you dream about?*
    What's your fav'rite fantasy ?
    What do you dream about ?
    Do you ever dream of me?

Verse:
We met in Tibet on a mountain trek
With our baggage on a yak
A Mongol horde laid ambush
They were poised for an attack

Build:
They dangled me by my fingernails
From a sheer cliff two miles high

Setup:
Then you dropped down on a length of rope
In the nick of time when I'd lost all hope
And as you carried me off I heard somebody say
"What a lucky getaway!"

(Repeat Chorus)

Verse:
We were lost at sea on a desert isle
Wearing suntans and a grin
You said that you adored me
You'd be mine through thick and thin

Build:
You held me tight and I held my breath
At the lust inside your eyes

Setup:
*(Then) A boat sailed by and you lit a flare
And I said No! No! Could we stay right there
And as they carried us off I heard somebody say
"What a lucky getaway!"

(Repeat Chorus)

LYRICS & MUSIC/PAMELA PHILLIPS OLAND

Pickup Notes: Please note that I have placed parentheses around the word *Then* to indicate that this word is a "pickup" note. A "pickup" note means an additional word comes in at the beginning of a line, prior to the line itself. It requires an additional note. In this case, *"A"* which would have been a quarter note becomes *"Then A"* which is now sung as two eighth notes. The meter of the rest of the line is unchanged.

2. *Some composers need a reference rhythm to compose to.* This requires you to read the lyrics into a cassette tape in the rhythm that you wrote them. It is helpful to tap out the rhythm as you are reading. (You can tap two sticks, a bongo drum, or whatever you have, to get the percussive sound that marks off the rhythm.) As you read, think of your dummy melody in your head, and speak the words in the rhythm you wrote them to.

3. *The type of dummy melody you choose will help establish the style of the song and the type of artist it might be suitable for.* Obviously, you wouldn't use a dummy R & B melody if you were planning to write a rock alternative song, and vice versa. Your dummy melody will set the mood and tempo and will put a particular singer or style of music in your mind. This will help you to create a lyric appropriate to that genre.

4. *Having a dummy melody in mind helps you structure your song evenly.* It helps you plan ahead for how long the verses should be and enables you to know how many lines and how many words you will need in each repeating verse. Also, it gives you some idea of how effective your chorus lines will be when put to music.

I must say here that very often the melody the composer comes up with isn't even remotely close to your dummy melody. And, even more often, composers don't want to know what rhythmic pattern you wrote to. They just like to get ideas from the words. In that event, the words have an orderly feel and sequence to them, and when the composer comes up with a wonderful melody to your first verse, he or she rarely has to look at the second verse and say, "What's this? It doesn't fit my melody!"

I want to point out that as hard as you work at structuring your song correctly for a composer to write music to, there are times the composer will interpret the words in a rhythm you hadn't thought of. In that case, it is possible your lines won't all work in subsequent verses. Assuming that what the composer has come up with sounds good, my advice is not to throw a tantrum or call the whole thing off and take back your lyrics, but to do whatever rewriting is now necessary to make your subsequent verses conform to the new structure.

If you're just plain unable to come up with a melody by yourself because that simply isn't what you're good at, there's a very simple solution. Choose a

UNDERSTANDING THE CRAFT ≡ 107

song that you love, and write a new lyric to it. To me that's the ideal use of karaoke tracks! There are many companies that now produce and sell these musical backing tracks to famous songs. While they are actually marketed for karaoke clubs and for singers to vocalize to, think what a terrific tool they are for us as lyricists: We can use their formulas as the basis for coming up with new lyrics. Since nobody will ever know what your dummy melody was anyway, your secret—the famous melody you used to give your new lyric a tried-and-trusted form and structure—will remain a secret.

One final perk to writing dummy melodies: Occasionally, even the best lyricists/worst composers among us write a terrific dummy melody and end up getting it recorded just as it is! In fact, one extremely good dummy melody that I wrote was recorded by Frank Sinatra (I guess you could call that *dummy luck!*).

THE FIRST LINE

Never underestimate the power of a first line to hook the listener into wanting to hear the rest of the song.

Consider a guy's song about a girl at a dance, with whom he senses mutual attraction. Perhaps the song could start out, "I saw you look at me across the room." Or maybe, "It would be so nice to meet you." But aren't those rather lame lines? A word such as *nice* is just that: nice. But it has no zest or pizzazz. It just sits there. In a song I wrote with Paul Janz, called "Come on and Break My Heart," my opening line deals with just such a situation. I wrote, "Your intentions shine like diamonds in your eyes tonight." This is a bold opening statement that sets up the sensual mood of the song from the start. It narrows down the concept to its most basic point. We know from this line that he is singing it to a girl who is attracted to him. We know it is night-time, which is much more often associated with romance and sex in songs than daytime. We know that she is a strong, assertive woman who makes no bones about showing her interest. We also get the feeling she is mischievous and playful and someone worth desiring. All of this just from that one line.

Never settle for just any first line, since your first line will definitely set the direction for the entire song. Here are some ways in which you can judge whether the first line you have chosen is the right one for your song:

1. *Has it created the kind of mood you intend to get across with this song?* If it has not strongly set up the appropriate mood, you'll have trouble ever getting the mood going in successive lines.

Think about what kind of mood you want to create and ask yourself what word picture would best express it. Understanding the mood will lead you into an appropriate first line and away from inconsequential ideas. Here are some examples of setting up a mood: "She doesn't know it now, but tomorrow she'll wake up in an empty bed"—this tells you right off the bat that the singer is planning on leaving; it is a melancholy idea. "Blame It on the Moonlight"—this asks the listener to excuse the singer's rash behavior and sets up a romantic mood. "I never saw the stop sign and I crashed head-on into you"—this sets up a reckless person out for a reckless relationship. The mood is brittle and promises excitement.

2. *Does it set up the person and time frame of the song?* Is this a song about "you" or "she" or "we," and is it now, in the past, or in the future? In order to have your listeners identify with the song, you can't keep them waiting to know the person and tense; most listeners will immediately pigeonhole the song as to a past or present relationship of their own.

3. *Is it written in the speech pattern of the style of song you wish to write?* Whatever market you're aiming for—Country, R & B, Rap, rock, whatever you choose—they all have their own idioms and colloquialisms. Make sure your first line—and every line—works in that style. A song immediately typecasts itself in the first line. For instance, in my song co-written with Todd Cerney titled "Good Taste in Bad Women," my first line is, "I wouldn't go so far as to sayin' that I never met a girl I didn't like . . . " This is by nature a humorous Country idea, and has to lead into a Country song. If I wanted a rock idea, I'd perhaps go with something like, "I'm blinded by the sight of the light in the eyes of any cold-hearted hot-blooded woman." R & B? More earthy, such as "I can't resist a lady who ain't actin' like a lady." All three lines talk about a man who loves women. However, each is phrased differently, to appeal to a different audience.

4. *Does the first line set a picture in the listener's mind?* The listener must be drawn into the story right away. As I mentioned above, the listener puts him- or herself right into the picture. The picture can be absolutely anything—a scenic location, a moment in the past, a dance floor, a love encounter, or whatever you choose. For example, in my song "Something in Your Eyes," co-written with Richard Carpenter, my first line is, "There was a certain face that filled a thousand nights . . . " We have all had many faces that have filled many nights of our dreams, be they actual love interests in our lives, or just fantasies. In this instance, the hope is that my listener superimposes a certain face into the song.

5. *Does the first line say something that is immediately understandable?* Songs must be conversational, and even if we use lines full of imagery in the body of the song to add color or interest, the opening line must be clear and straightforward. In a song once turned in to me by a student, the first line was, "I'm in a hot wind turning brown." I'm sure the student knew what he meant by this, but to me this was far too abstract to make anything certain out of, and I could only speculate as to his intent. In any event, by the time I was done speculating on that one line, the song was over and I'd missed the rest of it. A line like this one belongs in a poem. Poetry is *meant* to be

speculated on over and over again. It is *meant* to be wrapped around the tongue a dozen different ways. It is *meant* to suddenly inspire abstract ideas and concepts and bring you to a hundred "Ahas!" Not so lyrics.

6. *Does your first line make your listener eager to hear what follows?* If the first line isn't interesting, appealing, or colorful, the listener might tune out the rest of the song, which you may have labored long and hard over and may actually be better than the first line. How regrettable this is for those of us who really have written an excellent lyric with a slow beginning.

I'm not saying that if you have a boring first line everybody's going to stop listening. But I *am* saying that they won't be drawn into the song and may not pay attention to anything but the hook and the melody. Many hits, especially in the dance music genre, rely heavily on hook, rhythm track, and production values, but are weak on lyric content. These songs are here today, gone tomorrow. They can rarely be lasting copyrights unless they say something memorable.

A powerful first line is guaranteed to grab the ears of your listeners. You will develop your own style of constructing a song, and it may not be the same as mine, but you need to start off writing the song by writing an inspired opening line. This will lead you to all the wonderful lines that can follow a special thought. If you have to write five verses or ten before you come up with that great line to start your song, so be it. Put your best foot forward.

LAUNDRY LISTS

I once spent two years writing jingles. I wrote quickly. I had to! My boss paid me $25 for each lyric, so I knocked them out at the rate of about three a day. And I thought I was lucky to have the job! Like a true beginning songwriter, I held the common belief that any assignment was better than no assignment!

I can't say the work was thrilling. But I did learn a few lessons that have stayed with me until this day. One is that people often don't like what they think they heard when it isn't what they think they're looking for, and they instantly shut off their mind to it. Then if you play it for them another day when they have a different mindset, they don't recognize it as the thing they hated, and this time they love it! I once was called into my jingle boss's office and asked to come up with a jingle for a certain canned chicken. Off the cuff, without even thinking, my mind came up with, "The Trick in Pickin' Chicken Is Pickin' Which Chicken to Pick." "Pamela! No-oo-oo! Just go and think about it, and have something to present to the client tomorrow," he said. So the next day, I sat in the office and ate some canned chicken on a tooth-pick and dutifully extolled its virtues (what we do for money, eh!) and when my boss said, "Well, Pamela, give them your line!" I said, "The Trick in Pickin' Chicken Is Pickin' Which Chicken to Pick." The client jumped up and said, "That's terrific! I love it!" And my boss said, "Great, Pamela! Now why couldn't you have come up with something like that *yesterday?*"

But the other lesson was the really important one. It concerned *laundry lists*. It was so simply stated, but it had a profound influence on all my future work. It came up when I was trying to figure out how to write a jingle about a client who had a multitude of services to offer. So I wrote an adorable jingle with all the services listed in perfect rhyme and meter. When my boss read it, he said, "If you're advertising Heinz 57 varieties, you can't talk about the tomatoes, the beans, and the ketchup all in one ad. You have to just pick one and write about it!"

This holds true in songwriting, too. How often have you heard a song that lists all the reasons one is loved, or all the reasons one is sad, without ever getting to the point of what happened? This is a "laundry list," and, to repeat, love the beans or the ketchup, but don't write about them both in the same song. It is generally a disaster to try to capture all aspects of a subject in two verses and a chorus, even if you feel that they all are important. Make an effort to pick one that is good subject matter for a song, and leave the rest for later endeavors. You'll be amazed at how much you find to say on one subject if you don't clutter your page with *laundry lists!*

LYRIC-CRAFTING EXERCISES

1. *Rewrite a popular song.* As I discussed in the section on dummy melodies, this is a very tried and trusted method of developing songwriting skills. To recap: Pick a well-known song that you are fond of, and write a new title and a new lyric to it. You know that the song has already been a hit, so the form of the melody has obviously proven itself. Use the melody as a basis for creating a brand new song with just as much punch to it as the original. Later you can write a new melody to your lyric, or give it to a composer to write a melody to. (Again, don't tell your collaborator which song you wrote it to, as he or she may never be able to escape from the original tune!)

2. *Write different versions of your song.* This takes a lot of discipline, as you are likely to be enamored by your original draft. But the exercise is to take the same title and write two, three, even four *entirely different lyrics.* Try to tell each one as a unique and different story from the others.

3. *Practice using the thesaurus.* When you have completed a song, try replacing ordinary and simple images with more exotic and exciting ideas; with more complex images; with words that convey more interesting pictures. You may find that your original, simple images were better, but some might stick, and at the very least you'll have something with which to compare them.

4. *Update your past work.* Take a favorite lyric or poem written in the past, at least six months ago, and look at it now in light of what you have since learned. You will see holes in it that you can drive a tank through. So, as an exercise, retaining a copy of your original for posterity, see how you would

have written the same idea now. Chances are, you won't finish this exercise, as you will become so disgusted with how amateurish the piece now seems to you that nothing you can do will bring it up to your current standards of writing. This exercise is indeed an eye opener! It's very good for your morale, too, as you can really see how far you've come!

LET'S WRITE A SONG!

Now that you have all the tools at your disposal, let's walk through the writing of a song. Claudia Brandt, a brilliant Argentine composer, brought me a melody. She played it over several times, and I came up with twelve titles I felt fit the melody. We tried singing them all to the melody, and chose "Haven't I." Then we asked ourselves the obvious question: Haven't I *what?*

The follow-ups to that question included "Haven't I been good to you?" "Haven't I got the right to love you?" "Haven't I got the best man in town?" and so on. We decided that the words "Haven't I" were strongest when answering the question "Haven't I given you everything I can?"

The next step was to write the opening line. We pictured the singer as a woman who has given herself up to love, and is its unwilling captive, powerless to resist what she feels, and at a loss as to why it isn't working out.

The first line we agreed on was:
I don't know when it was I knew
All that I cared about was you
which led us to the thought for the next line—she has fallen somehow under this man's spell. The line we chose was:
Funny how quickly life can change
The next line was a statement of her reality as she sees it:
This isn't just a passing phase
The rhyme: "aze" led us to
All of my nights and all my days
The sound-alike rhyme for "change," and the captive concept led us to:
Love has me captive in its chains
Next came the "B" section. The idea was that she's trapped:
If I had wings, I'd leave forever
Followed by a line that turns that idea on it's head
But it's forever I want to stay . . .
Now the chorus, which had to start with our hook:
Haven't I . . .
The question was haven't I what, and we decided that this question needed to be answered with a list of what she had given to the relationship, so it was:
Haven't I told you how I need your smile?
Haven't I shown you we're so good together?

The next "Haven't I" needed to be more romantic and dramatic, to carry the song onward:

Haven't I laughed and cried and lived and died for your love?

And finally, the payoff line that all this was leading to:

Haven't I loved you enough?

Claudia then played the song through that far, and realized that the words "Haven't I" needed to be repeated for emphasis at the end of the chorus.

Haven't I?

Next came the second verse. I felt that this verse needed to state the why of it; to answer the question why she was trying to hold on to this man. The opening line we agreed on is:

All of the questions of my life—
I see the answers in your eyes

The question then was how to complete that thought so that it clearly tied up the revelations of her heart and made them strong. Our choice was:

There's nothing else I need to know

The second half of that verse needed to go to the cause of her angst, which is driving the song: the passionate plea, the needing to know. We wrote:

Why are you tearing me apart
When I'm a prisoner of your heart?

We then had one more line of verse to write, and we had to make it count. It had to have an "o" rhyme to rhyme with "know." It had to be bittersweet, and it had to touch the listener, and hopefully touch the heart of the man she was singing it to. What we wrote was:

How can you want to let me go?

What was missing in the story? Our second "B" section addresses the one issue that hasn't been brought up yet. Has she tried to understand where he's coming from? It all has to be said in one line. Here's how we did it:

I know your fears are walls between us

Then the completing line of that "B" section had to be a "springboard" into the chorus that says "Haven't I done all these things to try to make it work." In other words, we had to analyze what she would need to have to say to him to get him to reconsider. So, referring to those fear walls, we wrote:

Give me a chance and I'll break them down.

She is now gaining on her point, as she sings the chorus again.

We decided that in this song we wanted a bridge. What additional and important information needed to be brought to play in this story? We decided that this bridge has to convey her sense of desperation as she works to break down his resistance. Thus, our short two-line bridge starts:

I speak these words, but you don't hear me

The very last line we get to write in this song, the second line in the bridge, has to convey her love for him and her need to work this out, and we wrote a line that led strongly back into the chorus:

My life is all about you, what can I do?
The finished song is extremely powerful. The final chorus raises a step musically, and has a final ending on the poignant words "Haven't I." Here's the completed lyric in order:

HAVEN'T I . . . ?
I don't know when it was I knew
All that I cared about was you
Funny how quickly life can change

This isn't just a passing phase
All of my nights and all my days
Love has me captive in its chains

If I had wings, I'd leave forever
But it's forever I want to stay . . .

Chorus: *Haven't I told you how I need your smile*
            Haven't I shown you—we're so good together
            Haven't I laughed and cried, and lived and died
            For your love
            Haven't I loved you enough
            Haven't I . . . ?

All of the questions of my life—
I see the answers in your eyes
There's nothing else I need to know

Why are you tearing me apart
When I'm a prisoner of your heart
How can you want to let me go?

I know your fears are walls between us
Give me a chance, and I'll break them down

Chorus: *Haven't I told you how I need your smile*
            Haven't I shown you we're so good together
            Haven't I laughed and cried, and lived and died
            For your love
            Haven't I loved you enough?

Bridge: *I speak these words, but you don't hear me*
            My life is all about you . . . what can I do?

Chorus: *Haven't I told you how I need your smile*
          Haven't I shown you we're so good together
          Haven't I laughed and cried, and lived and died
          For your love
          Haven't I loved you enough?
          Haven't I . . . ?

WORDS & MUSIC/CLAUDIA BRANT AND PAMELA PHILLIPS OLAND
PROPERTY OF PEER SOUTHERN MUSIC (BMI) AND PAM-O-LAND
MUSIC (ASCAP)

5

THE ART OF SUCCESSFUL COLLABORATION

Collaboration could be defined as a joint effort combining the best ideas of two or more talents for the greater good of the project. But I confess that when I started out, there was no room in my life for sharing—I wrote 100 percent of my first few hundred songs. I needed to prove I could do it all: words *and* music. The truth is, I was always glib with words, but most of my melodies came to me with difficulty.

I adored words. I had written my first little story book when I was about five, and my favorite part of school was writing compositions in English class. As I grew older and joined clubs and organizations, all I ever wanted to do was be the "reporter." And as I wound my tortured way through violin and piano lessons, and studied to be a ballerina, desperately trying to master crotchets and quavers and tempos at the Royal Academy's high-pressure ballet school, my fascination with words continued.

When I first wrote songs, people attributed these leanings to a musical inheritance from my father, Max Phillips, a gifted musician who played marvelous violin, clarinet, and sax. I'd grown up with some of the best musicians in London, Los Angeles, and Las Vegas playing in our living room. But my true aptitude—words—was actually an inheritance from my *mother!*

Nobody guessed how I struggled to come up with melodies that even came close to the potential of the lyrics I wrote. Though I had some melodic aptitude for special material, when it came to radio-friendly pop, the natural aptitude wasn't there. The more I pushed myself to be a pop composer, the more I sacrificed my fluency with words.

Thus, my career may never have materialized, but fate stepped in in the form of my Aunt Anne, who asked me to sing one afternoon at her club. I took my guitar and sang all my folk songs. A gentleman approached me after the show and told me he had a son who was a music agent; would I like to meet him?

Inherent in collabora-tion is a great opportu-nity to benefit from the insights and wisdom born of somebody else's time on earth. One must treat a collabora-tor's point of view with great respect. It is a wonderful gift: the opportunity to see an idea through some-body else's eyes.

His son, Stan Milander, who was to become one of the leading agents in the music business, listened to my songs and said, "You need to collaborate. Let me introduce you to my friend Joe." The result was my first co-written song, my first collaboration.

Joe and I sat at the piano, and he started noodling around with some musical ideas. I found I was magically able to put words wherever there were notes. It was so much easier to do it that way than to have to write both words and music!

Of course, knowing little of the craft when we wrote those first songs, we just started at the beginning and finished up wherever we finished up. There was no pre-thought that went into structure or title. Nevertheless, it was a marvelous eye-opener, the beginning of what has turned out to be a way of life for me professionally: collaboration.

HELP WANTED: *COLLABORATOR*

In collaborating, I have learned never to forget that the end result of our combined efforts must be something we both love. Therefore, I must always be open to my partner's ideas and thoughts. I may have a very strong concept as to where I want to take my lyrics, but I have to recognize that my collaborator may have been thinking along completely different lines. It is very easy to be stubborn when faced with this dilemma. I, as the "lyricist," could intensify my position as to where the song has to go, and my partner would be equally insistent that it take some other twist. This brings up the following questions: Must I win this battle of wits at any cost? Must I sacrifice the integrity of my own ideas? Should I *blend* my ideas with his? Could I just *fall in* with a partner's idea? Could it be that [GASP] my collaborator has a *better* idea than mine?

For better or worse, you will discover, as I did, that there is no pat solution. Any of the above choices work, depending on how willing to bend each collaborator is. While there will be some cases where a co-writer needs to be right at any cost—even to the point of quitting the project if his or her ideas don't prevail—we must remember that collaboration works both ways. If both of us are too stubborn to see each other's point of view, we are defeating the whole idea of collaborating.

Inherent in collaboration is a great opportunity to benefit from the insights and wisdom born of somebody else's time on earth. One must treat a collaborator's point of view with great respect. It is a wonderful gift: the opportunity to see an idea through somebody else's eyes.

There are several ways collaborations are found and formed:

1. Attend seminars and conferences put on by your local Songwriters' Association. These groups exist all over the country, and if there isn't one in your hometown, there probably is one within driving distance. (Or it may be up to *you* to round up all your fellow songwriters in your area and get such an organization going.) Listen to the work of other members of the group, and arrange to collaborate with those whose work you admire.

2. Let your friends and associates know that you are actively seeking collaborations with other songwriters. You'd be surprised how many people know others with similar aptitudes and desires as yours in the music field, and they are usually be happy to arrange meetings among you.

3. Continually ask the publishers you deal with if they have any ideas regarding writers with whom you could collaborate. Sometimes they have staff writers who they feel should collaborate. Other times, they can put you in touch with other unsigned songwriters whose work they feel would blend well with yours.

4. Once you've begun networking with other songwriters in your area, ask them for recommendations. Perhaps they will have entered into a collaboration that was fruitless for them, for one reason or another, but they think that the two of you might be better suited to work together.

5. Put notices up—"Composer (or "Lyricist") Wanted!"—on the bulletin boards of local music schools, music departments of colleges or universities, recording studios, sheet music shops, record shops, and musical instrument shops.

6. Put an ad in *The Music Connection, BAM, American Songwriter,* or any other publication dedicated to songwriters and musicians. Seek out an interactive Internet site where you can find—perhaps even chat with—a potential collaborator. List your talents (lyrics, music, or both), perhaps your credits, where you live, and the style in which you want to collaborate. (More on collaboration styles on page 126.) Long-distance collaboration is easy, thanks to the telephone, the fax, e-mail, and snail mail. And recently, when I had only a few hours' time to write a song for *The Sopranos,* my collaborator Tom Harriman sang the melody down into my telephone answering machine!

YOURS, MINE, AND OURS

There is an art to collaboration, and when it's working well, you can't beat it for creative exchange, supportiveness, and just plain fun. After all, that *is* a big part of why we're writing, isn't it? For the fun of it.

But don't expect to be able to just get together with another songwriter and have it a smooth-sailing, effortless experience right from the start. There is a psychology to working with another person in a collaborative writing

> *Co-writers need to become friends, or, at the very least, friendly, first. After all, you are going about producing a work of art together that will take all of your combined talents and artistry, your innermost thought processes, and your dedication and best work habits to boot.*

effort, and there are definite unwritten rules to making it work.

For your part, you don't want to lose (1) your mind; (2) your integrity; (3) your originality; (4) your legal rights; (5) your perspective on the song; (6) your credits; (7) your friendship; or (8) your professionalism. It's a good guess that your collaborator wants to retain all of the above as well. So how do you approach working together with the optimum chance of being successful?

I think it's extremely important to get to know the other individual as a person before you ever attempt to work together. Assuming that your collaboration isn't stemming out of a long-term friendship that has gradually led you to write together, I am of the firm opinion that co-writers need to become friends, or, at the very least, *friendly,* first. After all, you are going about producing a work of art together that will take all of your combined talents and artistry, your innermost thought processes, and your dedication and best work habits to boot. It's going to expose some very vulnerable parts of you that you'd be less than likely to choose to show a stranger. Jumping into a writing situation "cold," without getting to know each other first, is like running a marathon without doing warm-ups. A bond of communication and understanding needs to be set up before a collaboration can ever be successful.

I was on a songwriting panel once with some highly successful songwriters (all men) who got very testy when I suggested that a friendly relationship is necessary before writing. They all felt that this was utter nonsense, that if you're professional, you simply say, "How do you do?" and sit down and write a song. I quipped that we're not talking about the sex life of the playboy bachelor! Personally, I fail to see the fun of creating art with someone else when there is no underlying friendly interplay between the two of you.

In any event, friends or not, there are some ground rules for collaboration that seem to make it all go a lot more smoothly. As one who has collaborated more often than not, I offer you the following strategies to help ensure that each co-writing experience is mutually beneficial and satisfactory.

Holding onto Your Sanity

Often the pressures of working with another individual create the need to "super-excel," to be incredibly witty and bright on cue, pulling out of thin air the most wonderful thoughts ever imagined. This is almost always the result of ego: For example, your own ego tells you that you need to show your stuff to this co-writer; or, in the alternative, the collaborator has a large ego that intimidates you and makes you feel you have to live up to his or her expectations. But you know what? If you start off by being intimidated, you'll never get anywhere, because you'll always be trying to please the other person instead of going with your own instincts that please yourself. This is a terrible trap to fall into, to try to live up to false expectations created either in your own mind or that of your writing partner. You know what you know, and you know how to do what you do. Don't get sidetracked into playing ego games with yourself and your co-writer,

Approach every collaborative song with the same calm understanding of your craft and style, the same trust in your personal skills that you would put into a self-written song.

as you will most likely fail to come up with something good. Either that, or you'll push yourself to such an extreme that you'll develop a serious case of hypertension and get all sorts of symptoms from the shakes to heavy perspiration to what appears to be total mind-block. And trust me, I speak from experience: The only cure for this condition is to leave the room, the house, and the collaboration!

THE REMEDY
Approach every collaborative song with the same calm understanding of your craft and style, the same trust in your personal skills that you would put into a self-written song. Know that there will be times your collaborator will dislike your work and turn it down flat. Ultimately, if you've done your best and given it what you know, you can safely conclude that you can't please everybody.

Maintaining Your Integrity
You learn early on that you must compromise to survive in a collaboration. Two different people with different backgrounds and perspectives on life and love cannot be expected to see life through exactly the same colored glasses. When you shut your eyes and visualize a scene, you both base your visions on the sum and parts of your own life experiences. We all choose to look at things differently, and that's what makes each of us unique. If we all looked at life exactly the same way, what a famine of interesting lyrics there would be, because nobody would ever give us anything new to think about. However, there's a point beyond which your integrity will not let you go. When push comes to shove, you must take a solid stand and refuse to roll over.

THE REMEDY
If your collaborator insists on an approach to writing the song or actual lines that you find impossible to live with, first try to understand his or her point of view to the best of your ability. Make sure you aren't passing up a really sound idea for the sake of getting your way. If you're convinced that your integrity is on the line, do the following:

1. Explain your reasons for being unable to go along with his choice and don't back down on an idea that you feel strongly about. Try to convince your collaborator of the value of *your* point of view.

2. If your collaborator is still adamant about a choice you cannot in good conscience go along with, explain that in collaboration all choices must be mutual, and discuss trying to come up with a third choice that is agreeable to both of you.

3. If your collaborator still insists on his idea and refuses to try to come up with a mutually agreeable solution, drop out of the project. The bottom line is that if you have a problem with the song at the time of its *creation*, you will *never* be happy to have your name associated with it.

Keeping Your Originality

If your collaborator's ideas are simply wonderful, welcome them! Always remember that the song is the star here, not the writers. As Quincy Jones once said, "Check your egos at the door." You can only *benefit* from exciting contributions by your co-writer. But if you're coming up with very interesting lines and your collaborator keeps insisting on changing them into less than wonderful lines, ask yourself if the collaborator truly knows what he or she is about. Don't cave in and let a wonderful line go, just to appease another writer's need to contribute something. Some writers, unfortunately, have not learned how to enjoy and welcome the sparks of creativity of others; they always feel they have to alter everything so that it comes out reflecting their own personal point of view. But since your talent is in expressing your own very special insights and perspectives on the subject, don't let your originality be stifled by a collaborator's need to write something—anything—as long as its his or hers.

Learn to recognize and develop your collaborator's talent and be humble enough to greet better-than-your-own ideas with enthusiasm. Just as you want to look good, remember that your collaborator will also want to have many opportunities to excel in the process.

THE REMEDY

Stand up for what you believe in, and fight for lines and concepts you think are vital to the success of the song. Don't be swayed from what you believe just to take the easy way out, known as compromise. On the other hand, be willing to listen to your partner's point of view. Don't be afraid to give up your own less-than-special lines in favor of your co-writer's great ideas. Learn to recognize and develop your collaborator's talent and be humble enough to greet better-than-your-own ideas with enthusiasm. Just as you want to look good, remember that your collaborator will also want to have many opportunities to excel in the process. After all, the true meaning of collaboration should be: *An exchange of ideas that results in a greater end product than either collaborator could have come up with alone.* The satisfaction should be mutual, and so you will either stimulate your collaborator to be more creative, or your collaborator will trigger some great ideas in you. The relinquishing of your own originality to hear the ideas of your writing partner is certainly not a thing to be afraid of. Collaboration is about doing it *together!*

Preserving Your Legal Rights

One of the most frequently asked questions I hear is, "How do you get back your lyrics if you don't like the melody someone wrote to them?" The answer is that you have to foresee this situation in advance and provide for it in the form of an agreement.

Retaining Rights to Your Original Work

The agreement may be in writing or oral, though a written agreement that is dated and signed is easier to enforce. *I am not a lawyer, and you may want to have one check this language,* but the agreement should basically say something to the effect of: "The attached lyrics, titled (title) are the sole property of (your name), and the music as written on the attached lead sheet (or, recorded on the attached [cassette][CD]) is the sole property of (collaborator's name). Should either of the parties hereto decide not to use the other's creative work product with respect to their ([words][music]) herein, all rights in and to said creative work product shall revert to the writer thereof." Since titles cannot by copyrighted, either party should be allowed to use the title. Many songs have been successful using identical titles, and this should not cause a problem for either song. However, as a courtesy, if your collaborator came up with the title in the first place and is very much against your ever using it in any other song, you would do well to acquiesce and avoid a fight. The world is full of titles; you'll find plenty more.

By the way, if you co-wrote the entire song, weaving back and forth between you, you're probably out of luck in terms of getting back any rights to your original work product. There's just no way to divide up the rights to such a song.

An effective way to salvage a song that has been co-written and is not satisfactory to the collaborators is to bring in a third songwriter to do some rewriting and polishing. The new writer will have a fresh perspective on where to take the song. It's better to split a song into thirds and have something you like than to own half of a song you will never play for anybody because you hate it. This way, both original co-writers remain involved, and the third writer has the benefit of both your ideas.

Splits

If you are co-writing with one or more collaborators, determine the percentage split before you start. These things can get very hairy later on when the value of the copyright has been established and everyone is greedy. You could end up with a small fraction of credit and ownership in the composition. I have been furious on occasion to see a record on which I've collaborated come out with as many as five names as co-writers. I've written 100 percent of the lyric, but have been informed at the last minute that I get one-fifth of the total income instead of the one-half to which a lyricist is traditionally entitled. Be sure your collaborator hasn't brought in a friend/lover/child to work on the song without consulting you. I wrote a song a couple of years ago that a collaborator suddenly informed me had a new *one-third percent* co-writer on the melody and track. He didn't ask me in advance, but simply brought in this new songwriter with whom he was smitten that week. He played me the tape and said something gooshy like, "Lynn is a co-writer; she put her marvelous little hands on the piano and came up with this bridge." Well, Lynn's marvelous little hands cost that guy a collaboration with me. I was very annoyed at having my writer's share reduced from one-half to one-third, without first being consulted—especially in light of the fact that I had written 100 percent of the lyrics and most of the melody on the hook. Of course, there was no reason in the world why he couldn't have written the bridge melody himself, except making points with the woman, which is fine with me, but not on *my* song!

Collaboration splits have changed a lot since the days of Tin Pan Alley. A song was a song, the composer got half, the lyricist got half, end of story. But we're not living in the age of piano-voice demos of thirty-two–bar songs. We're talking about five-minute epics with three verses, two pre-choruses, bridges, breakdowns, reprises, musical solos, and fades, seventy-two–track direct-to-hard-drive demos with umpteen layers of synthesizer overdubs, four tracks of background vocals, five tracks of drums, and ten mix-and-match lead vocals.

If all you've written is lyrics and it takes more than one composer to accomplish all of the tracking and melody, the distinctive bass line, and so on, you should be willing to relinquish an additional portion of your song share. Generally, if I have written 100 percent of the lyrics, I do not accept less than one-third of the total song, no matter how many composers are involved. The composers then share the remaining two-thirds, which they generally believe is a fair split. This is not so much pride as it is integrity. The bigger an artist is you're working with, the more honorable he or she is likely to be in recognizing your true split on the song. When I wrote the theme to the feature film *Burglar* with Jermaine, Jackie and Randy Jackson, Bernard Edwards, and others, they were very gracious about splitting two-thirds of the song among themselves.

An oral understanding regarding splits at the beginning is usually sufficient, though, as any lawyer will tell you, it never hurts to put your agreements into writing.

Copyright

To protect both you and your collaborator, register the copyright on a form P.A. with the Library of Congress in Washington, D.C. Formal copyright registration establishes a date of having written the work. It is generally agreed that "mailing a song to yourself" also known as "poor man's copyright" is a practice unlikely to hold up in a court of law.

Publishing

Though a collaborator may try to coerce you, never be in a hurry to sign away your publishing share on a song, unless perhaps there is an urgency that is time sensitive with regard to the song's use. Definitely don't be inveigled by a collaborator to sign away your own publishing share to the company at which he or she is a staff writer unless you feel this can benefit *you*. Some writers are pressured by their publishers to bring all the publishing of their collaborators into that publisher's hot little hands. Sometimes, the co-writer will actually— perhaps secretly—share in that publishing income. Your income! Feel under no such obligation. Only sign a song contract if it's of your own volition. And should your collaborator ever insist that you sign a song-publishing agreement with his or her own publishing company, you'd better ask yourself why you should give away your publishing share of the song. It could be very valuable to you—both financially and as a negotiating tool—later on.

Keeping Your Perspective on the Song

A collaborative song generally begins with a clear concept that each of you have in your minds. Since you are bringing that concept into the collaboration, you both have to try—in spite of the new twists and new meanings that arise from exploring the story idea—to keep the story on track. When you co-write, so many ideas can get thrown back and forth that it's easy to be swayed from what you set out to say. Unless the conversation leads you to what is actually a better idea, try to remember that you both lose if your focus gets lost.

THE REMEDY

Don't be embarrassed to keep on guiding the song back into focus. If you are the primary lyricist in the relationship, your collaborator will undoubtedly be counting on *you* to make sure the story grows in as powerful a direction as you had first discussed.

Keeping Your Credits

Sometimes within an ongoing collaboration, you'll write more on one song than another. If you are to have a longstanding relationship, it cannot be hampered by haggling over who did what. It is very common for writers to say, "Well, I did more of the music, so I deserve 60 percent or 75 percent on this song." But over the long haul, I believe it all comes out in the wash. Over the lifetime of the collaboration, each of you will have contributed valuable things to each of your works together and will benefit equally from the body of work. It is not always *how much* you invest in a song, it is the quality of *what* you put into it. For instance, in the Academy Award–winning song "Arthur," though four names were on the song as co-writers, whoever came up with the stunningly visual and original line, "If you get caught between the moon and New York City," certainly made an important contribution to the song. It would have been enough even if he or she had not volunteered another word or note!

THE REMEDY

As two collaborators work on their first song together, there is a process of getting to know one another. Perhaps in the first song you write, the contributions each of you will make will be genuinely skewed. In that case, agree to an amicable, if not equal split. However, make a pact that if you are to write more songs together, you must have equal splits across the board, regardless of who does what. Sometimes you will each carry the other; sometimes you'll contribute equally. Arguing over splits on credit and money is not conducive to healthy collaborations.

Maintaining Your Friendship

Writing a song is not worth losing a friend over. Who has the better idea is not worth hating somebody over. If your partner is unable to come up with anything that pleases you, it's not worth disdaining him or her over. Always put the friendship ahead of the song. If your co-writer is having a bad day, week, or year, show understanding and perhaps take a break from writing together, but don't take a break from the friendship.

Fighting Possessiveness

In my first major collaboration, I fell into the trap of letting my collaborator "possess" me, in that I felt guilty if I even *thought* about working with anybody else. On the few occasions during those years when I did go and work with other collaborators, I would tell her about them dismissively, deriding the songs I'd written with them as "not much good," so she wouldn't feel I had been unfaithful to the collaboration. It was an awful mental pickle to be in, as I also resented anybody whom she occasionally co-wrote with. I felt as if her wanting to work with others in some way would detract from the bond we had as collaborators.

In today's music business, I see what seems to be a very healthy trend toward multiple collaborations among a group of songwriters who are all friends with one another. Songwriters have found that they can be friendly without being competitive. Over a period of months and years, the same people work together in different combinations. They recommend demo singers, musicians, studios, equipment, and when they are working together as a duo and are stuck for a lyric or a bridge or whatever, they'll call on a third song-writer whom they perhaps both know and work with separately.

Perhaps this is an eroding of the old-time, one-on-one collaborative style that made such teams as Mann/Weil, Leiber/Stoller, Bacharach/David, Rodgers/Hammerstein, and Goffin/King famous, but it seems to work in today's highly technical, electronic-influenced musical world. It also doesn't preclude ongoing primary collaborations, with occasional co-writes on the side. What I'm saying is that co-writing outside a primary relationship can bring new color and depth to what co-writers do together. Once in a while, half of an established co-writing team might avoid becoming stale or feeling trapped in an ongoing relationship by branching out. Working with other writers can infuse some new stylings and ideas into their work.

The hardest thing to handle is often the feelings of guilt for wanting to work with somebody else. But remember: Whatever you do in your other co-writing relationships can only make you a better writer, who is capable of bringing more to your ongoing collaboration. The second hardest thing to handle is the letting go, when your co-writer expresses a need to work with others. Let's face it, if you make a scene about it and insist that he or she does-n't do it, it's only going to push you apart and ruin the relationship anyway. Remain calm—you'll find you lose nothing by being genuinely understand-ing and encouraging when your collaborators work with other lyricists.

Please do not take this to mean that if you have a really marvelous, exclusive collaboration that truly works and brings you both pleasure and great rewards, that you should sacrifice it to work with others and spread yourself thinner. If you're into something really special, stay with it as long as it's good. There will always be untold numbers of other writers you can meet and work with at a later date, should you so desire.

As for me, each of my collaborations has a special place in my life. I enjoy my wonderful collaboration-friendships so much that I cannot foresee ever choosing to give them all up for one exclusive relationship.

Maintaining Your Professionalism

If you feel that a writer with whom you are attempting a collaboration has poor work habits or is unskilled to the point of not being able to compete in the marketplace, I see no reason to continue working with this person. Your time is valuable and not worth wasting on pointless collaborations. I know one very successful rock songwriter who will stop in the middle of a verse and simply declare, "This is going nowhere. I'm not going to finish it." Brusque, perhaps; and I have met several writers who have found this behavior threat-ening and ego-bruising. But even if he doesn't do it with a good bedside man-ner, his point is well taken. If it's not going to be a great song or even a good song, why write it, spend the money on demo-ing it, and waste your own and your publisher's time with it?

In retrospect, I can see that I never should have bothered to write, demo, or submit a few of the songs that are gathering dust in my catalogue, though I'm sure my collaborators and I believed in them at the time.

But the lesson that I'd like to pass along to you as you get involved in collaboration is that, too often, "iffy" songs are the result of too much compromising for ego's sake and not enough commitment to making the *song* great. I have to say, knowing what I know now about the competitive marketplace, I would not bother to write some of those songs were I asked to work on them now. It's very hard to say *no* to a melody that someone you care about has offered you, especially when that someone really loves what he or she has created. On the other hand, on looking back, I can see that some of the collaborations were doomed at the point of that first compromise.

STYLES IN WHICH TO COLLABORATE

When the Track is the Record

While tracks used to be the exclusive purview of musical arrangers, recently there has been a trend toward writing lyrics directly to tracks, without any melody being provided. The first time I was asked to do this, by a rock artist, I listened to this slamming rock track several times, then called the composer and said: "This is a wonderful track, but there's something missing!" "What?" he asked, perplexed. "*The notes,*" I replied! He said, "Oh, I thought you could write to the track." In a case like this, a lyricist must either write lyrics into the shape of the bass line, as I did, or must by default write both words and music. Since the track-writer will want to claim credit for half the song, this becomes a muddy area for a lyricist to contend with. Today, much of what is being written can't be defined as "songs," so much as "records." Thus, the contribution of a hip, exciting track could well be the key to getting the song recorded. So even though you have written words and music, which is traditionally 100 percent of the song, if your collaborator(s) wrote the track, you may find yourself accepting a 50 percent or smaller share in the copyright.

Traditional Writing Styles

There are three traditional ways in which to write a song: (1) write the lyrics first, (2) write the melody first, or (3) write both lyrics and melody at the same time. I have no preference among these styles; however, most of my collaborators seem to work best in one style or another, so I try to accommodate them. Over the years I have learned to write equally effectively in any of these styles. You may have already found your favorite way of working; if not, experiment. Learning to be good at all of them will maximize your professional potential.

Writing the Lyrics First

Most composers believe they can write a melody to a lyric. In my experience, very few can take a lyric, *as is,* and write a melody that fits it syllable for syllable, making it come alive. I find this even though I have done my utmost to make every line scan properly in successive verses and used a simple dummy melody when setting up the scansions. For the composers who can, however, writing to a lyric is the simplest thing in the world and comes very naturally. I must admit I do find it tedious to develop a really strong lyric, only to hand it over to a composer who comes back a few days later with a melody that has no earthly relationship to my lyric. That means I have to completely rewrite and restructure my lyrics to fit the new melody. Sometimes the new melody takes the song light years ahead, and my new lyric is dramatically better than the original draft. Other times, however, the new melody has only weakened the quality of the lyric and changed its mood, because the composer never really considered what mood the lyric suggested.

In any event, when you decide to write "lyrics first," begin by coming up with a good title and developing the story line either mentally or on paper in an outline form. Go over the details of the story line with your collaborator so that he or she can give you input.

Working with a dummy melody, create your lyric to whichever song formula you choose. Make sure that any time a section is repeated, such as a second or third verse, every single word reads to the same scansion and meter.

If the first line of the first verse reads:
Don't *wait* till it's too *late,* 'cause I'll be *gone*

Make sure the first line of the second verse reads in the same meter, such as:
So *take* your chance, don't *let* it slip *away*

If the first line is a complicated scan such as this, with fifteen syllables:
If I'm *gon*na *be* your *ba*by, *don't you* be *tel*lin' me *lies*

You're in trouble if the first line of the next verse (also fifteen syllables) scans:
I *don't* want your *pro*mises, *you* know I'm *rea*dy for *ac*tion

You notice that though each of those two lines contains fifteen syllables, the number of words alone isn't enough to make them match, as the emphasis must be correct. It is an "in" joke but one you can count on, that we must avoid putting the "em-*pha*-sis on the wrong syl-*la*-ble!" As I've mentioned before, some composers will appreciate your reading the lyric in rhythm onto a cassette, so that they can have some idea of how the lyric works with their melody or track. Others want to try to find their own way.

When your collaborator finishes writing the melody, however, if you're not happy with it, ask him if he'd try something else. Of course, if he refuses, you must reluctantly tell him you'd prefer to take your lyrics back and save them for something else. You're not obligated to sacrifice your good lyrics to a mediocre melody.

Writing to a Track or Melody

First, listen to the melody many times to familiarize yourself with all its parts. Then, identify the hook line and imagine the title (if the composer has given you one) being sung to those notes. If they haven't given you a title, you have to set about finding one, which means singing dozens of lines to that melody until certain lines jump out as being a good match. Get your collaborator in on the title-choosing process if possible, as most composers want to be involved in choosing a title for their melody. Remember that inherent in a piece of music is an atmosphere, a mood that you have to discover. Is it about losing? winning? regret? romance? hunger? Is it sad, sexy, or humorous? Once you have pinpointed the story that exists within the melody, you can begin writing first a title, then writing the great lyrics that bring it to life.

When a suitable title has been selected, go over the basics of the story you want to tell with the composer. Provide two or three concepts that might fit this title so your collaborator can make a clearer choice. I have noticed that when the composer approves the title and concept in advance, I don't do as much rewriting!

Writing Together at the Same Time

This is the old theatrical Tin Pan Alley method of writing songs, and it's not always easy. It's a free flow of ideas back and forth that you bounce off each other. The song builds as it goes, the collaborators feed off each other's creativity. Country writers in Nashville do it every day. They start at ten, write through to lunchtime, go out for a bite to eat, and come back and finish the song. That's how thousands of songs a week are written in Music City, Tennessee. Don't worry, it becomes second nature once you gain confidence in your ideas.

Writing together at the same time requires concentration and a quick-working mind. It helps to be a good listener, paying attention to where your partner is taking the idea, and seeing where that leads you. Unfortunately, sometimes it isn't helped by the fact that your collaborator will be sitting looking at you expectantly while you're trying to think; naturally, this makes your brain fly out the window and you couldn't come up with a line to hang the wash on! It is, however, extremely rewarding to work this way.

Just hang in there with the process. Throw all your ideas out there, say them out loud, keep talking, and suddenly you'll spit the right one out. Both you and your collaborator will hear it at the same time, and smile with delight!

In a creative environment, where the two of you are on the same wavelength, you can't beat a together-at-the-same-time type of collaboration, as some of the work you will come up with will surely be inspired. So if you're going to do it that way, be in a comfortable environment. Don't worry if you go off the track and talk about romance or current events or your car insurance bill during the process. You'll need to take breaks from the pressure of working together so hard. Sometimes, if you go out for a meal and get off the subject, you'll come back refreshed and ready to finish the song. In my considered opinion, it's better to try to finish a draft of a song written in this style (regardless of the number of interruptions or breaks) in one stretch—one afternoon, evening, or day.

INTUITIVE CHOICES IN COLLABORATION

One of my favorite former students, Alan, called me from Canada to say he had made a major breakthrough in his songwriting. "I've stopped pushing so hard," he announced proudly. "I suddenly understand you have to just let the ideas come to you."

Alan explained that he had been writing with a collaborator and, as usual, he had been driving himself crazy trying to come up with lines. Like all of us, he wanted to prove himself a worthy collaborator and was trying to carry his weight in the songwriting relationship. The woman he was writing with was being quite prolific that day, and the ideas were flowing from her. Alan was so interested in what she was coming up with that he forgot to have his usual anxiety attack at trying to perform on cue. As a result, he had let ideas just come to him as an instinctive reflex, instead of forcing them.

We are not performing seals. Nobody ever said coming up with brilliant ideas was going to be easy. Instilled in all our psyches is a will to prove how clever, quick, and interesting we can be, and at no time is that need to prove one's dexterity with ideas greater than during a face-to-face collaborative writing effort.

Alan was delighted to learn that in a collaboration of ideas, it was not the responsibility of either of the collaborators to come up with *all* the great moments. Rather, it is a shared experience that permits each individual to respond to the other's input.

Psychologists sometimes put patients through a Rorschach test, which requires them to look at an ink blot and say the first things that come into their heads. This is used to evaluate and interpret their psychological disposition. In songwriting, imagine that your collaborator's comments are Rorschach blots, and your role is to respond to them in the first way that comes to your mind. This is a great mental

In songwriting, two heads are often better than one. Though it can sometimes be a two-headed monster, it can also put eyes in the back of your head so you can see what's going on on the other side of life.

game and can be a lot more fun than the private agony of trying to come up with wonderful ideas all by yourself, just to prove that you can! Thoughts that your collaborator might come up with could trigger exactly the right direction for the lines you're seeking. Even if your co-writer is a composer and not a lyricist, he or she will be able to help you direct your thinking if you open up. Your collaborator may not know how to say the thought cleverly—that's why you're there—but still may have a strong grasp of the concept and direction it should take. Your partner can help you shape your thinking by making thoughtful comments, discussing the scenario you're trying to paint with your lyrics, and perhaps even seeing aspects of the scene that you have overlooked. Believe me, you will be eternally grateful for any comments that steer you onto the home-run course.

Over time, you will learn to differentiate between your collaborator's truly bad ideas, the ones that are slightly off base, and the ones that are in the ballpark. It's an intuitive kind of thing; you'll just know it's right, that's all. You'll have to guide your partner's thinking just as he or she is guiding yours, until between you you've hit on the best direction for the song.

But all the effort you put in is worth it, because as I've said, when a collaboration is great, nothing can top it. It's exhilaration at its finest. It's juices flowing and eyes sparkling. It's an exchange of ideas and points of view. It's a way of rising to a challenge to work better than ever, and it's a system of checks and balances wherein you have somebody there to tell you you can work just a little harder—someone with just as much at stake in the race as you have, who wants to see the song succeed as much as you do. In songwriting, two heads are often better than one. Though it can sometimes be a two-headed monster, it can also put eyes in the back of your head so you can see what's going on on the other side of life. Quite simply, collaboration gets you away from yourself and back to communicating.

FEAR OF COLLABORATION

Many people fear that in collaborating they will lose something of themselves. They fear that their creativity will be stultified by the input of another writer, that they will lose their individuality or point of view. They fear that they will no longer be recognized as "total" creative writers.

I'd like to be able to say that none of this ever happens. But it does. Except it only happens in the wrong collaborations. When working in a demeaning or suppressive relationship, one's creativity may indeed suffer and wither. But mirroring normal interpersonal relationships, if one is in any worthwhile writing collaboration, it needs to allow both parties to grow and learn to be strong. We all know that nobody flourishes or grows when they're being manipulated. I have been through, and have watched friends go through, bad collaborations that cut off the flow of confidence and smother all feelings of self-worth. But these scenarios don't have to happen. You may have heard the saying, "You create what you fear." Go into a collaboration with a healthy attitude, and you'll have nothing to fear.

Negative Collaborations Produce Burnout Look-Alike

I've had the curious experience of feeling completely untalented and dry of any ideas when working with certain people. There have only been a few instances of this, but it's always the same thing. They drain me like vacuum cleaners, sucking me dry of all creativity and energy. I have forced myself to work in certain of these situations that I thought might benefit my career, but I've discovered that all it does is shake me up and make me doubt my abilities.

One young composer who was new to the business but by some great luck was working with all the great lyricists you can think of, kept throwing in my face the names of those he was working with. He intimidated me so much by telling me that my work had to be at least as good as theirs, that I couldn't come up with a creative line to save my life. He sat on the sofa and stared at me as I tried to do an umpteenth rewrite to please him, and I felt my bowels constrict, my throat go dry, and my extremities begin to shake. My head felt as if it were filled with cotton, and not a single word would come to my mind. Finally, I told him I thought we'd better give it up, as it wasn't working out. He was relieved, as he thought I was a lousy lyricist. When he walked down the pathway away from my house, I started gathering inner strength, color came back to my face, and I felt as if I'd just had a jail sentence commuted! I started dancing and singing around the house, kissing my husband, cooking, laughing, and acting as if I'd just found the answer to the meaning of life, so great was my relief to see his departing back! Oddly enough, he was a nice fellow; I enjoyed having lunch with him. However, when it came to collaborating, he was a jinx to my art, as he undermined my self-image.

On another occasion, I worked with a very sweet recording artist who kept me doing rewrites for almost a year on a song that had a title suggested by something beautiful in one of her diaries. She finally approved the lyrics and I brought the melodist to her home to finish the song for her forthcoming album. She suddenly decided she *didn't* like the lyrics and started throwing out dozens of contradictory concepts, so fast did her mind work. I was totally unnerved but tried to keep up, though the sound of her secretary making travel arrangements, her maid vacuuming, and her son playing Michael Jackson through studio monitors in his bedroom down the hall gave me an advanced case of the heebie jeebies. I couldn't think of one word, let alone a line. It was as if my brain had taken a vacation. When I finally left, I drove down the street and stopped at the nearest liquor shop, where I purchased a huge Three Musketeers bar. I jammed it in my mouth and consumed it in about a minute flat. (I think that's known as a chocolate fix.) And I'd been off chocolate for a year! When I got home, my husband stared at me in disbelief and asked, "What is all that chocolate on your dress?" I looked down, and my dress was literally covered with squished chocolate from top to bottom. "I earned it!" I said.

The next day, I met the recording artist in a restaurant with the idea of finalizing the lyrics. She didn't give me a minute to even sit down and catch my breath, let alone eat my food, but commenced with the rewriting once more, in the exact same hurried, overwhelming fashion. In retrospect, I realize I should have told her she was being impossible. Was I just trying to prove to myself that I could handle it? What nonsense if I was. Anyway, when she finally raised the coffee cup to her mouth, after about half an hour, I took the moment to talk about something human, real, ordinary, NOT LYRICS! "I just today got confirmation from my publisher," I told her, "and they want me to write a book about how to write lyrics for the commercial marketplace." "How wonderful, dear!" she said, *genuinely* enthusiastic. "Now let's see why it is we think we can write a book about how to write lyrics!" I looked at her, and suddenly I laughed inside. The preposterousness of this comment broke the spell. In fifteen minutes I had all the lines she wanted. She's a very bright and articulate woman, but I'll *never* write another song with her again. We could be friends, I realized, but the chemistry was all wrong for collaboration.

Thus have I learned to stay away from uncreative associations. They slow down my thinking process and steal my self-confidence. I'm sure you have all had similar experiences if you've done any collaborating at all. I don't think you have to be Einstein to figure out that it isn't working. You just don't always want to acknowledge the signs. Start getting in touch with those real, physical symptoms of discomfort: the faintness; the upset stomach; the trembling; the desire to be on the moon, in Siberia, *anyplace* but right there. Recognize the effects on you of this collaborator's criticism, whether you can analyze it and see its merits or whether you *just don't want to hear it*—even if he or she has won a shelf full of Grammys! I am firmly convinced that collaboration often boils down to a matter of attractive or repellent chemistry between two individuals.

But whether it's different chemistry or different points of view, different levels of professionalism or different styles, I advise you to stay away from any collaboration that doesn't make you work at full power, energy, and creativity. Take steps to extricate yourself from any collaboration that seems to bring out the worst in you. Why go on with it if all it does is undermine your talent? So be friends, be lovers, be siblings, be spouses, but *don't write together!* What do you want to bet that what you thought was "burnout" was simply lousy working chemistry!

Breaking off a bad or stultifying work relationship is never particularly easy to do, but you have to do it as soon as possible, so as not to waste your own or your collaborator's time. It's hard to imagine that your collaborator isn't feeling the same way about the situation, so he or she will most likely welcome your polite efforts to end it and move on. "I don't think this is working, no offense . . . " That's all you have to say. Leave it simple and neat; no lengthy explanations or insults are necessary.

The unfortunate consequence is that the severance of ties, especially where the two of you have made a committed effort to trying to make it work, can leave writers feeling very bewildered and "out on their own." The obvious answer is to get right back in there and start networking, meeting new people, and establishing new collaborations. Because when you do find a great collaboration, you'll know it was well worth the wait.

6

STREET SMART
AND MARKET WISE

O nce upon a time, there was popular music. And that included just about anything anybody loved to sing, hum, or whistle. It was *always* melodic, *always* had catchy lyrics, and was usually simply sung, often with a minimum of accompaniment.

In the late fifties and early sixties, Country, pop, R & B, and soul, as well as orchestral songs, novelty songs, folk songs, and almost any other format you can think of, shared the spotlight on the radio. You might have heard Buddy Holly & the Crickets one minute, Tennessee Ernie Ford the next. The hits came higgledy-piggledy from a diverse lineup of artists, including Elvis Presley, Frank Sinatra, Ricky Nelson, Lawrence Welk, the Shirelles, Marty Robbins, Pat Boone, Johnny Mathis, the Ronnettes, the Percy Faith Orchestra, Patti Page, and the Purple People Eater. A good song was just a good song, and all a songwriter had to worry about was writing a great melody and a catchy lyric, and she'd make the Top 100.

I'm not sure what happened along the way to divide music into so many subcategories, but we now find ourselves looking through *Billboard Magazine* and finding an array of so many different music charts that our eyes glaze over. What do all these charts mean to a songwriter? Well, they mean we need to direct our songwriting toward one genre or another. We can even be as specific as trying to custom-write the song for a particular artist within the format we've chosen. There are no longer a panoply of artists who cover the latest songs and provide us with two and three almost simultaneous cover versions of the same song on the charts.

At one time, if you liked a new song, you could go to the local record store and find it by twenty-five different artists, from Nat King Cole to Tony Martin, from the Gordon Jenkins Singers to Joni James. You weren't buying what we now refer to as "a production" by a certain artist; you were buying, wonder of wonders, *the song!* You just wanted it sung by your favorite singer.

I heard once that Jimmy Webb's composition "By the Time I Get to Phoenix" was recorded some 850 times. I feel thrilled these days if I can get a song covered more than once, which is very sad, considering the amount of work and love that goes into each song. But the truth is, we live in the age of the Disposable Song. Most songs have one life on one album and then vanish forever because they were written for one specific format. Furthermore, many—particularly Hip-hop and Rap—are written starting with a rhythm track rather than starting with the lyrics and melody line. The words and music are frequently added just prior to recording, and are more about stream of consciousness than craft. This type of song rarely has long-term value as a copyright, or "standard," since what the artist has created is not so much a song, as a *record*. The fact is that if a song doesn't hold up without the record's production values, it's short-lived as a copyright. The most it can hope for is not a cover version, but that some part of it will later be sampled by another artist, and used as a clip in another song.

When you decide to use a "sample" of somebody else's record, be aware of what that will mean to you:

1. The record you are sampling already exists as a copyright and has attained some level of success in its own right;
2. The original owner and music publisher of that sampled work consider that your new work, which incorporates the sample, is not a separate entity, but an amalgamated, blended song, in which the writers of the original sample become participants.
3. Because of the existing success or profile of the sampled material, the owner/publisher of that work is in the position of deciding how large your percentage of ownership will be in this new blended song, regardless of how small the amount of sampled material may be. Some owner/publishers request a reasonable split, others have been known to request as much as 100 percent ownership of the blended song. If that should happen to you, your income on the song, even though you've written a whole new song around the sample, would amount to zero.
4. The incorporation of a sample in any original song written for a motion picture immediately disqualifies the whole song from eligibility for Academy Award consideration.

If we are to be competitive in the songwriting business today, we can maximize our efforts by being market wise: directing a song we're writing toward a particular style and chart. Few if any artists record the old thirty-two–bar song format. Those who do—with the exception of jazz and "music of our lives" formats—rarely get any radio airplay to promote album sales. So what that means to "standard," "middle-of-the-road"–type of artists—once the largest user of traditionally written songs—is that they are not likely to get signed by major labels, and instead need to go with private or independent distribution, possibly make distribution deals with Internet record companies. The great loss to the listening world at large is that sweeping strings, harmonious chorales, and mellifluous voices singing the melody "as written" are rarely marketed to or heard by the masses any more.

Therefore, in my view, to maximize our songwriting time, we should (1) attempt to write for an artist of our choice; and (2) have a firm footing in the style in which he or she sings. Writing in an unfamiliar style or a "pseudo" style often leads to discouraging rejection when trying to pitch a song, and who needs to subject themselves to that!

> If you're going to write in a particular style, you must become extremely familiar with it. Remember: There are umpteen people writing in that style who *do* know what they're doing, so do your homework, or your attempt will surely suffer by comparison.

That doesn't mean that you can't learn to write in more than one style. You certainly can, but it takes a concerted effort. Therefore, if you're trying to write in an unfamiliar style with the intention of becoming professional in it, the best thing to do is immerse yourself in the style—researching it thoroughly, listening to everything you can get your hands on. Write several things until you get the hang of it, until it becomes second nature. Don't be upset if you aren't brilliant at first; remember that, until you master it, this is all part of the learning process. It doesn't mean you're no good or you can't write, it just means you have to learn the language of this style. For instance, it is not enough to drop a "g" off the end of a word (lovin', wantin', needin') to make your lyric right for a Country song! To write good Country requires getting comfortable with writing from the point of view of rural Southern folk.

The next step in getting good at a certain style of writing is to subject your songs to thoughtful scrutiny by publishers or other writers who specialize in the style. They'll be able to give you constructive comments that will tell you where you're going right and where you're missing the boat.

Frankly, you'd do yourself a big favor to write in a style that you love and listen to all the time, as it will come to you much more naturally than trying to feel your way around an unfamiliar musical world. Also, if you're *collaborating* on a song that's being written in a certain style, you'd better make sure that your collaborator is either a natural at that style or has really worked at it. The big trap in writing outside of a style that's comfortable for you is that you tend to get gimmicky, thinking you are emulating the style, when really all you're doing is parodying it. It helps for you to be realistic about your expertise from the outset, as the artists and producers looking at your songs will recognize an imitation as quickly as a diamond cutter can spot a cubic zirconium.

A STYLE GUIDE

There are so many formats today that you could think of writing in, discussing them alone would fill a book. Many of these formats are genuine musical styles with a history and roots and a long line of musical exponents who have worked in that particular art form. A good many of them, however, are simply radio format labels that some enterprising disc jockey or promotion type came up with to sell a particular station's sound, to differentiate it from other stations with a similar format.

Many names of musical styles are recent coinages. *Black music,* for instance, is an outgrowth of the term "R & B," which means "rhythm and blues," long a mainstay of popular radio. *Black music* was a phrase coined to represent black pride in the cultural contribution to our musical heritage of African-American composers, lyricists, musicians, vocalists, arrangers, and producers. Black music is still also called R & B, and R & B is still also called Black music. The term *Urban music,* which applies to the exact same material, was coined by pop radio stations that wished to include Black/R & B music in their formats. "Crossover" refers to a station that plays the Black/R & B/Urban format plus pop. Oddly enough, crossover programming gives the listeners a greater diversity of material to sample and it's reminiscent of the "old-style" format of all-encompassing radio.

Pop, Hot 100, and *hit radio* all mean approximately the same thing, as they tend to play what's on the "Hot 100" pop charts as listed in music trade magazines. *Adult contemporary, easy listening, MOR,* and *soft rock* are virtually the same, though specific play lists vary, reflecting how adventurous the program directors are in their selection of mid-tempo songs.

Needless to say, there is a certain amount of confusion among writers as we try to determine what format we are trying to write for. If the pop charts and pop radio are also playing Urban music, and if pop stars are winning awards in the R & B categories and Black stars are winning pop awards, how do we determine what to write for whom? There is no easy answer to these questions. The best we can do is study an artist's individual style and music and try to write good, strong lyrics that make a contemporary statement. Ultimately, the producer chosen for the project will determine the exact slant of the record, which could move the song over from one category to another simply by altering the arrangement and interpretation. One thing is certain, though: A demo can't try to be more than one thing at once. There must be a distinctive sound on the demo, something that conveys at least one definitive style in which the song could be presented on record. Then the producer can take it from there and decide whether the songwriter's way or some other format might best present the song.

A good song is still a good song, whatever the category. Radio formats change and evolve as often as the clothes on a shop window mannequin. What do they all mean? Absolute definitions are hard to come by, because everyone has their own interpretation. All *you* have to worry about is studying the one you're working on today.

STUDYING RADIO AND MUSIC VIDEOS

The more you listen to different formats on the radio, the more aware you become of how vast the industry is. You also get a handle on how good your work is going to have to be in order to be competitive. It's good to have an idea what you're up against, but don't let it threaten your self-confidence. Every writer of each of those songs started just where you did. If they can be successful, why not you, too? So listen to as much music as you can absorb without feeling threatened or intimidated by it.

I find music videos fascinating and hypnotic. Once I turn on a music video network, I get caught up in it. I don't know if I listen to the songs as much as I watch the visual interpretations and study the faces of the artists. Videos provide a wonderful slice of life, because they are incredibly imaginative. I cannot imagine anybody being active in the music business, let alone writing songs, and not keeping up with videos. Also, since so many singles are accompanied by videos, it doesn't hurt to "think video" when writing lyrics.

A&R people are always saying, "I want something like [blank]," which means the latest No. 1 song. What they really mean is, "I want something that is as original/knocks me out as much as/is as good in its own way as [blank]." This is because it's been proven over and over again that the songs that rise to the top are not copies of others that have been successful. The ones that make it are usually unique and fresh in their approach.

In any event, the time that elapses between a song's being selected and its receiving airplay is usually substantial. It must be presented to the artist, the artist's management, and the A&R (Artists & Repertoire) director at the label, and considered against all other material submitted; a producer must be selected, an arranger's charts must be written, the recording dates must be set. After it has been mixed, mastered, pressed, distributed, and promoted—whatever song those A&R people said they were looking for way back when is yesterday's news. It's cold. In the intervening weeks or months, they have made the same comment about twenty-five other songs.

The biggest pitfall in studying what you listen to on the radio and TV is that sometimes it's easy to inadvertently copy what you hear. And stealing a melody, even inadvertently, will subject you and your publisher to an expen-

It is your job to become an original, to say old things in a new way. But until you know what's been said before, and embrace the rich history of popular music, you will likely write trite, repetitive ideas.

sive copyright-infringement lawsuit. The one thing you can steal pretty much without getting caught, however, is the *feel* of a song. The feel of a song is a combination of its tempo, rhythm, groove, meter, bass line, motion, lilt, and pocket (the "pocket" is the comfortable way the song sits in its rhythmic track). In fact, a songs *feel* is quite literally what the song makes you feel. If a feel appeals to you, you can write a new lyric over it. The composer you work with may never know how you arrived at the verse pattern you did, but he or she will instantly recognize that, for-mat-wise, it *feels* like a hit.

Finally, listening to music or watching music video clips often stimu-lates the sluggish writing momentum. If you've hit a wall on a song you're working on, sometimes watching MTV or other music video channels gets your creative juices flowing, and suddenly the answer for your own song comes to you, you turn the tube off—and get on with writing your own hit!

THE COMPETITION

A little (very little) narcissism goes a long way in this business, and usually too far. Excessive egotism with regard to your own work can be a terrible trap, and many writers have been hoisted on their own petard—done in by their own brash overconfidence.

So saying, we've got something important to discuss: You know all those famous names, such as Diane Warren, Max Martin, Baby Face, L.A. Reid, Barry Mann, Cynthia Weil, Will Jennings, Lamont Dozier, Willie Nelson, Ashford & Simpson, Bernie Taupin, Carole Bayer Sager? Well, you know the ones. Did you ever stop to consider that your songs are *in competition with theirs?* Eeek!

It is common for beginning writers to compare themselves only to the writers in their circle—their friends and peers. So listening to the demos of well-known writers, knowing they're being listened to side by side with your own, can really put a dent in your confidence. But that's reality, so there's no point in pretending it somehow doesn't affect *your* career. The sooner you deal with recognizing the competition, the sooner you're going to become a professional in this business and a peer of those great writers.

Study the Greats

Get to know the music of artists who are successful in the style in which you want to write. Listen to the radio—you'll find clues in the music you hear both on current and "oldies" stations. Borrow or buy all the CDs you can to familiarize yourself with the type of lyrics, the feel and format of the songs. This would also be the place to suggest that you download pirated music from Internet sites. Yet, in good conscience, I cannot suggest you support Web sites that are preventing artists and songwriters from earning their due royalties.

I believe that it is crucial to delve into and study the work of successful writers who have come before you. Get to know the pioneering pop writing of Fats Domino ("I'm Walkin," "One Night," "My Happiness"), Buddy Holly ("That'll Be the Day," "Peggy Sue," "True Love Ways"), and Chuck Berry ("Johnny B. Goode," "Maybellene," "Roll Over Beethoven"). Determine for yourself why John Lennon and Paul McCartney's writing for the Beatles ("Yesterday," "Hey, Jude," "Strawberry Fields Forever") was so phenomenally successful. If you're writing rock, read the casual arrogance of the Rolling Stones' lyrics ("Satisfaction," "Sympathy for the Devil," "Wild Horses") and be moved by the mystical quality of the Doors' lyrics ("Crystal Ship," "Riders on the Storm," "People are Strange.") Think you're the first person to ever sing the blues? Try listening to Big Mama Thornton (she wrote and sang the original "You Ain't Nothin' But a Hound Dog"), or pioneering blues writers such as Mississippi John Hurt ("See See Rider," "Stack O' Lee Blues,"), Charles E. Calhoun ("Flip Flop and Fly," "Shake, Rattle & Roll,"), Bessie Smith ("Hard Time Blues"). Or go to the wonderful Harry's Blues Lyrics Online Web site with its more than 3,000 lyrics printed in full, as well as more than 1,500 30-second blues sound clips, which will provide you with hours of insights into the history of the blues.

Want to write a musical? In my view, writing show music without ever being thrilled by the lyrics of the likes of Cole Porter *(Anything Goes, Kiss Me Kate, Can Can)*, Oscar Hammerstein *(Showboat, The King & I, Oklahoma!, Carousel)*, Lorenz Hart *(Pal Joey, Babes in Arms, The Boys from Syracuse)*, Dorothy Fields *(Annie Get Your Gun, Sweet Charity)*, and Alan Jay Lerner *(My Fair Lady, Brigadoon, Camelot)* is tragic. The point is this: Whatever you can say, it's likely to have been said before by one of these great lyricists or their peers, and in a turn of phrase that will knock you out. I don't doubt that you've already have figured out that it's your job to become an original, to say old things in a new way. But until you know what's been said before, and embrace the rich history of popular music, you will likely write trite, repetitive ideas.

The Development of Ideas

It's no accident when a song comes out right. It's the result of carefully developed songwriting. Only through thoughtful analysis of the subject matter, the style, and the approach will you write an excellent song. It's not enough just to hum a cute melody and write a driving track and hope that the lyrics will sort of slide by. One of the first songs I ever had recorded, called "Words," was sung by Lola Falana. She did a lovely job of the vocal and gave it her all. The trouble was, I had written the following sequence of lines: "Words . . . don't get it said; I never heard a word that said what's in my head; why do you always seem to give me words instead . . . la la la, la la la." Wait a minute! *"La la la, la la la???"* Give me a break! The very professional Ms. Falana sang those *la la's* with more feeling than most singers can muster on a "you're breaking my heart." But I gave her nothing to work with! It was my fault that the song fell flat in the middle. Oh why oh why didn't I just say, "I need you to show me!" instead of "la la la"? I guess I just didn't know any better. I hadn't yet trained myself properly in the development of ideas.

An artist I am working with, Juan Placenscia, is also an accomplished soccer coach. He shared with me a comment he offered to a young female player: "Play with Purpose." It's such a strong statement, that I thought I would offer it to you in the context of songwriting. "Write with Purpose!" Have a vision and a plan in mind.

Ask Yourself Why These Hit Songs Work

Look at the lyrics of the successful songs you're studying, and find what is creative, clever, unusual, interesting about them. What fraction of these lyrics are ordinary everyday lines? What portion of these lyrics are "important-sounding" statements? How many times does a preachy line get past? How many of the lines are introverted and intensely personal? How many of the lines sound pompous or self-indulgent? How often does the lyric refer to "they" as opposed to "we"; "he and she" as opposed to "you and me"? How many songs have negative or depressing messages? Look at the structure of the verses, the way they lead into the choruses. And if there's a bridge, look at the way it's used to add dimension to the song; that is, what does it do, if anything, for the story?

It's very easy to think your own lyrics are the best ones ever written on the planet. It's a trap we all fall into. I thought my lyrics were *primo* right from the very first one. It was only as I improved that I recognized how poorly written the earliest ones were. In fact, as I reached new levels of proficiency, I would look back at the prior few months/years of work and discover distinct improvements in approach and understanding. That continued all the years of the learning process, through more than two thousand complete lyrics and parts of lyrics that I wrote. Interestingly, in my work today, I'm able to recognize what's wrong with the lyrics at the moment of their creation, often before they ever get as far as the paper I'm writing on. My years of study of "what works" have paid off, as I am able to judge (my criteria being years of instinct at this point) whether a line sounds "right" to my ear or not. And this is very clear: There is no gray area of "maybe" anymore. That's not to say that I don't write down some mediocre lines once in a while. It's just that when I do, I recognize them for what they are and have no illusions. Furthermore, when a line is contrived to be "clever" or "original," unless it is truly breathtaking, I have no pretensions about its greatness. I have seen too many lines to fail to recognize what is good, what is mediocre, and what is just plain awful!

Identify Your Heroes

Having now made a study of the work of those who have been successful, it's time to identify your favorite writers, the ones whose work again and again hits home, feels comfortable to the ears, and tells a story you can relate to. There are as many different opinions as to who the great writers are as there are great writers. It's all got to do with individual style and taste.

> *Learn to listen to your songs as an objective observer, and enjoy whatever you write that's truly wonderful!*

Personally, my breakthrough occurred when listening to Carole King's *Tapestry* album. The King/Gerry Goffin collaborations sparked my interest because of their straightforward, down-to-earth approach to storytelling in songs. I had always written about love in a rather fanciful manner; the Goffin/King songs said things about how real people felt.

Once you've identified the who and why of your songwriter heroes, applying the same "how does it feel to the ear" standards to your own lyrics will be a natural and obvious step. Learn to listen to your songs as an objective observer, and enjoy whatever you write that's truly wonderful!

Study Your Own Best Work

Be brutal with yourself—take your own best work apart line by line, word by word. See how it compares structurally and content-wise with that of the successful writers you admire or are competing with (not always the same ones!). Try to imagine how *they* might have written this line. Try to imagine how they would have reacted, had you been collaborating with them on this song, if you had presented this particular line, what would have been their criticism? What would they have loved about it? Would they have kept it in the song? But, ultimately, decide based on your own intuitive opinion of the merit of your own work.

I say study your *best* work, because only by reaching a standard of excellence and then exceeding it knowingly can you grow as a writer. Only you can develop your own instincts as to what is "commercial," by constantly comparing and contrasting your work with successful, well-written songs by writers you admire.

Get in the Race

You can't win a race if you're not even in the running. You can't have a hit song, make a fortune, and retire to Tahiti unless you write and submit it. Now that you have acknowledged the parameters of your interests, talents, abilities, and perspectives, go about writing the very best song you can. Now don't say you're not going to bother to compete! Where's your spirit?! You have just as much right to try to earn a place on that album as any other writer does, including today's most famous writers. There is no reason on earth why you can't do what they do and did, and maybe even top them. Did I neglect to mention that they're only human? Ah, well, they are! They have the same notes and the same vocabulary at their disposal as you do. They have the same thesaurus, dictionary, rhyming dictionary, and ambition. The only traits and qualities that separate them from you are how well they've developed their writing skills: art and craft, professionalism, self-criticism, knowledge of the marketplace, contacts, refinement of songwriting expertise, and quality of demos.

I have never sold myself short. Unfortunately, I believed early on that my work was better than it was, so it took me quite a few extra years to become as skillful a lyricist as I thought I was in the first place. At first, I used to save my "best" songs to submit only to specific artists. Then I finally got the idea that it was not for me to be so choosy in "casting" my own songs. I remember being concerned when an artist named Whitney Houston, whom I had never heard of, was about to record my song "Nobody Loves Me Like You Do." If I hadn't kept my mouth shut, I might have tried to prevent the recording! Imagine (umpteen million album sales later) how I'd have felt if I had insisted that song be kept off the album to wait for a "bigger" artist. Ouch!

Always keep your self-esteem and your ambition strong. Your break may be just around the corner, any time, any day. The right song may connect with the right project at any time, but you'll never know if you don't write it. Competition may be frightening, especially when it's top of the line, highly gifted competition. However, all those other writers had to start somewhere, just as you do. They honed their craft, learned from their mistakes, and competed with their betters until they were their peers. You can, too!

EVALUATING YOUR POINT OF VIEW

A writer just naturally writes from his or her own viewpoint. Having a viewpoint is what makes you want to start writing in the first place. But you'd be amazed how many lyricists really have never bothered to identify how they feel about most of life's basic issues. Since these feelings will be reflected in a great many of your lyrics, it's important that you examine them from all angles. With this in mind, I suggest that it would be extremely worthwhile to delve into some introspection, and take a look at what's important to you:

• *Love*—Have you loved deeply? Have you been loved in return? What is your fantasy of a perfect love relationship? Are you cynical about love?

• *Hurt*—How do you think hurt becomes an issue in a love relationship? How have you responded to being hurt? How have you inflicted hurt?

• *Relationships*—Do you get along with people? Do people seek you out? Do you look for or see flaws in others' relationships?

• *Hate*—Are you given to violent, stormy encounters, or are you a softie?

• *Connecting*—Is it easy or difficult, comfortable or awkward for you to meet people?

• *Friendship*—Do you volunteer your friendship and offer it freely, or does your friendship come only with restrictions and limitations (i.e., what *you* are going to get out of it)?

• *Giving*—Do you love to give? Do you hold back part of you? Are you capable of accepting love or only giving it?

• *Sex*—Are you a giver or a taker, the seducer or the seduced, active or passive, traditional or experimental?

• *Commitment*—Do you believe in it for you? for others? What's your experience of marriage? Is it right for you? Has it worked for those you care about?

• *Emotions*—Are you cool or hot? Do you prefer logic over emotions, or vice versa?

• *Control*—Do you need to be in control, to be controlled, or to share control?

• *Conversation*—Are you a good listener? Are you frequently too busy thinking of what *you* want to say next to listen to the other person? Do you learn from others? Do you feel that your opinion will benefit others?

• *Passion*—Is passion something you start within yourself, or do you need someone else to inspire you? Can you inspire passion in someone else? How?

• *Humor*—Do you look for the humor in life, or do you have a serious nature? Do you like humor that is subtle, blatant, slapstick, sexually ribald, scapegoat, droll, ethnic, intellectual?

• *Time*—Are you easygoing or always in a hurry? Do you look at your watch a lot? Are you usually late or early for appointments? Which do you believe: "When it's right it'll happen" or, "Nothing happens unless you make it happen"?

• *Politics*—Are your opinions liberal, conservative, somewhere in between? What issues do you feel deeply drawn to?

• *Tradition*—Are you old-fashioned, contemporary, or progressive in your attitudes toward relationships, "the sanctity of marriage," sexual expression in the workplace, and social issues such as equal rights for women (in the home and/or the workplace), gay rights, etc.?

• *Spiritualism*—Are you devout to an established religion? Are you a believer in or attracted to psychic phenomena, fortune tellers, spirit communication, astrology, mind reading, ESP, crystal power, mental healing, metaphysics, or other spiritual possibilities?

• *Fate*—Do you believe in fate or free will?

• *Money*—Is money important? How important is it compared with other things? What other things are more important? Are you entitled to money? How much is enough? If you spend money freely, do you believe that more will come to you?

• *Ethics*—What is your concept of morality? Do you have a clearly defined sense of right and wrong? Can you justify "white lies" or manipulation of the truth, and, if so, under what circumstances?

• *Social Conscience*—Do you feel committed to drawing others' attention to a wrong that exists in the world? Do you feel that you could help make it better? Do you put your needs or those of others first?

• *Forgiveness*—Do you forgive easily? How long do you hold grudges?

• *Adultery*—Is it ever right? If so, under what circumstances? Have you ever committed it? What feelings and emotions did it arouse in you? How would you feel if your partner committed adultery?

• *The Now*—Are you living in the here and now emotionally and mentally, or do you tend to live on memories of a better or worse past? Do you live for the future, i.e., for what could or might happen in days to come?

• *Happiness*—Are you happy? What does it, or would it take to make you happy? What would be your ultimate happiness? Are you aware of anything you do to bring happiness to others?

There are no right or wrong answers to these questions in this context. There is no preferable point of view for you as a songwriter. It's simply important for you to identify and be thoroughly clear on your own perspectives on life, so that you can write about what you know.

7

REWRITE? MOI?

A s writers, we have to evaluate our own work before it gets into anybody else's hands. It's critical that we see beyond what we *want* to
see and be deeply honest about how the song stands up to criteria
set by the successful songs of the day.

Once we've talked ourselves into how good a song is, we find it very
hard to fix or change, as we feel that altering even one word or note will ruin
the song. We want to convert everyone else to *our* way of thinking, instead of
bending to what others think. But before a song is ready to be submitted anywhere, you still have a chance to make it better. A realistic look at your song
might turn up the realization that it either:

- Is a *living room hit* (which, unfortunately, doesn't guarantee that a publisher, producer, or record company will see it in the same light)

- *Lacks commercial appeal* (which could mean that you are happy with the
song artistically, but it doesn't have the strength to make it to radio)

- Is *unfinished* (it's surprising how many songwriters submit partially developed ideas and incomplete songs, expecting delighted requests for the songs
to be finished immediately—requests that all but never come)

No songs in any of these categories are ready to be submitted in the real
song marketplace.

I want you to be able to read your finished lyric objectively and know
that you have accurately targeted it toward an artist or style of music. I also
very much want you to be able to look for obvious problem areas that could
cost you the attention and interest of a potential buyer. So let's take a look at
the common areas in which songs fall down before they really have a chance.

LIVING ROOM HITS

It's human nature to look for praise and give a wide berth to criticism. Who wants to be told (by anybody at all) that the song we've been slaving over for two weeks just doesn't make it?

So we often fall into the trap of only listening to the good stuff, the praise. Unfortunately, a lot of times that praise is from people whose opinions come only from love and good intentions. When you play your new song for your lover, your mother, your sister, your brother, your best friends, your church group, your cronies at the local club, or in many cases, even your manager or your own band—in spite of the enthusiastic response, "It's a hit!" or some variation thereof—the song may be nothing more than a *Living Room Hit*. When we've had so much positive reinforcement from these supporters of ours, we are often lulled into a false sense of believing the work is great. Based on and armed with this confidence, we fall into the trap of rejecting advice from qualified industry professionals, stubbornly believing that our songs are perfect as they are.

As you'll learn later in this chapter, there are various types of criticism. Sometimes you can't trust industry pros' opinions any more than you can your family's, so before you take any criticism to heart, you must evaluate the source it comes from. But I have to tell you here: The same applies to *positive* critiques.

I remember turning in a song to my publisher that cost $1,178 to demo, an outrageous but true expense. The budget for the session included two lead singers, three background singers, a 24-track studio, a guitarist, and a $250 cartage bill for my partner's keyboards and equipment to be lugged to the studio and set up. To our utter dismay, the male lead singer we'd hired just couldn't get the passion we wanted in the vocal. And, believe me, we wasted several hours trying to motivate him. He had a pleasant voice and good technique, but passion, after all, is not something you can teach someone. My collaborator and I worried a lot about the finished demo. We knew the tracks were dynamite and the song was a killer, and both our publishers said the demo was fine and the vocals were okay. But in our hearts we knew the vocal didn't move us, and even *we* didn't want to listen to the song very often.

We asked our publishers whether we should re-demo the song, paying the extra (around $370 for vocals and studio time) out of our own pockets, and both said absolutely not, the song was fine. But we had to trust our own judgment in this case. *Even though the response was positive,* we booked studio time and hired a singer and asked both publishers to immediately stop sending the song out until the new "improved" demo was turned in.

The bottom line is this: If you think the song is not happening—even a little tiny question flittering around in the back of your brain that makes you squirm as you try not to deal with the hunch—the truth is you're probably right. Unfortunately, or perhaps fortunately, you just can't fool yourself!

Oh, and by the way—you know that line you sing extra soulfully so that people will think it's more meaningful than it really is? *Change it! Rewrite it!* Trust your heart; you know you're trying to talk yourself into how good it is, and that line will nag you until the last day you sing it.

Invariably, the line I end up having to change in a song is the one I was "iffy" about when I turned in the lyrics to the composer, who pounces on that line like a cat pounces on a lame mouse. So I've learned to police my own work and be brutal about changing things before they even get as far as my co-writers or my publishers, let alone A&R people, producers, and artists.

The times I let things slip by, I always regret it. Every time I hear the demo, when that awful line comes up, I surreptitiously dart a look at the listener's face to see if he or she caught it, to see if the eyes flicker or the eyebrows raise.

Exceptions to the Rule

Of course, Living Room Hits are great for the ego. And sometimes your Living Room Fans are right on target and what you've written is a bona-fide hit. Also, there is definitely a certain type of song that appeals to the Living Room Audience that is not commercially viable—but who cares?

These are special songs from the heart, about personal subjects; they're very "artsy" and not particularly commercial, but they can be touching when performed before a small, appreciative audience. Sometimes, we feel strongly that "If the world hears this song, it can't help but weep! It's gotta go straight to the top!" It's always hard to accept that record companies don't regard as viable this type of emotional and philosophical work, when it's pitched by songwriters. When the writer is also the artist and has some say in what goes on his or her album, especially in the "alternative" or "folk" formats, these songs do sometimes get recorded.

My honest suggestion is to keep on writing those songs because they, like the poetry that I hope you are still writing in your spare time, are a true reflection of your deepest feelings and thoughts, your expressions of what is important to you in this life. It really doesn't matter whether anybody else likes those songs, as they are cathartic to write and they are important to *you*. Since *the process is the purpose* here, those beautiful, moving, artistic songs should be written simply because you *need* to write them to please yourself, regardless of "commercial" considerations.

I advise you *never* to stop writing something that you need to express—whatever it is! Whether it's a line, a few lines, a verse, an entire song—whatever—follow through on the thought. In fact, some of your best commercial ideas will start that way, ger-

I advise you never to stop writing something that you need to express—whatever it is! Whether it's a line, a few lines, a verse, an entire song—whatever—follow through on the thought.

> *To make a lyric as commercial as possible, it has to be easy to sing and easy to listen to. It must be comfortable to the ear, and it must be about something that as many people as possible can relate to.*

minating at one moment, only to be reconsidered and finally explored to the fullest at some later date for some other song you're writing.

IS IT COMMERCIAL?

In the early days of my career, when publishers would listen to a song of mine that I thought was fabulous and remark, "It's not commercial," I would be fuming! Don't they get it—how great it is? Don't they see the subtlety of the lyrics, the moodiness of the melody? I mean, do they have cotton in their ears or what?

I swore over and over again, "I'm not going to write commercial songs; I won't prostitute myself!"

But you know what? All *commercial* means is People Like It. Period. That means, of course, that not all commercial songs are good, and not all good songs are commercial. Commercial songs just have a common thread running through them that's easy to listen to, easy to tap your foot to, a hook that's easy to remember and hum. A commercial song, ideally, could be recorded by R2-D2 the Astromech Droid, and *still* stand up, because it's that ear-tickling.

Through the last few decades, different types of songs have been commercial. Styles change continually.

There are always some so-called commercial songs that you and I don't particularly care for. But who are we to fight what's commercial? If it appeals to the masses, there's something about it we must study and learn from if we are to remain contemporary songwriters. We cannot arbitrarily dismiss anything that's on the radio; we must mull over what it is about that song that has makes it so well liked.

If I don't like a song, I discuss it with people and find those who *do* like it, and I pick their brains. I want to know why that song is a hit and what I am shutting my ears to. What is it I'm not getting?

In fact, songs quite often come in a flavor of the month. The styles come and go very quickly, as do the musicians, artists, and producers who are their purveyors. Producers like Quincy Jones, who have moved effortlessly from style to style for years, are in the small minority. For others, it easy to get trapped into a particular sound or style, and not be able to break out of it when it becomes dated.

Look no further than the Beatles' songwriters Lennon and McCartney to see how songwriters can keep growing and expanding in their musical range by constantly setting new trends. None of their numerous albums repeated the sounds and stylings of a previous album; they always broke new ground.

What does this mean in terms of "copycatting" a new song that is on the radio? As I've noted elsewhere, it means that by the time that copycat song is written, recorded, and released, the sound will be as overripe as week-old fish. Originals are far more successful than imitations.

> When Whitney Houston's first album came out, it was a reversion to really classy, tender, and tasteful songs, simply delivered by a wonderful, big voice. The first reviews I read (and I read them avidly, since I had written one of the songs) absolutely panned the album as "mushy and overly sentimental" and indicated that the style of the album had no audience. Guess what! It sold more than 14 million copies worldwide. Suddenly, everybody in town was trying to write songs "à la Whitney Houston," at the request of every A&R person in the known world.

What is it about a song that makes it commercial? Some producers just say, "I know it when I hear it." Some think it's the beat, some the lyrics, and almost everyone will tell you it's the melody. Many people think that a good melody with a bad lyric can be successful; and most will tell you that if the lyric is good on a good melody, that good lyric is the element that takes the song all the way. I don't care how brilliant the track and the melody are or who played the sax solo. As far as I'm concerned, *without a great lyric, it's only half a song!*

To make a lyric as commercial as possible, it has to be easy to sing and easy to listen to. It must be comfortable to the ear, and it must be about something that as many people as possible can relate to.

A common criterion for a very commercial song is that you want to play it again and again, and you never get tired of hearing it. In a way, that's what I was told the first time I ever submitted a song to a publisher. The publisher was at A&M Records' AlmoIrving/Rondor Music (the same company where I later worked as a staff writer for five years). He sent me back my tape with a little note that said, "Why don't you go out and buy the top ten records and play them over and over again and then you'll know what I'm looking for." That wasn't very helpful at the time, since I didn't know what I was supposed to be listening for, but I figured it out in time.

So what *do* all No. 1 songs have in common?

• They've got a powerful hook

• They're simple

• You can't get enough of them!

In other words, they're commercial.

IS IT FINISHED?

Some songs, although we can't quite finish them, are coming along so well that we want to submit them for a project anyway so as not to miss the opportunity. There is a big temptation among songwriters to turn in a song somewhere, sometime, with a little note that reads, "It's not quite finished yet, but . . . "

Naturally, this is an unprofessional thing to do, and these songs are rarely if ever taken seriously. The only exception occurs when the unfinished song is purposely being submitted to be co-written by the artist or producer. Other than that exception, if you can't finish the idea yourself, what makes you think the listener is going to go for it? It probably isn't finished because you are stumped about where to take the story or the melody next.

One thing you could do would be to evaluate the title all over again and re-outline the song. Then, try to restructure the areas that are weak, using your new knowledge of craft to do so. If you are stuck for a direction, you might ask another songwriter who you know has good ideas for some input. You might simply need direction as to what aspect of the story the final verse needs to address, what details the bridge needs to fill in and how long it should be, whether the chorus is too long or too short, or if there's a better way to use the hook. Any of these questions well might be answered by a fresh set of ears.

You also have to make sure you haven't mixed tenses, jumping back and forth between past, present, and future, such as, "She came into the room and walks over to me." *Came* is past tense and *walks* is present tense. You have to make up your mind about which tense you want to use.

Another red flag area to watch for in checking your work is mixing the "person." First person is "I/me/my/we/us/our." Second person is "You/your," and third person is "He/she/it/they/him/her/it/them/his/her/its/theirs." A common mistake in songs is to set up in the verse "She was the prettiest girl I ever knew," and then in the chorus say "I miss you so much." Stay with the same "person" throughout the song.

If the song is for a project and you are late because you couldn't finish it, you must call the company for whom the song is being written, apologize, and offer a firm delivery date of a finished song. When you're boxed into a corner and you have a deadline to meet, sometimes it's better to bring another writer aboard to try to finish it than to scrap the good opportunity altogether. In most cases, projects are never on schedule, and the chances are that, even late, your song will still be considered.

TARGETING A LYRIC

There are many things to consider before deciding that a lyric is finished and in its best possible form. Though you may be happy with the overall lyric, it still may have a long way to go before it's ready to demo and submit.

I offer you the following yardsticks by which to evaluate whether your lyrics are truly at their most moving and thought provoking, and whether they are realistically competitive in the professional songwriting arena. Remember that these are not hard-and-fast *rules* but only measures by which to evaluate your own work. (I am sure that sometimes you will find that you have gone totally against all that follows in this section, and yet have written a breathtakingly brilliant song.) Art is inexact, and at its very best it is the result of individual expression. I think a songwriter must ultimately learn to judge and evaluate a song within its own context, not strictly according to how it relates to so-called rules for songwriting.

Nevertheless, I believe that most lyrics can be measured against the following criteria:

Is the Language Appropriate?

We have to recognize our own limitations in terms of worldliness. Though we might like to think we can converse and be comfortable in many types of sociological, cultural, and ethnic groups, we are probably fairly limited by our upbringing, background, job opportunities, and ongoing friendships.

Therefore, when we try to write in a style that's not a natural outgrowth of our experience, our words lack a certain flow and become stilted and uncomfortable.

So when you're starting to write an R & B song, a Country song, a Rap song, or a Heavy Metal song, ask yourself if you are truly conversant with this type of language. I can't express too frequently that if you're not comfortable with the music in the genre you are attempting, it will be readily apparent to its true aficionados.

Believe it or not, *getting even one word wrong* (*wrong* meaning *inappropriate*) can actually spoil your chances of getting a song cut! So my advice is to make sure that somebody else who is familiar with the genre reads it before you spend money on a demo and waste good contacts shopping an inappropriate song. Better still, collaborate with specialists if you plan on tackling lyric areas with which you are unfamiliar.

I have had invaluable insights from my collaborators who understand a market better than I do. I remember the first professional press release that I ever wrote: It was for exhaust baffles for Kawasaki KZ1000 motorcycles. I did my best, considering that I didn't know the front end of a motorcycle from the back! I studied the literature and wrote a pretty good press release, but the giveaway of my ignorance was that I called the KZ1000 a "cycle"! My partner Bill Estay called me up laughing after reading the press release and quickly explained that in biker-speak *cycle* referred to a bicycle, and *bike* referred to a motorcycle. Collaborating with a knowledgeable partner saved the day for me.

Though I've written hundreds of R & B songs, I am keenly aware that conversational urban language changes continually. Thus, I frequently look to

> *It is important to use simple language and to be careful about incorporating catch phrases "of the moment," as the moment changes, and the sayings become passé.*

the composer I'm working with to go over a line and tell me, "No, that's too formal," "That's not 'street' enough," or "I can't really hear anyone saying that." This is valuable input and ultimately makes us both look good.

Will the Language Hold Up?

It can take a long time to get a song placed—sometimes months or even years. It is important to use simple language and to be careful about incorporating catch phrases "of the moment," as the moment changes, and the sayings become passé.

Words and phrases such as *groovy, far out, the cat's meow, sock it to me, get down, cool, hot, heavy, too hip, let's split, trendy, let's book, outta sight,* and *chill* have all had their moment of popularity. In fact, they come and go, regaining popularity and then going out of fashion again. Thus, if you're going to spend several hundred dollars on a demo featuring the Hip Words of the Week, keep in mind that if you can't get a cut immediately on the song, this dated demo will represent a lot of time, money, and effort right down the drain.

Singability

Certain words do not sing well; others do not sing at all. Try singing "I feel listless," for instance! Seriously, a word may look perfect on paper but be impossible to wrap around the singer's tongue when sung. Lack of singability is one of the primary causes of rewrites. Try not to use words in your writing that have no musical or artistic value, or words that are dull and lackluster. Yeah, there's a good word not to use. Imagine trying to sing, "Your love is lackluster." In fact, do more than imagine trying to sing it: Make a point of singing every line you write *out loud* to test how well it "sings."

Repetitive Hooks

A hook, as you've heard a thousand times by now, is the part of the song that you remember, the part that you walk away singing, the part with the title—or is it?

Certainly, the title should also be the major hook of the song, repeated so many times that only an imbecile would have to ask at the end, "What was it called?" However—and this is important—*the title doesn't have to be the only lyrical hook!*

Consider the following lyric:

STARTING TONIGHT
Blame it on all the love songs
You know they . . . they gave me something to dream

Waiting in every love song
I thought I . . . I heard a promise for me

I've had my sweet nights
My share of broken hearts
To get where love starts here with you

Chorus:　　Secondary Hook:
　　　　　　This time we're falling in love together
　　　　　　Two hearts believing we've got it right
　　　　　　We can make it happen
　　　　　　We can make it matter
　　　　　　From now on . . .
Hook:　　　*Starting tonight*

Maybe it was the moonlight that caught me
Maybe the stars in your eyes
Someday it simply feels right, somebody
Just makes you glad you're alive

And this is better than any love song
'Cause it's about you and me

(Repeat Chorus)

Bridge:　　*Ev'rybody's dreaming love will come someday*
　　　　　　But you've got to know it when you find it
　　　　　　Our chance is here and now, don't let go
Hook:　　　*Forever's Starting Tonight . . .*

(Repeat Chorus and Fade)

MUSIC & LYRICS/PAUL CHITEN AND PAMELA PHILLIPS OLAND

This song has two hooks: "This time we're falling in love together," and, "Starting tonight." Because, musically, the chorus seems to pay off the idea best at its end, Paul and I chose to use the final line of the chorus as the title. We then re-used it at the end of the bridge to give it one more pitch, but the *opening* line of the chorus could arguably be the hook of this song instead.

While a bass line or piano figure that runs through the song could also be used as a melodic hook, another secondary hook could be using a repeated line at the beginning or end of each verse. A memorable hook could also be a *background* line, sung over and over behind the lead in a repetitive fashion.

Contrived Rhymes

Did you rhyme that line that way because it was a wonderful expression of what you wanted to say, or did you rhyme it just because it rhymed? Did you rhyme *silent* with *violent* because that was the only word you could think of that sounded the same? Did you rhyme *luck* with *buck, cluck,* or *stuck* because you'd set yourself up with an *uck?* What you did, like Little Jack Horner, was paint yourself into a corner, looking to pull out a plum. But all you got was corn.

So what do you do when you have a wonderful rhyme set up, and nothing to go with it? You have two choices:

1. Rewrite the first line to give yourself something better to work with

2. Use a *sound-alike* rhyme that will give the song some real meaning, instead of a silly, shallow, embarrassing rhyme

I was working on a song titled, "Show Me the Way to Your Heart" for Scott Grimes to sing. Richard Carpenter had found the melody in Japan and asked me to write an English lyric to it. I had the lyric all done and was really happy with it; then he threw me a curve: He changed the last line of the second verse melody, forcing me to rhyme a word I had never intended to rhyme. The word? "Shoulder." I spent three days searching for actual or oblique rhymes for the line, "We've laughed and you've cried on my shoulder." I came up with the following lines:

- How I long for my arms to enfold you
- There's so much that I've never told you
- 'Cause my longing for you just gets stronger
- I don't wanna be sister and brother
- That I don't look at you like a brother
- 'Cause I don't wanna be like a brother
- As the fire in my eyes starts to smolder
- As the fires of love start to smolder
- That my warmth for you's starting to smolder
- There's a fire beginning to smolder
- There's a warmth for you starting to smolder
- 'Cause I can't keep this secret much longer
- 'Cause you can't keep me waiting much longer.

As you can see, I was really going crazy looking for this rhyme, but I knew they were all wrong, every one of them. Even the sound-alikes I tried didn't work, as they were all so contrived. I definitely hated the lines that ended in "smolder"—boy they were awful! And the "sister and brother" routine didn't make it by a mile. What I ended up with, which everybody liked a lot, was the following finished couplet:

I guess you think you really know me
I keep all the secrets you've told me
We're such good friends . . . that's where it ends
But at night when I'm dreaming, you hold me . . .

Maybe we've known each other too long
We've laughed and you've cried on my shoulder
Why can't you see this change in me
Won't you say it's not too much *to hope for?*

From "Show Me the Way to Your Heart,"
Lyrics/Pamela Phillips Oland, Music/Ryo Azuka

Why didn't I do as I say you ought to, and just change the "shoulder" line to something else? Oh, but if only I could have! Unfortunately for me, that was one line that was inviolate, since the producer liked it (which reminds me to remind you of the popular axiom regarding rewrites: *"Don't fix it if it ain't broke!"*). If the producer likes a line, you don't rewrite it; you work around it until you get hives and chew off your fingernails, but you *never voluntarily change anything* once it's approved!

In any event, look at the finished couplet. Isn't it better to have come up with something that didn't quite rhyme but at least had some meaning in the song rather than to stick in an icky line just to get a real rhyme?

Wandering Ideas

It's very easy for a song to drift away from the original intent of the title. You can avoid this pitfall by writing an outline of the topic and story before writing the actual lyric. If you know what it is you intend to say, you'll have an easier time coming up with the words. If you have only a title or a basic concept but no direction as to where to take it, you will find that by the end of the song you are miles away from what you wanted to get across.

Sometimes, your finished song will be much more interesting than what you set out to write. It is neither right nor wrong, of course, because you're the boss, you're the writer, and you get to decide what your song says. However, if you were intending to make a certain point that never got made, or if you were going to tell a story that somehow never got told and you wish it had, you should have been very certain at the beginning about what you wanted to say. Then, as you proceeded with the songwriting, you should have referred back often to the words and ideas you had already written.

In fact, any time you feel you're getting off the track in a songwriting effort, if you lose your train of thought, or your mind wanders, you should stop writing and read the song through from the beginning to as far as you've gotten several times. It is profoundly important to stay in touch with your story.

The Story Needs to Grow

A significant pit all songwriters fall into at one time or another is the tendency to repeat the same aspect of a story over and over again in different words. The reality is that if you tell an aspect of a story in the first verse and then reword it for subsequent verses—and sometimes even for the choruses and the bridge—you have not done your job. Good songwriting requires story development every bit as much as writing a screenplay. In fact, think of a song as a mini-film, wherein the story arc develops, peaks, and gets resolved in two verses and a chorus, instead of 120 pages. Sometimes it's not even readily apparent that what you've done is repeat your core idea instead of developing your story. You realize something is wrong with the song, but you feel the lyric writing is strong, so no matter how many times you reread it, you don't get what's missing. What's the remedy?

1. Study the story in the first verse and paraphrase it into a few words.

2. Paraphrase each subsequent section in a few words and see how close they are to the story line in the first verse.

3. See which of your sections *best* encapsulated your idea, and use that *or* a reworking of that as the opening verse.

4. Scrap the rest of your song and start a new draft from the second section onward.

I know it's hard—even painful—to give up something you've written that you really are attached to. But you've got to know that if even *you* can see the flaws in your writing, the industry professionals who will be looking at your song will also see them and probably call you on them. Just remember that a boring song doesn't play favorites. It bores everyone.

Rick Beringer and I crafted a story song that provides a good example of not repeating an idea, but always taking it one step further. The song is called "Same Old Song and Dance." In it, the story not only develops like a movie, but the same chorus applies in three different ways to various stages of the story's development, as expressed in the three verses.

SAME OLD SONG AND DANCE

He wore a white coat
As he swung the girls to a fiddle and a Bob Wills tune
Over his shoulder
She caught his eye by the light of a Harvest full moon

Chorus: *He asked her once . . . she told him no*
               He turned around as if to go
               She heard her heart say, "Put your right foot first
               There ain't no second chance
               Let him lead you the same old song and dance."

He brought a white rose
As he swore to her she was never gonna cry again
His voice was breaking
"You've put up with me so long, don't let our love end."

Chorus: *He asked her once . . . she told him no*
               He turned around as if to go
               She heard her heart say, "Put your right foot first
               There ain't no second chance
               Let him lead you the same old song and dance."

Bridge: *In the circle of their arms, there's no room for changing partners*
               'Cause their need is strong for the same old song and dance

She wore a white dress
As he asked the band play a fiddle and a Bob Wills tune
Their kids were smiling
After fifty years he was acting like a blushing bridegroom

Chorus: *He asked her once . . . she told him no*
               He turned around as if to go
               She heard her heart say, "Put your right foot first
               There ain't no second chance
               Let him lead you the same old song and dance.
               Let him lead you the same old song and dance."

WORDS & MUSIC/PAMELA PHILLIPS OLAND AND RICK BERESFORD

LEARNING TO EVALUATE CRITICISM

To alter an old adage, "Those who *can, do;* those who *can't, become critics!*"
Now that you're sure your song is as good as you can make it, you're ready to

put it out there like fresh meat for the vultures! Criticism is all very good and sometimes it's extremely helpful. However, any songwriter who intends to stay in the industry for more than a week needs to understand that there are different types of criticism, some of which are valuable and constructive, while others are hurtful and of no value. They can be broken down roughly as follows:

1. Informed critique

2. Mean-spirited criticism

3. Jealous or competitive criticism

4. Opinionated criticism

5. Positive or constructive critique

6. Detrimental criticism

7. Uninformed criticism

Informed Critique

Informed criticism comes from people who know from experience what they're talking about. These people generally have become successful by understanding the marketplace and studying what makes a song work, what makes one song a hit and another a miss. Major music publishers, record company A&R directors, successful recording artists, much-recorded songwriters, and in-demand record producers usually fall into the informed category.

An informed critic will study your song and give you a meaningful evaluation of why it works or why it misses. Often such an expert can go through the song with you line by line and tell you how he or she feels about the power of the hook, the melody of the verses, and the necessity to keep, remove, or add a bridge. The informed critic will have a feel for the tempo; the length of the song; even the impact of the musical approach to the demo.

If you are going to listen to anyone, try to make it an *informed* critic. At the very least, this person's opinion is based on real experience and offers you the benefit of hearing it from the point of view of actual working knowledge; at the very most, his or her criticism can help you turn your problematic song into a hit record. Whether you want to accept or agree with the informed criticism is another matter entirely. But at least you can accord it proper weight in the decision whether or not to rewrite.

Mean-Spirited Criticism

The main motivation behind mean-spirited criticism is to force a power play. For some reason, many professionals in the industry think they look better and show strength by giving heavily negative criticism to aspiring songwriters. Once, years ago, I went to a low-level publishing manager at Chappell

Music with a series of new songs, which I sang and played for him. Each time I would start, I'd be ten bars into a new song, and he'd say, curtly, "Next." So I'd turn the lyric sheet over and go on to the next song. He would repeat this cold appraisal for each song. He did this for all thirteen of my songs, finally asking me, "Have you ever thought about becoming a plumber?" I was so mortified that I could barely contain my tears. I drove blindly to my late friend and colleague Hod David's house and, crying bitterly, told him what had happened. Hod hugged me and sat me down and reminded me of all the wonderful songs we'd written together and of all the terrific people in the industry who *did* believe in me. "You can't let *one* mean-spirited individual count more than everything else you've ever done. His opinion is only his opinion, and nothing more." Hod was right, and I will never forget his kindness: Because he cared to point out the good, I am where I am today.

Jealous or Competitive Criticism

It is human nature to be competitive, but while some people can appreciate the work of their peers, others are aggravated by anyone else's success. That's just the way it is. Therefore, a lot of destructive, jealous, or competitive criticism gets tossed around in the name of being helpful. It can be very hurtful to the recipient, and when it is not well intended, it serves no useful purpose at all.

You should listen with a skeptical ear to unconstructive criticism by other songwriters. Perhaps the individual doing the criticizing is having a hard time in his or her own career, and seeing your excellent work is just the last straw. So rather than accept that perhaps you are equally talented and also deserve a break, this writer might put down your work in a pretty merciless fashion. Consider the source before you take to heart any jealous or competitive criticism.

Opinionated Criticism

This is a case of what my husband would call, "The wrong way or the Army's way!" Some people cannot conceive that they could possibly be wrong. They are thoroughly convinced of their position.

Songwriting is just not that absolute of an art. One person's dud is another person's hit, and you can bet there are thousands of songwriters who have success stories to back up that contention. I personally have had songs turned down by the best in the business, only to have the same songs, unchanged, surface triumphantly under somebody else's aegis. Beware of the *absolute* type of opinionated criticism, which allows no room for doubt or question. Nobody knows everything; those who think they do know even less.

Just remember: You are under no obligation to listen to criticism by anybody at all, let alone take it to heart. You should listen with a skeptical ear to criticism by other songwriters that is not particularly constructive.

Positive or Constructive Critique

Positive or constructive criticism is a way of saying, "Yes, the substance is good, but it still needs work, and here is how I think it could be improved."

The *positive* critic will first evaluate the song on its own merits, trying to understand the style and what the writer was going for. Then within that context he or she will try to find the weak points of the piece and offer positive input as to what the songwriter must do to make the song stronger overall.

Positive criticism is the kindest that one can hope for, other than no criticism at all. But it does have one pitfall: The critic is not necessarily being totally honest. Or, to put it another way: The critic is offering positive ways to improve the song but is neglecting to say whether, in his or her opinion, the song has any chance of success *whatever* you do to fix it.

So, since even *positive* criticism is suspect, make sure that it has gotten to the meat of what you need to know: Will this song work commercially? Even if you're getting positive feedback, ask the critic, "If I fix it, does the song have a chance? Am I wasting my time pouring any more energy into this lyric?"

Detrimental Criticism

This is, of course, just the opposite of positive criticism. It is the totally one-sided kind that only picks out what is wrong with a song and never points up what you've done right. People who take the time to evaluate your work but offer only detrimental criticism are to be avoided, as they can seriously affect your desire to continue writing. After all, it stands to reason that if an "expert in the know" doesn't have one good thing to say about your work, it has to make you doubt your talents altogether. I believe that because this type of criticism fosters loss of self-esteem and nothing more, it is not helpful and therefore is of no value. Even the weakest lyricist needs to know *something* he or she has done well. Whether it's formula, picking a good title, coming up with an interesting story, one good rhyme in the entire song, a good opening line—whatever—the writer needs to know about it in order to build from there. It may be a slow, painstaking process to become a *great* lyricist but, like a house, you cannot build your talent overnight. Each insightful brick of the foundation needs to be laid with care. Steer clear of people who offer only *detrimental* criticism and have nothing good to say about your work.

Uninformed Criticism

This is a dangerous variety since, positive or negative, uninformed criticism is based on personal criteria that may have no value in the music business.

The uninformed criticism of family and friends, however well intended, can be absolutely the most wounding of anybody's. You're putting them in a position of power over you, which they will learn to wield with amazing alacrity. If you show them a song in progress, be ready for a barrage of personalized critiques. Most people can't "hear" a rough version of a song, but it's amazing how their opinions change when they hear the same song—unaltered—in a full-scale demo. Suddenly they love it.

But the point is this: It doesn't matter what they think, as they are *uninformed* critics and may have other reasons for being critical than just that they don't like the song. If you are asking for their opinion, in my opinion, you are asking for trouble.

> *Learn which criticism is helpful and which to ignore. Be more selective about who you play your songs for, and don't put yourself in the position of being open to unnecessarily hurtful criticism.*

THE POSITIVE SIDE OF UNINFORMED CRITICISM

All this is not to say that if your mother, your sister, or your best friend picks out a line that she feels sounds awkward, you should disregard her comments. She may bring up a very good point. Though she isn't an expert, she does know what she likes. If the uninformed critic is making a genuine comment that you feel you can relate to, sometimes that person may spot a trouble area in the song before you invest any more time and energy in the demo-ing and presentation.

So the bottom line is this: *Consider who gave you the criticism* and how much validity you want to accord that person's opinion. Try not to take criticism as a personal affront. I know it feels as if they've just said your children are ugly, but you have to weigh the source of the critique against what you truly believe about the song in your heart. Learn which criticism is helpful and which to ignore. Be more selective about who you play your songs for. Don't put yourself in the position of being open to unnecessarily hurtful criticism.

Although there are many times when you will choose to ignore the criticism you receive, there are times when you cannot escape the "Big R"— Rewriting!

REWRITING

I know that there is no more thankless feeling than to have sweated out a lyric, honing and crafting, sketching and etching till you feel you've perfected it, only to be told that it has to be rewritten. I know the series of feelings: indignation, followed by incredulity, followed by anger, followed by resentfulness, followed by doubt as to the critic's mental capacity. That person who has set him- or herself up as the paragon of good taste when it comes to knowing the right lyric is now in a position of power over you as the writer. So now you have two choices: You can rewrite, or you can leave it as is.

As you know, the first question you have to ask yourself is, "Who is the critic?" Then consider, "What does he or she know about songwriting?" and "Do I respect his or her opinion?" You already know that you must beware of Living Room Hits. You also know that positive responses from family and friends, while most heartening and certainly necessary to keep your ego from

Take the rewrite as a challenge to your artistry and inventiveness, not as a blow to your ego.

sagging when opposition presents itself, may not be entirely reliable, however heartfelt. By the same token, the instinctive delight your personal support group voices at a certain phrase or hook may be a very good sign that you're onto something extraordinary. Watch for the reaction to specifics, and beware the blanket approvals.

But not all experts are right, either. An old friend of mine once called a certain publisher "the supreme arbiter of taste," because even though he was not a writer himself, he seemed to think he had all the ideas as to what constituted a good song. Often we felt he asked for rewrites just for the sake of saying *something*. And while sometimes he really was right, he often (in our joint opinion) was not, so it became difficult to determine which suggestions were important and which ones were ego-speak.

Let's look at people whose requests to rewrite you should consider seriously:

1. *The artist you're pitching the song to.* The artist knows what he or she wants to sing about. If you want this artist to record your song, *listen* to how he or she wants you to rewrite it. A song is of no use to you if nobody ever hears it, and if you've gotten it as far as an artist who actually is interested in recording it, you're halfway to home plate. Accept the suggestions enthusiastically, not with a scowl. Discuss ideas with him or her so that you clearly know what the artist has in mind. Assure the artist that you can write it the way he or she wants it. Make yourself available for further rewrites, if necessary. Usually, the artist will like most of what you've done but will have problems singing certain lines. Unfortunately, sometimes all he or she likes is the title and the melody, so you have to come up with a whole new approach to the lyrics.

2. *The record producer you're pitching the song to.* A record producer's interest in your work can have the far-reaching consequence of a long-term relationship. If the producer likes the way you write, he or she may ask you to work on future projects. Though you may slave over who-knows-how-many rewrites, they may fall on deaf ears. So (before you sic the Terminator on the producer!), complain to your mother, complain to your diary, complain to your dog, by all means; but rewrite until you get it the way he or she wants it. Remember that the record producer is in the driver's seat: This person is the user of material, and you are a provider of material. Hopefully, the producer's fingers are on the pulse of the music scene at the present time, and he or she knows what's hot and what's not, what's stylish and what's past. If you're not too busy feeling irked that you have to alter your work and nursing your bruised ego, you may just find you can learn something from this person.

3. *The music publisher.* Since music publishers deal with songs day in and day out, they are in a position to look at your work and find its glaring faults. They can spot a poem from a lyric at a hundred paces and will tell you so immediately, though as I've noted, they can't always say *how* they can tell the difference. They've heard fifty-two versions of every trite line ever imagined and will point out to you in which verse of what song your marvelous "original" line has been used before. A music publisher will sit down and painstakingly analyze with you which lines are breathtaking and which ones stink. (We all sometimes write stinkers.) He or she will run through the development of your idea with you and point out to you its weaknesses and strengths; will tell you exactly what needs rewriting and why. And after saying all that, I want to add, emphatically: *Don't take the publisher's word as gospel unless you believe in that particular publisher.* Get a second opinion, or a third, or a fourth. Take it to every publisher in town if you want to until you are satisfied that you have a publisher whose insights hit home. (If I'd listened to that bozo at Chappell, I'd be installing toilets today instead of writing this book!)

4. *Your collaborator.* Since collaboration is a marriage of ideas, rewriting is often the result of compromise. Without sacrificing the integrity of what you want to say in your lyrics, try to benefit from your collaborator's unique point of view. This additional input from somebody whose stake in this song is as strong as yours and could add a whole new dimension to the subject matter. If your collaborator is the artist or producer, your vision for the direction of the lyrics may get overruled, so you must be prepared to throw yourself into rewriting—in the best possible language you can muster—with the idea of achieving what he or she feels strongly the song should say. The idea here is to write what he or she would have said if he or she had done it him- or herself. Is that prostitution of your art? Not at all. One may know *what* he or she wants to say, but obviously, would rather have you say it, because he or she likes your way with words. Take the rewrite as a challenge to your artistry and inventiveness, not as a blow to your ego. If you disagree with their comments about what needs to be revised, say so, and explain why. But if you have to explain why for more than about a minute and he or she still doesn't get it, you'd better hang it up. Chances are, it just *doesn't* work if you have to explain *why* it works.

Don't be hostile to requests for rewriting. The change can put a needed polish on the song, sharpen the perspective, make it more commercial, get to the point quicker. Sometimes in the rewrite you get a better handle on the song, even though you had thought you did an exemplary job the first time. The song may "sing better" to the melody after you've cut out and replaced words that sounded awkward when sung, even though they looked good on paper.

> *If you could write something that you were as proud of as your first draft, you are capable of writing something even better. You are a wellspring of ideas that has no boundaries.*

Don't compromise your integrity if you really believe in something and you have been asked to rip it asunder. Sometimes it's just better to sigh with regret and stash that song away for another time, when you can find someone else who believes in it.

In the final analysis, it always comes down to *your* decision. After all, it is your song, and nobody can force you to rewrite a single word. Weigh the benefits of rewriting against your own personal belief in the inviolability of what you have written. But take my tip: If you're seriously looking for a career in songwriting, *don't engrave in stone anything you write.*

The bottom line is this: Nobody likes a Prima Donna. Be willing to rewrite, or you'll get a name as somebody who is difficult to work with, and too sensitive to call on. Remember, always, that if you could write something that you were as proud of as your first draft, you are capable of writing something even better. Or at least different. You are a wellspring of ideas that has no boundaries. Your talent is an unexplored treasure. Stand on your head and you're standing on a gold mine—all you have to do is work it! Lots of paper, sharpened pencils, time, patience, and a little sweat: These are the ingredients of rewriting.

MAKING REALITY PALATABLE

Sometimes you need to write a complete draft of something very personal just to get it out of your system. Though it may even be written in proper lyric-writing form, this lyric still can be too personal to be well received by the buyers and users of music, such as publishers, A&R people, and artists. Also, though the story is important to *you,* it may not relate well to the everyday experience of the average listener. That leads me back to a small but important fact: When you say "I," you're speaking for the *listener.*

The self-indulgence of writing this type of song is obviously good and cathartic for you at the time, but you might need to do a complete rewrite before the song is presentable as a viable commercial entity. At the very least, the slant of the story will have to change considerably to take it outside of its strongly personal, but basically unrelateable, first-person-singular angst style to a style the audience can more easily associate with. Sometimes you might be too close to the subject to clearly see its universal dimensions. In that case, it's often better to ask another lyricist to take another approach to it.

As songwriters, we're very lucky we are able to express our anger and frustration when we want to fight back; words are our weapons. I remember when my friend Barry Bregman came to me with a draft of a song he had titled "Nowhere to Run." The song was about a personal hurt he had experienced, which he had felt driven to write about. Since it dealt with the loss of a deep friendship, writing the following lyrics helped him express his feelings.

NOWHERE TO RUN

When we started
Happened all so casually
Felt so free

Open hearted
As far as I could see
You almost fooled me
I took you by surprise

Chorus: *(You got) Nowhere to run*
           You're getting in deeper
           (There's) No place to hide
           You feel like you've been cornered
           No place to go
           You're going to have to face me on your own
           On your own . . .

I never doubted
You played it all so perfectly
I couldn't tell
Desperation
Finally broke you down
The light is burning out
The weather's getting cold

Chorus: *Nowhere to run*
           You're getting in deeper
           No place to hide
           I've got you in the corner
           No place to go
           You're going to have to face it all alone

Bridge: *We have built this bridge on trust*
           That never should be broken
           But now you're turning it to dust
           And taking my emotions Can't you see . . .
           You're almost out of time

(Vamp choruses)

Lyrics & Music/Barry Bregman

I read the lyrics and told my friend that they were well written, but far too right-on for my taste. He asked me what lines I would change, but for me the change was not any line in particular. What he had written hung together for the most part just fine. It was just that I felt the approach needed to be more subtle. I told him he was too close to the subject to be objective about what happened. In doing so, he had created a song he and those close to him would understand, having been privy to the events and the real players, but not one that would appeal to the average listener's memory bank. It was about such a specific hurt that, even though the actual events were not documented in his lyric, it was obviously painful to go through—a cross between hurt and anger, dominated by the need to see the foe brought to his or her knees. The lyric may have been personal, but the theme and basic story were universal and gave me a lot to think about.

When Barry asked me what I would do with this lyric, I said I'd take a different approach altogether, starting with the title, as I felt it was both too obvious and had been used too many times. After tossing around a few titles, I came up with "Wars of the Heart," which he immediately loved. This was a strong title because it was (a) original—or seemed to be, (b) catchy, (c) powerful, (d) an interesting mental picture, and (e) a provocative concept.

Barry okayed me going off on my own and writing a new lyric, subject to his approval. We had worked together in this fashion in the past, and he trusted my judgment lyrically. I told him that if he didn't like what I wrote he had no obligation to use it.

The Rewriting Process

THE APPROACH
First I had to consider the driving nature of the melody and track. They were just wonderfully moody and inspired the need to write a lyric with an "edge."

THE FIRST VERSE
I decided to set up a picture that told us right off the bat that the singer and the subject were no longer friends, and that the singer knew that the former friend was suffering—if not remorse, then at least sadness at the loss. My build ended the verse with an irony that I felt led well into the title.

THE CHORUS
I wanted to make full use of the concepts of "wars" and "of the heart." These were different from wars between countries, and yet shared similarities in their physical destructiveness. I also wanted to get in the irony of how, even when something is totally, irredeemably over, we universally

nurture the memories of what once was and what could have been. I wanted to suggest the human fantasy of turning back the clock to just before "it" happened, somehow thus preventing the crash. Finally, I was fortunate to fall into a well-known saying regarding war, which fit perfectly into this context.

THE SECOND VERSE

I began by openly doubting that the relationship had ever been what the singer thought it was. As one link in the chain was faulty, it gave rise to the theory that all of them might be. Since I had liked Barry's original line, "You almost fooled me," immediately on reading his lyric, I borrowed this line. But I let my singer be strong and show that he had discovered the treachery in time. My build in the second verse throws all the guilt and blame onto the other party, but in a very simplistic phrase that almost says, "Amazing—I trusted you so much, what on earth did you do it for?"

THE SECOND CHORUS

I followed this verse with the word *Now* leading into the second chorus. Since this was a pop song, I felt the chorus should be the same the second time around instead of using new answer lines. In this way, the repeated hook lines could be, so to speak, "hammered home."

THE BRIDGE

I had suggested the "bridge of trust" idea to Barry in an earlier conversation about relationships breaking down. My approach to this resolution section of the song was to use the concept of burning a bridge, but not just any bridge, this time *a bridge of trust*. It occurred to me that the wrongdoer in this situation had probably considered him- or herself in the right at the time and somehow justified every move, never thinking it through far enough to realize that inflicting such a great hurt might be the stuff of future nightmares. I drove the thought home with a concept Barry had tossed out in general conversation on the subject, which I had felt was very clever. He said something like, "That guy's gonna find out it's a great big world, but it always leads to me." Finally, I led back into the final vamp choruses with a question of futility.

FINAL VAMP

In the process of recording the demo, it felt very natural to suggest to the singer the ad-lib line, "Nobody wins . . . these wars of the heart."

The "I" in this song became anybody who had ever been wronged but managed to get out before it was too late, leaving the wrongdoer to feel bad. This is a resolution we would all prefer to see for any bad-ending relationship. And yet, the "I" also knew that victory was sometimes incredibly sad.

What pleased me, finally, was that Barry was very happy with the final lyric, and he said it still captured the original story very clearly for him. Everyone else I've played it for sees a situation in their own lives. The lyric, when read back, had become a song about *any* broken relationship—not just friendship, but also love.

As such, it went from a very specific song of anger about a particular situation and relationship to a very universal song that can be heard on as many different levels as there are listeners.

WARS OF THE HEART

Verse 1:   After midnight
I drove past your house tonight
Your light was on
Saw you crying
Life's not always black and white
And love is long gone

Build: Nobody wins the fight . . . but

Chorus: *Wars of the heart*
Tear us to pieces
Blow us apart
While memories still tease us
Endings are so hard
We win the battles and we lose the Wars
Of the heart

Verse 2:   Did I know you
Or was it all a big charade
I don't understand
You almost fooled me
Almost but not quite
I didn't play into your hands

Build: You threw it all away . . . now

(Repeat Chorus)

Bridge: *When our bridge of trust was burned*
You never dreamed it would hurt you
Though you may travel round this world
You'll find it's just a circle back to me
Tell me . . . why do there have to be . . . these

Chorus:　*Wars of the heart*
Tearing us to pieces
Blowing us apart
While memories still tease us
Endings are so hard
We win the battles and we lose the Wars . . .
Of the Heart
Nobody wins . . . these Wars of the Heart
(etc. . . . fade)

Lyrics/Pamela Phillips Oland, Music/Barry Bregman

KNOWING IT WHEN YOU HEAR IT

If you learn nothing else from this book, I hope you'll learn to trust your own instincts and intuitive ideas. In spite of the deluge of praise, criticism, adulation, and advice you'll receive from the massed contingents of supporters and detractors, professionals and laymen, I hope you will see that the song is in your hands to make or shape as you wish. Obviously, if *you* don't believe in your own creative decisions, you can never sell them to anyone else. That doesn't mean you should ignore the input. What you need is to find a way to balance the cacophony of opinions with the trusted sound of your own inner voice. Weigh everything you hear, and separate the useful from the unproductive.

AN A TO Z TARGET CHECKLIST

Targeting a lyric requires you to consider a great many questions, including those just discussed. This is a good time to recap all the various ideas and topics we have covered, but this time from the point of view of re-evaluating your finished work. Here's a handy list of items to check against your song, to make sure that you have done all you can to review and reconsider your lyric before demo-ing and submitting it:

A.　Is the language appropriate for the style?
B.　Is the lyric conversational?
C.　Will the slang or contemporary language hold up?
D.　Do all the words "sing" well?
E.　Is the hook strong? Does it repeat?

(continued)

F. Are there additional hooks in the song?

G. Are your rhymes natural or contrived?

H. Have you said what you set out to say, told the story you intended to tell?

I. Has the story developed and unfolded throughout the song?

J. Have you reflected the attitude of the artist you want to pitch the song to?

K. Are you able to visualize the characters who populate the story of your song?

L. Does the song paint the singer in a sympathetic fashion or as a loser?

M. Have you used any words for which you don't know the exact meaning?

N. Are there more than two verse sections in a row?

O. Do you need a bridge?

P. Has the story suggested by the title been told well? Does the hook pay off?

Q. Would a story like this belong in a genre like that?

R. Are there any adjectives, adverbs, or other parts of speech that could be more colorful or more interesting?

S. Have you been "too clever" with any words or phrases?

T. Have you used an easy-to-sing formula?

U. Do all the verses scan well with each other?

V. Have you allowed your intuition to guide your writing?

W. Have you inadvertently copied another song?

X. Is the title the hook?

Y. Have you written a lyric or a poem?

Z. Can you say anything better than you've said it?

This is a long list and it encompasses a great deal of what I've talked about up to this point. After a while, all these points will be second nature to you, and when they are, you'll be able to write great lyrics almost every time.

8

Now That Your Song Is Finished

Rather than go into depth about how to shop songs, make record deals, evaluate publishing contracts, and the like, I offer you some off-the-cuff practical information as to how to gain a competitive edge in a very competitive business. There are no hard-and-fast "do's" and "don'ts" that apply to every single person who writes songs. Finding your way is, of necessity, a very personal experience, and it's based as much on luck and the ability to make and impress the right contacts as it is on talent.

THE DREAM

I know no two individuals who have followed the same path to success. Some songwriters are successful with their first attempts, and others pursue their goal for many, many years before success finds them. One thing's for sure: If you don't try, you don't make it. No matter how many let-downs and turn-downs come your way, you must never give up the dream. Because if you do, you'll never know how close you came to your own personal moment of recognition.

THE REALITY

We all need to be able to switch hats from being "songwriters" to "business people." We need to leave our vulnerability and creative souls home at the piano, and become sharp, knowledgeable, astute entrepreneurs. We must see ourselves as the creators of a product (songs), and we must learn to market and sell this product, recognizing and making the best possible deals for ourselves, learning to promote and create a demand for our product.

Just as our very survival depends on our writing songs purely for the love of the process, we must also be able to face the realities of songwriting as a career and a business.

> *We must see ourselves as the creators of a product (songs), and we must learn to market and sell this product, recognizing and making the best possible deals for ourselves, learning to promote and create a demand for our product.*

THE DEMO: A LYRICIST'S PERSPECTIVE

Make the best possible demo of your song that you can afford to. It isn't enough to write a great lyric, hand it over to the composer, and hope for the best! As a lyricist, you have an obligation to your song to put it into the best form you are capable of—especially in light of the fact that a portion of the cost of making a demo comes right out of your own pocket.

In my early days of song demo-ing, I relinquished complete control to my writing partners. I was somewhat intimidated by their seeming comfort and familiarity with recording studios. I knew little or nothing about how a studio operated, and therefore, I was at the mercy of my collaborators and their recording engineers. When I walked into a studio, I immediately felt ill at ease, probably thinking my ignorance was likely to be discovered at any moment. How much smarter I would have been if I had invested $40 or so for an hour of 16-track studio time, wherein I would have asked the engineer to explain, in the most basic of terms, how everything works and what all those mysterious buttons, knobs, and black boxes with colored lights are for! I wouldn't have required a six-month course in recording engineering. I wouldn't have had to sit in the engineer's chair and do his or her job myself. All I needed was to learn what gadgets and equipment were available to me—to find out what is a *limiter,* what is a *fader,* what is *delay* and how is it used. How do you *compress* a vocal, and why would you do that? Are there track positions on the master you should and should not put vocals on? How many tracks do you need for recording live drums? And how are they broken down?

It isn't necessary to become an expert. In fact, my favorite engineer, Michael McDonald of L.A.'s Private Island TRAX Studio, once said to me, "It's better that you don't become an expert on all the electronics. Every session needs at least one pair of fresh ears to just listen and go with gut feelings." Michael remarked that one unfortunate side effect of our electronic music age is that sometimes the producers get so wrapped up in getting the sounds perfect that they lose sight of the heart of the song. But a passing knowledge of the available electronic wizardry can't hurt. If your engineer suggests some special effect, you'll know what sort of sound that means and what using this effect will afford you.

When you record a song demo, make sure the singer sings the first verse and chorus *as written.* In these days of "vocal gymnastics," singers want to start riffing on the first line, but how will the artist you are pitching your song to ever know what the real melody is, if you don't establish it in the first verse and chorus? Take control of your demo session, and get the song down the way you want it. Listen to the suggestions of your musicians and singers, and pay attention to the wise counsel of your engineer. But, in the end, it's your song and your reputation as a writer on the line. Live and die by your own choices!

Is That Song Worth Spending Money on?

Our songs are like our children. Once we write them, we become attached. So if we finish a song, play it around a little, and get excellent responses from those we play it to, we're immediately ready to go in the studio and cut a demo—though some of us prefer to save up three to five songs to get a better break on the musicians' time. But should every song we write have the benefit of a professional demo to present it? Of course not. The best among us still write drivel some of the time. So the question is, how do we decide which ones are worth demo-ing?

Since songwriting is such a subjective art, there are no hard-and-fast rules to follow when making this decision. Early on in the writing game, it's simpler. If you can't decide when you're first starting out which song among your catalogue is the best one to demo, there probably isn't any one at all that you should spend the money on yet. It's a good bet that they all may have good parts in them, but what you're perceiving as collective, overall excellence may well be something missing in all of them.

For more experienced writers, the issue isn't so simple. You have to evaluate your own song with cruel detachment. The song has to pass all sorts of judgments when it comes out into the marketplace. You're doing yourself a huge favor when you try to eliminate all the pitfalls in a song before it ever gets in the hands of a publisher/producer/manager/etc.

The first thing to do before demo-ing the song is to try to find what, if anything, is wrong with it. Here are ten checkpoints to consider once you complete a song:

1. *Are the verses equal in cadence, meter, and length?* Read each verse aloud to the same rhythm and check to make sure each one could reasonably fit over the other. (If one verse is four lines long, for instance, then all subsequent verses should also be four lines long.)

2. *Does the hook repeat in an orderly, regular fashion?* If it's a verse-chorus–style song, does the hook appear in the chorus at the same place or places each time? Is the hook always the same length each time it appears? In an "A-A-B-A"–style song, is the hook always used in the same way in the same place?

3. *Is the story set up properly before the first hook?* (Unless they're mad about the song, most industry professionals will not listen past the end of the first hook. Count on it!) If you don't grab the ear of the publisher/A&R person or other industry listener by what you've said by the end of the first

chorus, he or she probably will not be interested in listening to see if you've said something clever in the rest of the song. Don't save the best for last. Let there be great stuff at the end of the song, but also write something wonderful at the beginning. Draw your listener in and make him or her want to stay for more.

4. *Is the ending working as a fade? Should it simply end? Or vice versa?* "Fades" began as a contemporary convenience to get out of a song that the songwriter could not figure out how to end. While they have now long been accepted as a good and proper way to end a song, it is always a challenge well met when you come up with a stunning way to end a song instead of simply fading it.

On the other hand, is your ending contrived and uncomfortable? Does it cut off the flow of the chorus and leave the ear wanting more, wanting to just feel the song drift away rather than jar your ear with a final ending?

5. *Has the hook line been made to pay off in the best conceivable fashion?* Think about what you wanted to say with this hook/title. What is the real meaning you were hoping to get across? Did you do it? Did you do it well? Could you do it better? If you're unsure, you should take some time to experiment with reworking it and making sure there isn't a better way of expressing it. If you find that the hook really makes an impact, you probably don't need to rewrite it at all.

6. *Will the story interest anybody besides you and your immediate circle?* Will a lot of people find the story meaningful? (Make sure you have used the best *voice.* For instance, if it's "he and she," could it work better as "you and me"?) Try out the lyrics on some disinterested parties: Let them read them and see what reactions you get to the story.

7. *Is every word used correctly, according to its accepted meaning?* Look up any word you're not sure of in the dictionary. Make sure the correct syllables of the words are emphasized. The dictionary will give you pronunciation information.

8. *Is the song too long or too short?* Can you live without that extra verse, that extra fade chorus, half the bridge? Is anything you've said redundant? Do you have a feeling that something's missing, something has been left unsaid that should be covered?

9. *Is the point of the song clear to any listener?* Have you expressed yourself well? Has your idea come across? Can a listener visualize the people who populate the story of your song?

10. *If you were the publisher/producer, would you want this song?* You're close to your song. Obviously, you love it or you wouldn't consider it finished. Listen to the song objectively, as if you were about to choose between it and others that had been submitted, and ask yourself if it holds up.

Is there something irresistible about the song, some magical quality or some touching story that makes you feel totally confident that the song is a winner? Can you imagine the song being sung on the radio by an artist, and would that artist really sing that sentiment? Try to find any weak spots in the song, and fix them before you make the demo.

> *Listen to the song objectively, as if you were about to choose between it and others that had been submitted, and ask yourself if it holds up.*

How Much Will It Cost?

Once your song has passed the test, you must decide how much you can spend on the demo. Very simple demos can be made for as little as $75 by certain demo services; however, they can cost as much as $2,000. You will need to consider the following factors in preparing a budget:

• What is the hourly studio rate for the number of tracks you require?

• How much does the singer charge? Does the singer charge extra for background vocals, or is the fee all-inclusive for lead and backgrounds? Will additional background singers be required?

• How many musicians will you need, and how much do they charge? Some musicians charge per song, some by the hour. I must advise you that the musician's union (the American Federation of Musicians) frowns on musicians charging low demo rates and sets a recording studio rate that is applicable for this purpose. However, this is a very high rate for songwriters to put out for the purposes of "on-spec" demos, so as a practical matter, a great many musicians either are not members of the union or offer to work "off the books," as they can use the extra income. This is always with the understanding that should, by some chance, your demo be used as an actual recording, the difference between their demo rate and the union rate will be made up to them.

• Consider the cost of tape, depending on the studio equipment: an A-DAT cartridge, a 2-inch master tape for 24-track recorder, 1-inch tape for 16-tracks, or 8-track or 4-track master tape; quarter-inch tape for the mix-down, and DATs, CDs, or cassettes to make copies on.

• Some musicians have a lot of equipment and hire cartage companies to disassemble it at their home, lug it to the studio where they reassemble it for the session, then take it back to their home and set it up again. Cartage can be expensive and so, for demo purposes, try to get your musicians to bring only what they can carry themselves.

• While most small studios include the engineer in the price of studio time, many of the larger studios charge extra for the engineer. If you have a favorite engineer you wish to bring in on a session, plan on his or her fee.

Once you have worked out what you need and compared it with what your budget is, you may have to do some paring down. You'll have to call around to work out the best possible deal you can get for demo-ing your songs within your budget. For example, my budget for demos at one point soared from $400 or $500 to an average of $800. I've spent as much as $1,200 for one demo, which is entirely too much when you consider spending that on a regular basis. Demo-ing your songs must be cost effective. If I could play or sing on a session, it would bring the price down considerably, but I have to pay for everything unless my collaborator is a musician or singer whose voice is appropriate for the particular demo. One reason your demo budgets may sometimes be so outrageously high is that many of your collaborators will be record producers who want to be able to offer the 24-track demo master to the record company that picks up the song, in the hopes they can also produce the record. Remember: You co-own the master if you co-paid for it.

If you are a songwriter who plays no instruments, it would behoove you to find a keyboardist who not only plays on the demo session, but can act as the arranger, providing the feel of the song for you as well. Some will be happy to do it for the normal demo fee; others will charge extra. Be explicit as to what you want the song to sound like. If there is a song on an available album in release that has the same sort of feel as you envision for your song, bring it along and play it for your musicians, so that they can try to duplicate the feel of the "groove."

If your budget is tiny and you can choose between doing three or four second-rate demos or one or two first-class demos, the choice should be clear. If you're not sure which songs to keep and which ones to leave out, study the songs carefully to see which are the most memorable, hummable, have the most interesting lyrics, and have the catchiest titles. Think about your avenues for trying to sell your songs, and who will be listening to them. Pick the songs that are the most accessible to your contacts. Most of all, pick the best of what you have. And if you suddenly look at the songs and say, "These aren't really ready," by all means save your money and wait until you have something that really knocks you out—something you'd stake your reputation on.

Don't forget the "Three Song Rule." It is fairly common practice to submit no more than three songs on a demonstration tape. That is both to show off songs to publishers and producers, and usually to show off a new artist's work also. So unless it's requested, don't make an endless tape, since producers probably won't listen beyond the first three. Once again, *less is more:* If you don't wow them with the first three, why would they want to listen further anyway? And if they like what they hear, believe me, they'll be begging for more.

Pitching on CDs versus Cassettes

An A&R woman who is a friend of mine asked for some songs for a project, remarking, "I'll play the CD in my car." "Do you mean," I asked, "that you want me to go out and buy a CD burner, just to send you these two songs??" "That's all they use any more," she told me. On hanging up, I made several calls and found a unit I liked. It's by TASCAM, is freestanding and doesn't require running through a computer to record from any source. It's easy to operate and great for making up my own multiple-song masters.

Is this financial investment worth it? Is it a luxury or a necessity? Only you can decide. As for me, I don't know how I did without it!

Whatever you do, DON'T MAKE EXCUSES! *Shame on you* if you send in a song with a note that says, "I'm afraid my tape recorder wasn't working properly that day" or "I had a cold that night and my voice didn't sound its best" or "My sister borrowed my guitar, so I had to play piano, but I'm not really a pianist." Do these excuses sound absurd to you? Well, they are used every day. Just as bad are the following: "I wasn't sure whether to end the song with him coming home to her or him staying away forever, but I can change it if you like" or "I haven't quite finished the chorus yet, but I'm working on it," or "The demo singer usually sings musical theater, but please try to imagine my song with a Hip-hop artist." The moral: *Do it right or don't do it at all!*

SO WHAT'S THE DEAL ABOUT PUBLISHERS?

When your demo is complete, you'll then want to start shopping it around. Your first stop will probably be music publishers, as you will want to develop a relationship with a publisher or several publishers not only to get this first song placed, but—especially if you're not a performer yourself—for placing your future work. One of the reasons I have suggested making good-quality demos of your songs is to make your material competitive with other songs that publishers regularly receive from professional songwriters.

Once you have an ongoing relationship with a publisher, you might be able to get away with playing new songs "live" in their offices. You might even be able to present inexpensive piano/voice demos of new material in order to get the publisher's approval to demo them more fully at the publisher's expense. The point is, since first impressions last, you want to get on the best footing possible with your new allies, the publishers. So if you want them to be truly excited at discovering you and your work, you don't want them to be the least bit distracted by poor quality demos.

I suggest you first try working on a "one song at a time" basis with various legitimate publishers. Many publishers guest at songwriter conferences around the country, and have listening sessions where they are presented with new material. A great deal of this material is "picked up," and frequently the publishers are able to get it recorded. If you don't

Do it right or don't do it at all.

live in a city that plays host to such seminars, I suggest you look at the list of songwriter organizations in this book and elsewhere, and find the closest one you can affiliate with. It's worth making the trip now and again.

Writer/artists are in a separate category. Publishers frequently will sign you and bankroll your demo for a record deal, even using their connections to help you to shop for and obtain that record deal. Early on, many independent writer/artists hold onto the bulk of their catalogue, offering one song at a time to publishers hoping to get records with other artists, so that when they are ready to record themselves, they will still have a sizable song catalogue available for negotiating their artist deal.

Ultimately, you might want to find a staff-writer situation, which would pay you an annual advance against royalties, plus pay the costs of your demos. The plus side of a staff songwriter deal includes:

1) Having someone to oversee and develop your career;

2) Having someone with an established reputation and contacts, to introduce your work to the industry at large;

3) Having someone to make introductions between you and other writers and producers, connecting you to projects; and

4) Getting monetary advances that free you up to be a full-time songwriter.

The downsides of a staff deal might include:

1) If songs don't immediately find a home on a record, they can get shelved behind all the new songs you and other writers turn in;

2) It is normal for writers to do a great deal of the pitching of their own songs themselves, even when they are staff writers; yet this may disturb some writers;

3) There are certain TV and film projects in which the users of material (Disney and Paramount, for instance) require a 100 percent publishing share.

Negative possibilities notwithstanding, many reputable publishers offer exciting "development" deals to new and promising writers.

Where Do You Start Looking for a Publisher?

Since anybody with a song to publish can set him- or herself up in business as a music publisher, it is your job to decide whose opinions you trust and respect. There are as many opinions on how commercial a song is as there are publishers. That, in itself, doesn't determine the credibility of the publisher, but as is the nature of opinions, it largely depends on nothing more than personal taste.

There are lots of places where you can look up names of publishers: tip sheets, songwriters associations, songwriter magazines, and general books on songwriting available in most major bookshops, on the Internet, or by mail order. Just be careful of the little ads in magazine classified sections that ask for "song poems" to be made into songs. They will write music to your "song poem" and demo it, for a fee. Many of these operations are not reputable. I know it's tempting to answer one of these ads if you have a great lyric lying around and you need a melody to be written to it and don't know who to give it to, but check out the operation before you get involved.

You don't want to go out shopping for a publisher without a frame of reference to evaluate those you come across. Believe me, it's a two-way street. We writers have a tendency to be flattered if we are even vaguely smiled at with interested eyes. But it's important to keep in mind that the interest we read in a publisher's eyes is directly in accordance with what we are perceived as having to offer. The decision whether to work together as publisher and writer is definitely a mutual one, and feeling flattered isn't a good enough reason on which to base this important decision! As a writer, it's as much your choice who you want to have represent your work as it is the publisher's choice to want to work with you.

In that spirit, there are a number of factors that will help you in your search for the perfect publisher.

1. *Find out what the publisher's credentials are.* What hits has the company been credited with, and furthermore, what hits has he or she personally been responsible for?

2. *Is the publisher a well-known entity with a reputation in the music community?* Examples include Warner-Chappell, Universal Music, Peer, Chrysalis, EMI, BMG, Sony/ATV, Famous, and Tree. A large national or international publishing operation can be a wonderful ally. If they are ready to take a personal interest in you, they can do marvelous things for your career. Consider the viewpoint of a record producer or artist receiving a new song through the mail. If it bears the name of a reputable publisher, someone on whom they have always been able to count or whom they have sent appropriate songs for prior projects, this inures greatly to your benefit. Considering this respected source, your songs definitely are going to get a sincere and earnest listen. A publisher's reputation for having "great ears" goes a long way.

3. *Is the publisher a small but hands-on outfit?* Sometimes a small but energetic publishing house—often a one-person operation—may take you on as a personal project and crusade. They can put endless hours and tireless efforts into pushing your songs and building your reputation as a writer. They can give your work the kind of personal attention that no large, busy publisher has the time or inclination to invest. They can be your best friend and father confessor, your courage and your shoulder to cry on, and the source of valuable critiques and ruthless criticism.

So what's the answer? Do you prefer being a small or medium-sized fish in a large pond, or a big fish in a small pond? Ultimately, it depends on how many people go fishing at that pond! You might want to place different songs in different hands and see who does the best for you.

4. *Is the publisher willing to pay you even a token amount of money for the right to publish your song?* Is the money deliverable on execution of your single-song publishing contract? And if you are offered an exclusive staff writer deal, is the money the publisher is offering you going to make it worthwhile to give up your independence? If not, what is the incentive for you to sign? If you're considering a reputable and high-energy publisher, you might find that what the publisher can offer you outweighs the initial outlay of cash. However, if there is no money and no effort, *be sure your contract gives you a way out!*

5. *Is the publisher asking you to pay the company for the privilege of publishing your song?* IF SO, PUT ON YOUR TRACK SHOES AND RUN FOR YOUR LIFE!! THIS IS AN ABSOLUTE VIOLATION OF ALL THAT IS FAIR AND HONORABLE IN THE MUSIC PUBLISHING PROFESSION! *NEVER PAY TO HAVE YOUR SONG PUBLISHED!!*

6. *Do you feel comfortable with this publisher's suggestions and ideas?* Do you feel that you have a "meeting of the minds" on how you perceive life in general, and the way you word your lyrics in particular? Is this somebody you would like to work with on an ongoing basis? Can this publisher express what he or she feels "works" and "doesn't work" about your lyrics in a way that you can relate to? Does this publisher inspire confidence?

7. *Do you get a feeling of strangulation when reading the proposed publishing contract?* Is your firstborn being tied up in the fine print? Do the rights to your song(s) revert to you at the expiration of, say, three years, if the song is not placed on an album or single that is commercially released? Not every publisher will grant you a reversion clause, but please get your attorney to ask.

8. *Does this publisher balk at your hiring an attorney to go over the contract and negotiate it for you?* If so, don't deal with this character, as he or she is going to try to stick it to you as sure as gum sticks to a sneaker. It never hurts to hire a music lawyer, a specialist in his field, to give you a bargaining edge when negotiating your contracts.

9. *Does this publisher want to own 100 percent of the copyright?* Ah, interesting subject. In the early days, I was constantly warned by other writers (also unsuccessful) to hang onto my publishing share of the song at all costs. "The publishing is worth big dollars," I was warned. "It's like giving away a fortune." That's good advice—or *is it?*

Single-song publishing contracts are usually fairly standard, with a lot of "boilerplate" language, meaning basic obligations are spelled out for both sides, and the royalty payment structure is clearly outlined. These contracts are generally printed forms that the publishers acquire from form printers, personalized with their name printed along the top. Publishing deals will not usually deviate from the basic provisions printed into the contract unless you or your attorney requests specific changes. You can send for a copy of the Songwriters' Guild of America single-song contract, which many regard as the fairest to songwriters of all form contracts. You can compare the contract you have been offered against the provisions of this one, and you can try to persuade your publisher to use it instead of his or her own printed forms if you are unhappy with the contract you are being offered. Songwriters' Guild of America has an office at 6430 Sunset Boulevard, Suite 317, Hollywood, California 90028, (213) 462–1108.

The *Business* of Music

A) The ownership of a song is divided into two portions: 50 percent is the writer's share and 50 percent the publisher's share. There is no reason that I can think of to ever give anyone rights to any of your writer's share.

B) A money advance given a staff writer against songwriter royalties to be earned is always *recoupable* but *not refundable. Recoupable* means that when your earnings are collected by the publisher, the publisher will first *recoup*, or pay itself back the advance it gave you, before you see any profits. *Not refundable* means you don't have to *refund* what your songs don't earn; the advance is yours to keep. Any publishing contract will also stipulate that the publisher receives an "administration" fee for collecting your royalties and licensing use of your song(s).

C) The publishing share is the 50 percent of the song's income any portion of which a music publisher might acquire from you by the song contract. (If you are one of two writers on the song, your percentage of the writer's share diminishes to 25 percent of the total song, and the publishing share, which is yours to negotiate away, also dwindles to 25 percent of the total song. Your collaborator owns the rights to the other 50 percent of the songwriter and publisher's shares, which he or she is free to negotiate.) Ownership of the "publishing," as it is known, entitles the publisher to try to get the song recorded and to earn a penny for every penny, a dollar for every dollar, which you earn as the writer on the exploitation of the copyright. When you sign away the publishing of your copyright, it is usually forever, unless you are able to negotiate a reversion clause, as I discussed above. Retaining a piece of your publishing simply means that you don't give away the entire portion of publishing that's yours to give. When you build up a track record as a songwriter, it will be easier for you to make a "split" publishing deal, whereby you can retain a percentage of the publishing share and increase your income. Publishers usually make this type of split publishing arrangement on staff songwriter deals, in which they feel that the songwriter will be making an equal effort, based on the songwriter's contacts and reputation in the industry, to get their own song recorded.

So the answer to the question, "Should I hold onto my publishing or give up 100 percent of it?" depends on many factors. It does represent a good chunk of money if you have a hit. A great many talented and successful songwriters in the industry much prefer to remain "independent," that is, not affiliated with any publishers other than placing an occasional song in their hands to work. Many independent songwriters have developed relationships with A&R people and artists throughout the industry and feel that they are just as good at securing cuts on records as publishers. They prefer to hold onto their publishing share, signing it over only when necessary to get on a project, and take care of their own publishing needs with the help of an "administrator" to handle collection and licensing.

The downside of being your own publisher is the amount of time consumed by maintaining your copyrights. Staff writers prefer to concentrate on the writing and leave most of the song-running to the publishers.

There are other pros and cons both to being independent and to having a publisher. If, for instance, you are an independent writer and you secure a cut with a recording artist who is not asking you for a piece of the publishing as an incentive to record your song, you're in clover. More and more, however, producers and artists will ask for a share of your publishing if they are going to record your song. Your publishing share can be an important negotiating tool for you to use in getting a song recorded.

Major publishers will not usually relinquish any share of the publishing in order to secure recordings. Their position is that their investment in the writer, and in demo-ing and marketing the song, entitles them to retain control of the copyright. Because publishers are respected as major sources of good, screened material, producers and artists usually record their songs anyway, even without sharing in the publishing. So the question ultimately is this: Do you hold onto your publishing to be free to give it away as an incentive on a song-by-song basis, or do you sign it away in order to establish a relationship with a major music publisher?

ADMINISTRATION

In any event, I would be remiss if I didn't emphasize here that if you do decide to remain independent, you ought to make a deal with a reputable publisher to administer your portion of the publishing. The fee for that is usually 10–20 percent. This means that they collect all your "mechanical" royalties for you. They'll track down and pay you the money for sales of the record your song is on worldwide as well as collecting money from sheet music and folio sales. Believe me, they are well worth the percentage you pay them. Almost any publisher you approach can handle administration for you; also, there are independent companies that handle only publishing administration, and some music lawyers have staff who take care of this.

So good for you if you can hang on to your publishing share—you'll make twice as much money on the deal; but please don't think that by signing over your publishing to a reputable publisher you are committing a dreadful error. Publishers are not "the enemy"; for the most part, they are there to help you advance your career. If they place a song, you make money, they make money, and everyone is happy.

Remember that publishers are in the business of *publishing songs!* If they are going to get out there and invest time and energy in placing your song; if they are willing to advance money for the demo costs, absorb the costs of long-distance phone calls to, and lunches with, producers/artists/managers to try to plug your song(s); and if they are going to invest their professional reputations in the music industry, which ride on the presentation of every song they bring in—well then, a share in your publishing (and if you are an unknown writer with no track record and no professional reputation for them to trade on, a 100 percent share of your publishing) is a fair exchange. The publisher is there to develop you as a writer. If he or she can create a favorable reputation for you within the music community, the affiliation with you will be very valuable both financially and in terms of your ongoing relationship.

In the extreme cases where your publisher is not pitching songs, merely collecting royalties for you while you develop your own career, then what you are essentially doing, of course, is borrowing money (your advance) with your songs as collateral; the share of publishing interest that the publisher receives becomes, in effect, the interest rate on your loan.

Nevertheless, if a reputable publisher is eager to sign and work one of your songs, my advice is this: Don't act as if this song is the key to your career. There are many more in you where that one came from. You're foolish to get hung up on the fate of one song. A better use of your time and energies is to take courage from the interest that you have received in that song, sign the publishing over to a publisher who can make the copyright count, and direct your energies into writing one even better! Sometimes owning 100 percent of your publishing can work out to be 100 percent of nothing. And that's nothing to write home about.

HIT 'EM WITH YOUR BEST SHOT

Presentation is everything. You only get one chance to grab your listener's attention and sell your song, so you need to be sure beyond sure that you're going to get the best listen possible. We've talked about making your demo competitive, and not sending in a sub-par presentation. Clearly, negative attention does not beat no attention at all! In my view, it's kind of like not wearing brown shoes to a black-tie event: The less you distract people with extraneous things to criticize, the more they'll focus their attention on what's right about what you're presenting.

You want to have your work considered the equal of the best that's being presented by others. At least have presentation going for you! You may have written the greatest masterpiece since "White Christmas," but if nobody ever bothers to pay it the proper attention, alas, it will simply never get its proper shot. There are thousands of people writing songs. It is realistic to acknowledge that far more songs are being written than there are slots on record dates. If your song is to be considered as a viable, competitive entity in the selection process, it has to be, at the very least, presented in a fashion in keeping with industry standards.

To find out who is looking for songs at any particular time, just ask music publishers to give you an idea of the artists they are seeking songs for and the style they're after. The secretaries working in record company A&R departments should be able to tell you who is currently recording. Trade publications, too, such as *Billboard, Black Radio Exclusive,* and *Cash Box,* often provide clues as to which artists and producers are searching for material.

It's okay to send simultaneous submissions of the same song to a variety of artists. You should only have the problem that Whitney Houston, Brandi, and Mariah Carey all want to record your song at once and you have to choose among them! The A&R (Artists & Repertoire) staff of a record company are always looking for that one special hit, and they don't care if it comes from you or Godzilla. All they care about is the song, and they won't waste any time putting it on hold for their artist. Study *Songwriter's Market* for some clues to help you decide to whom you want to submit. You will be submitting your three-song-or-less tape presentations to A&R people, publishers, and perhaps artist management companies. Make each mailing count.

YOUR PACKAGE

Use your opportunities wisely. Realizing that you're competing with songs by everyone from Eric Clapton to Jewell should make you want to take that extra step to make sure your presentation package is competitive and attractive.

The music business has become extremely sophisticated, and although you may contend that you are writing songs, not producing records, keep in mind that most industry people who will listen to your songs will be hoping to get casting ideas from your demos. To accomplish that, the demos cannot afford to be too generic; they must suggest a style of record. Obviously, your own style and character should come out in your demo. But you certainly want to do everything you can to make sure your demo hits its target. Record producers receive hundreds of tapes a week from all over the country. Some will not listen to unsolicited material, but many have "listeners" on their staff, whose job it is to weed through the material that arrives in the mail and select what sounds as if it should be considered. These people don't have time to sit down and try to make heads or tails out of what you've sent them, so take the guesswork out of it for them. So what are the don'ts?

- Don't make your demo sitting in the living room singing into a cassette tape recorder, because that's what it will sound like you did.
- Don't hand-write your lyrics.
- Don't hand-write your cassette or CD labels.
- Don't fill your cover letter with disclaimers and excuses.
- Don't sing your demo yourself, unless you are a good and tuneful singer, and, even then, unless the style of the song matches the style of your voice.

Quality Mailings

Since your contact will receive tons of mail every day, make sure your mailing looks thoroughly professional, and always type and never hand-write cover letters and address labels.

- Write a short, pleasant cover letter to accompany your tape and lyric sheets. If you have a certain artist in mind for a song, indicate that in the letter. Try to avoid turning the cover letter into a personal biography.
- It's okay to include a copy of your résumé or discography, if you have one, which the recipient can choose to peruse or not.
- Use an 8½-by-11-inch rag bond for typing your lyrics and cover letter, and fold it one-third up from the bottom and one-third over from the top if you are using legal-size letter envelopes. Don't fold it at all if you are using 9-by-12-inch envelopes with a piece of thin cardboard to keep the packet from bending. If you are using a padded mailing envelope, fold the paper in any size that's compatible with the size of envelope, either in thirds, as described, or in half and then in quarters. For small padded envelopes, first fold the sheets of paper upward in half then fold in the left side one-third, and then the right side one-third.
- Use personalized printed stationery, if possible. Create your own letterhead on your computer if you prefer (more on this below).
- Don't try to cram too much into an envelope—buy a bigger envelope or send less.

• Properly box and label your CD or cassette. If you are not using a padded mailing envelope, purchase a roll of small-quilt packing plastic at a discount stationers, and cut a piece to fit around the CD jewel box or cassette box, taping it with scotch tape.

• Take it to the post office and have your package weighed to make sure you have used adequate postage. Your contact will be furious if he or she has to pay excess postage on receipt!

• Make use of the post office's certified return receipt requested service if you want to know when, and by whom, your package was received.

• Make sure to include your name, address, and telephone number on every lyric sheet and on the CD or cassette label, not only so that there can be no doubt as to who wrote the material it contains, but also, of course, so that you can be contacted if there's interest in your song. You would be amazed at how many dozens of lyrics and cassettes I have personally seen that are missing the writer's name and contact information! A writer cannot assume that the publisher will keep the demo and lyrics together with the mailing envelope that contains the address of the sender! The lyrics and tape usually get separated, and you can count on the receptionist tossing out the mailing envelope.

• If you have conversed with the addressee or his or her representative, mark the envelope to that person's attention with the words, *By Request.*

Cover Letters

Do not ramble on and on in a cover letter. Get to the point as soon as possible. What's the purpose of the correspondence? How did you decide to write to this person? What's enclosed? What do you want? Thanks for your time and interest. Very truly yours. Always include an "SASE" (a self-addressed stamped envelope), if you ever want to see your tape again, should your song be turned down. (Note: In reality, it's unlikely anyone will return a CD or cassette to you, or the photo you've sent in, if you're an artist. So the moral is this: Never send an original or your only copy of a demo, photo, or anything else of personal value!) For sample cover letters, see pages 197 and 198.

Lyric Sheets

Let me repeat! Don't even think of sending hand-written lyric sheets! Nothing is more of a turnoff to a publisher or artist than receiving a ratty piece of notebook paper scrawled in illegible handwriting.

In fact, there are some wonderful inexpensive printers on the market, and I think you should invest in one, and type your lyrics on a computer.

While probably no two writers type up their lyrics in the identical manner, here are some examples and guidelines.

• Always but always print or type your lyrics on either printed 8½-by-11-inch letterhead or good-quality bond paper (preferable twenty-pound rag content, but copier paper is acceptable).

• Be sure to include your name, address, and telephone number.

• Type the title in all capitals, and underline it.

• Type the names of the writers in upper and lower case, either at the top of the page under the title, or a few lines below the end of the lyrics. Some examples would be:

> Lyrics/Pamela Phillips Oland,—Music/Rick Neigher
> or
> Words & Music by Pamela Phillips Oland and Wayne Tester
> or
> Music by J. P. Dunne,—Words by P. P. Oland

• If you are a member of a performing rights society, such as ASCAP, BMI or SESAC, make that notation. If the song has been published and copyrighted, you may want to make that notation also (i.e., By Pamela Phillips Oland © 2001 Pam-O-Land Music [ASCAP])

• Center the lyric on the page.

• Choose a style, such as all capitals or upper and lower case, and keep it consistent.

• Don't make ink or pencil corrections; retype it if you made a mistake.

• Set the lyrics up so that the parts of a song stand out. The verses can be marked "Verse 1," "Verse 2," or not, according to your preference. The chorus can be in all capitals, bold typeface, block indented or flush left, but always identify it as "Chorus." A bridge can be set out in block indention or flush left, can be all capitals, can be in parentheses—this is a style choice. The main thing to remember is to label the chorus and the bridge. It is optional but not necessary to retype a chorus that has identical wording. Just "Chorus" or "Repeat Chorus" or "Chorus Repeats" or some variation thereof is sufficient. (See pages 199 and 200 for sample lyric sheets.)

Your Own Letterhead

Never underestimate the power of stationery in presenting your songs. I actually think that some people think the lyrics are *better* because of how nice they *look*. You can either use generic paper stock, such as the inserts that come with blank cassettes and CDs, and blank to-from address labels, or you can have something that reflects you personally.

How much of an investment do you have to make to have your own letterhead? Something simple costs just a few bucks at an instant print shop. Or be creative and use the fonts on your computer to create and personalize your letterhead. You might even want to ask an artistic friend to design a logo (a symbol of your name or company name) and have a set of custom stationery printed, which will cost you in the vicinity of $200–$300 for a large supply. You'll need to personalize the following: (a) 8½-by-11-inch letterhead on twenty-pound rag bond; (b) 4-by-9½-inch legal-sized envelopes; (c) mailing labels to use on packages; (d) CD and/or cassette labels; and (e) box inserts (j-cards) for cassette boxes, or inserts for CD jewel boxes. Actually, there are programs available for making custom CD inserts and labels in full color, using computer graphics. These should have the name of your personal publishing company on them, if you have one, plus your name following the word "Contact"; otherwise, just type your name, along with address and telephone number. There should be room for you to type out the names of the songs enclosed. Why do I place such importance on clarity of presentation? I'd bet money that more than once a perfect song for a project has been submitted—but the writer couldn't be identified.

If you feel you can't justify this expense at this time, in lieu of printing these things, you can simply type them neatly. If you don't have a typewriter, borrow one, or pop into a stationery store and quietly use one of the nice electronic demonstration word processors with daisy-wheel printers while no one's paying attention!

Take it from me, it always looks better to have a typed label on a cassette, and that means not just the "A-side" and "B-side" labels that are standard with every cassette box, but the full labels that you buy on a sheet of twelve. They're available in white only, along with blank CD labels, blank professional audio cassettes, DATs and CDs, and all other audio supplies, at Project One Audio-Video, 6613 Sunset Boulevard, Hollywood, California 90028, (323) 464–2285. You can mail order what you need, or you could ask your local stationery store how to order them.

Your Demo Package

When assembling your song tape, do not make spoken introductions to the songs. Let the typed cassette box insert do the talking.

- Unless you have top-quality recording equipment in your home studio, avoid sending home-taped, "guitar-voice" demos when submitting to publishers. Invest in a professionally produced (however simple) demo in a properly equipped recording studio to maximize your vocal and music tracks. Remember that most modern recording studios offer you the ability to insert and edit by "punching in" over mistakes.

- Unless you are a qualified performer and musician, professional singers and musicians will get your song across far better than you can. An amateur performance, in fact, can cost you your shot at getting your song recorded.

- CDs are more popular than cassettes for pitching songs. If you must send cassettes, use high-quality, low-noise cassettes; never send old-fashioned reel-to-reel tapes—most publishers don't have recorders to play them on.

When assembling your song tape, do not make spoken introductions to the songs. Let the typed cassette box insert do the talking.

- If you only have one song you believe in 100 percent, only send that one. Don't waste the listener's time with less than your best.

- Don't feel frustrated at sending no more than three songs. If they love your work, they'll call you and ask to hear more!

Use your one chance to make a first impression with well-typed lyric sheets that make a good visual presentation and either a CD or a good-quality cassette tape of the best demo you can afford to make.

Calling First

It is always a good idea to call first, before sending in a presentation of songs. Make contact with somebody in the office, and get an authorization to send the package. Otherwise, it will likely be returned to sender as "Unsolicited." Once you have made the contact, you are able to mark the package "By Request." Even if you don't talk to the publishing company's professional manager, but an assistant or secretary, the contact with that person will endear you just enough that he or she might bother to open the package and take a moment to listen!

Keep in mind that professionals would rather deal with other professionals, plain and simple. That's why publishers have fairly short attention spans toward people who insist on sending in unprofessional presentations and amateurish material.

Then, once you've gotten past the professional packaging, they have to find something worthwhile inside when the package is unwrapped! So if you want to impress a publisher, only send in something that really shows off your promise as a writer. Get the publisher excited about you. Even if the song isn't what the publisher is looking for that day, you want that door to stay wide open for the next time you have something to submit!

PROFESSIONALISM

If you want to succeed in any business, you have to adopt a professional attitude that will mark you as somebody worthy of attention. The music business is certainly no exception, and there are a number of ways in which one can make good and lasting impressions on the members of the industry who are our life's blood. How we are perceived by producers, A&R folks, artists, managers, music-industry lawyers, music publishers, and fellow songwriters, is going to make the difference between making a strong, positive impression and making just a tiny dent in their memories.

One thing you can do to further your professionalism is to educate yourself by reading up on the industry. A lot of excellent books and magazines are on the market to help aspiring songwriters. They cover every conceivable aspect of the business end of the business, including basic legal information, the art and craft of composing music and writing lyrics, and all the peripheral areas such as getting record deals and finding publishing situations. Some books educate, some merely entertain, and many do both. Industry magazines bring you up-to-date on current music affairs, opportunities, and who-did-what-and-how stories. Ask your local bookstore about new releases. Subscribe to industry magazines, read on-line publications, or read the latest issues in a publisher's office. Remember that everything you learn will make you a stronger competitor, a more discerning writer.

Something else you can do to boost your professionalism is to join organizations. The Songwriter's Guild of America (SGA), the Nashville Songwriter's Association International (NSAI), the National Academy of Recording Arts and Sciences (NARAS), and other organizations are there to help you learn your craft, meet your peers, network with the industry, and feel part of the music business. Take advantage of becoming a member of your preferred professional organizations, as well as a member of your local branch or chapter of a songwriters' organization. It is much more rewarding and satisfying to pursue your goals with the support and admiration of your local songwriters' group. I have been a guest speaker for several such groups and have always found them to be warm, friendly, compassionate, and extremely helpful to their members. They give the local writers a sense of belonging—not being alone in "the struggle" for recognition.

Most important, it's never too soon to start developing professional work habits. And sometimes, with so much else to think about—writing, the quest for career, love lost and love found, paying the rent, and so on—we have little time to remember that with everything we do we are laying a foundation of little building blocks that will eventually support the house of our successes.

Ground Rules for Making and Keeping Appointments

CALLING OR WRITING FOR AN APPOINTMENT

Sometimes it's hard to get past the receptionist of a company, let alone get through the secretary or assistant of the executive you want to talk with. A receptionist's job is partly to filter out unwanted calls, and a secretary is always very protective of the boss' time and energy. When you place a call to a professional music office, be it publishing or A&R, this is no time to dither or be uncertain. Be clear about whom you want to talk with, and offer no unnecessary or unsolicited information. If you start telling your life story, you'll find your listener's attention span will be very short. Be confident and sharp, and present yourself as an important person would, not as a nonentity.

When you get the executive on the phone, be cordial and assertive, not overwhelming; say who you are and what the songs are you wish to play. If you don't live in that city and will be making a special trip, explain how long you will be in town and ask for an appointment to show your work and meet this executive. Don't be disappointed if he or she sets you up with a person who is on a lower rung of the company's hierarchy. Be grateful for an opening, and be ready to maximize the opportunity. Oh yes, and make sure that if you are planning a "live" piano-voice demonstration, the office has a piano! But always bring copies of your demo tape, as they may ask you to leave one even if you perform live.

Buy An Appointment Book

Even if you have very few business appointments, start keeping an appointment book to keep track of where you are scheduled to be. Also, keep track of the times and dates of all mailings pitching songs and all outgoing calls to industry people so that you can follow them up. Staying on top of everything you do that's music-connected is a good work habit and will help you to remember names, dates, and places, for all your contacts. These business records will help you to judge when and how to follow up your meetings. Accurate records will have the additional benefit of helping you prepare your income tax returns.

Do Your Homework

Bone up on the information you're likely to have to discuss at a meeting. If, for instance, you're meeting a record company executive, try to find out in advance from the promotion department which artists record on that label, and be familiar with their style and most recent works if you are expecting to pitch songs to them. Buy their most recent records or spend hours listening to the appropriate radio stations.

If possible, try to know a little about the person you are going to be meeting with. Regular reading of the "trades" or a chat with the secretary can be most informative. Be subtle when you ask questions. Familiarize yourself with the language of the field in which the person you are meeting specializes. If, for instance, he's a publisher, it wouldn't hurt to understand terms such as *exclusive writer, reversion clause,* and *recoupable royalties.* Again, there are books that cover such subjects.

Be On Time

Busy people don't like to be kept waiting. Being on time for appointments is a great attribute. I tell you this while admitting that I struggle to get places on time. My life is Murphy's Law in practice: It seems that just as I'm walking out the door, I'll invariably get a long-distance call I've been awaiting for weeks. If I'm in a hurry, you can bet my last pair of hose will rip, I'll misplace my car keys, or the gas gauge in my car will be on "E." If not that, a traveling proselytizer will bang on the door and engage me in a discussion about the future of life as we know it, or the dress I'm ironing will develop a glaring coffee stain I didn't notice, right down the front. There's always something that tries to make me late, no matter how earnest my intentions. But however polite people are about it, nobody likes to be kept waiting. So try not to put yourself in the position of holding them up. One common cause of tardiness is not planning ahead. Learn to give yourself enough "get ready" time, in case of the unexpected. If you are going to be unavoidably late, call as early as you possibly can to say how long it will take you to get there. Sometimes your contact might prefer to just postpone the meeting altogether rather than wait for you, and if you're going to be late, you owe your contact the courtesy of letting him or her make that choice.

NEVER UNDERESTIMATE THE VALUE OF A SECRETARY

In a business that is famous for hiring from within, today's tape copier, receptionist, or secretary can be tomorrow's chief executive. People with entry-level jobs often take them as a way to enter the industry and learn all facets from the ground up. Those with obvious talents and abilities cannot be kept down. The result: *promotion.* Thus, those among you who find it necessary to be superior or supercilious with the person who answers the phone and is unable to help you the moment you call, will have a long time to regret your egoism. In the first place, a valued secretary has a valued opinion, and that opinion of *you* will quickly be communicated in the very quarters in which you were hoping to make a great impression. "He sounds like an arrogant creep!" will already be echoing in the ears of the executive you were hoping to impress. If you get a meeting, instead of listening to your presentation, the executive will be busily evaluating your personality from a prejudged point of view.

And by the way, don't think bad first impressions somehow fade away. People have elephants' memories when it comes to those things. Furthermore, any time your name happens to arise in casual chatter, your reputation will precede you.

DON'T BE A SYCOPHANT

Diametrically opposed to the crime of being high-handed is that of being a sycophant. There is a way to be polite and charming without bootlicking. While executives enjoy holding their guests in rapt attention whenever they're speaking, they also don't want to feel that the person is incapable of expressing his or her own mind, hanging on every word as if it were straight out of the Bible. Ask sincere questions and converse enthusiastically. Some meetings are lively and some are quiet, so you have to feel out the person on the other side of the desk, and work at making both of you feel comfortable with the meeting.

BE ORGANIZED

Don't waste a busy executive's time by coming to a meeting unprepared. Have your paperwork neatly typed, and have all your photocopying done in advance of your meeting, rather than expecting some harried assistant to run around making copies for you. Have all your tapes neatly labeled and lyrics in the order in which you wish to show them.

BRING A CURRENT RÉSUMÉ OR DISCOGRAPHY

If you have had any activity whatsoever in the industry, type it up professionally to give it the best possible presentation. List all your credits, who has recorded which of your songs, and include chart positions if there are any. List any musical honors or awards you have received, as well as any musical or lyrical training you may have had, and if you like, include the names of collaborators, ways your work has been showcased, and what your music business career goals are.

DRESS FOR SUCCESS

No, this doesn't mean you have to go out and buy a three-piece suit! But be aware of what other professionals are wearing. Some people feel most comfortable in casual clothes, while others, like myself, like to dress a little more formally. Whatever's comfortable for you is fine—that is, in terms of *style.* Unfortunately, many writers look like slobs when they go to meetings. Your attractive appearance should be a given: It should be one thing they don't have to think about. You should simply look pleasant and comfortable in your chosen mode of dress. If you like to be outrageous and eccentric in your clothes, that's terrific. Just make sure it makes sense and makes some sort of statement about who you are.

LIMIT YOUR PRESENTATION

Play your best songs first. Don't force your listeners to "wait for the best stuff," as their ears will be turned off long before you get to it. It is generally an accepted custom to submit or play no more than three songs at one sitting, so show 'em your best and make every moment count.

KEEP GOOD RECORDS

Not everybody enjoys keeping a business diary or journal, as it is time-consuming and can become a

Developing your own sense of professionalism is something that will happen over a period of time. Experiment with your presentations, your scheduling, your phone personality, and your most comfortable appearance.

nuisance. However, it can also be a marvelous tool on which to build relationships and follow up on connections. Those of you who have home computers can list contacts by name in your database, and each time you have a meeting or phone call with a contact, you can immediately record what transpired, what compliments or criticisms you received, what projects he or she may have asked you to work on, deadlines, and the names and phone numbers of additional contacts he or she may have suggested. If you don't have a computer, you can keep a similar log by hand.

Developing your own sense of professionalism is something that will happen over a period of time. Experiment with your presentations, your scheduling, your phone personality, and your most comfortable appearance. Use common sense when it comes to making impressions; use good judgment when it comes to following up contacts. Know when *no* means *no;* learn when a *yes* is accompanied by reservations; always write a brief thank-you note after a good meeting, but don't call and write so often that you become a pest.

Finally, remember that the person you are going to be meeting with has a heart and soul and mind, too. Don't be so consumed with your own importance that you forget to be interested in those you deal with.

SAMPLE COVER LETTERS

Adrienne Ashby
1200 Brook Lane
Rapid City, South Dakota
Phone: (605) 000–0000

May 8, 2001

Mr. Ricardo Venardi
Professional Manager
Sound Music Publishing Company
9999 Hollywood Boulevard
Hollywood, CA 90028

Dear Mr. Venardi:

Re: 3 Original Dance Songs for the Johnsons

I am a songwriter working in South Dakota, and I am aware that the Johnsons are looking for some new dance material for their upcoming album on TJ Records. I understand that you are in a position to present new material for this project, and I hope that you will consider the enclosed three songs, titled, "Love For You," "Making Up," and "Whatever You Want."

The songs are in a rough demo form, and I would be happy to go into the Sound Factory, our local 16-track demo studio, to fully demo any of these songs you might think are suitable for this Johnsons project. Publishing is 100 percent available on all songs, and I am interested in signing single-song publishing contracts on this material with Sound Music Publishing Company.

I appreciate your time and interest in my songs.

Sincerely,

Adrienne Ashby

Enclosed: tape/3 lyrics/SASE

THE JOHN HARDING MUSIC COMPANY
1550 East Oakey Boulevard
Las Vegas, Nevada 89102
(702) 123–4567

9 February 2001

Ms. Jennifer Laws
Vice President, A&R
TELLATALE RECORDS
575 57th Street
New York, NY 10012

Re: Ballad "I Need More" for Anita Brown Album

Dear Ms. Laws:

I understand that you are looking for strong R & B ballad material for Anita Brown's forthcoming album. As I discussed with your secretary this morning, I am submitting a CD and lyric sheet on my song titled "I Need More" for your consideration. I hope this is the song you're looking for! Thanks for taking a listen.

Yours very truly,

John Harding

Enclosures: CD and lyrics (SASE)

SAMPLE LYRIC SHEETS

This first example includes three verses, a chorus and a bridge, a musical break and B sections (builds) in the verses. I've starred the B sections to show you where they are. However, since the person who'll receive these lyrics may find it far too confusing to read a separate annotation of "B section," I suggest you show the "B's" simply by dropping down an extra space and block indenting.

PICKIN' UP PIECES OF BROKEN HEARTS
Lyrics/Pamela Phillips Oland, Music/Dana Walden

Verse 1:   Pictures on the wall
Of the feelings they could never say
Further down the hall
Someone's gonna sleep away another day

Now that he's gone
She can't be strong
Till a new love comes along

Chorus: *And they're pickin' up pieces of broken hearts*
Shattered dreams on the road of life
As they try to mend what has come apart
Working from nothin' where do you start
Someone needs someone tonight

Verse 2:   Children of the night
Are alone again to greet the dawn
Who was choosing sides
Tell me, when the battle lines were being drawn

Cries in the void
Visions destroyed
Frames of truth on celluloid

(Repeat Chorus)

Bridge: *Tears will run like rivers*
Till the storm subsides
Man debates and God decides

(Musical Break)

Verse 3:   On the street of dreams
All the lonely strangers pass and never meet
Playing private scenes
Why are all the perfect endings always incomplete

Tearful mistakes
Passion divides
Man debates and God decides

(Repeat Chorus and Fade)

© Irving Music/Pamalybo Music/Zadoch Music (BMI)

"Nobody Loves Me Like You Do" utilizes the simpler formula, verse-verse-chorus-verse-chorus. However, all I have labeled on this example is the chorus. More is unnecessarily cluttered.

NOBODY LOVES ME LIKE YOU DO
Like a candle burning bright
Love is glowing in your eyes
A flame to light our way
That burns brighter ev'ry day
Now I have you
And Nobody Loves Me Like You Do

Like a leaf on the wind
I could find no place to land
I'd dream the hours away
And I'd wonder ev'ry day
Do dreams come true?
And Nobody Loves Me Like You Do

Chorus: *What if I'd never met you?*
           Where would I be right now?
           Funny how life just falls in place somehow
           You've touched my heart in places that I never even knew
           'Cause nobody loves me like you do

I was words without a tune
I was a song still unsung
A poem with no rhyme
A dancer out of time
But now there's you
And Nobody Loves Me Like You Do

(Repeat Chorus)

LYRICS/PAMELA PHILLIPS OLAND, MUSIC/JAMES PATRICK DUNNE
PROPERTY OF ENSIGN MUSIC CORPORATION

Whatever style you choose to type up your lyrics, I always think it's nice to be consistent; that is to use this same style for every lyric you send out. If you have an attractive type style or computer printout style, those who regularly receive your work will come to expect it to look a certain identifiable way, and this will be one more subconscious way in which they will remember you.

9

YOU CAN DO IT!

rom a songwriter's point of view, no effort ever seems to move smoothly enough, no question of "will it or won't it happen" can be resolved quickly enough. But if becoming a successful songwriter can be a slow process, along the way there are innumerable perks. We songwriters are in a position to meet and work with a host of incredibly talented people, to illuminate and uplift our lives with music and song, and most of all, we receive the gift of a unique kind of satisfaction that only comes from the dawning of an inspired idea.

If you are primarily wishing to be in this industry for some instant gratification, immediate acceptance, fame, and money dropping into your lap like pennies from heaven, you may not be able to hang in long enough to see your wish fulfilled. Although I hope, for your sake, that your career is smooth sailing from day one, you have to be prepared to work hard, cultivate contacts slowly and thoughtfully, demonstrate your good work habits, and gain friends and allies in the business who want to work with you. Take your career a day at a time. Reward yourself for staying with it, and do a little something every day toward your ultimate goal, even if it's only making one phone call or writing down one title idea. Over 365 days, that can amount to a substantial investment of time. It can mean a lot of phone calls and new contacts, and a veritable treasure chest of ideas!

ATTITUDE IS EVERYTHING

To become professional in your approach to your career, be a willing worker, open to constructive ideas and criticisms when you're on the job. Nobody likes to work with somebody who's surly, self-centered, and resistant to change. There should be no such words in your vocabulary as "I Can't Do It."

I'd like to relate to you an amusing story about a song that the producer Leon Sylvers III asked me to write lyrics for. The title I was given was

"Shakedown." The song was for Evelyn "Champagne" King, our three-way conversation went something like this:

Producer Leon Sylvers: This track is called "Shakedown," and we need it by tomorrow around noon . . . [It was 9:00 P.M.]

Evelyn: What does the title mean to you?

Me: Er . . . I don't know, a police bust?

Sylvers: Right! But make it a love song!

Evelyn: Yeah, and make it somethin' I can dance to!

So, armed with the above information, I set out to write a love song that you could dance to about a police bust.

A challenge, yes. Impossible, never. Lesson Number One: *The artist is always right. The producer is always right.* It is their project, they know exactly what they are looking for, and it is not within your domain to tell them otherwise. Your great insights as to what they should sing about and what direction they should take lyrically are not always welcome, so the sooner you learn to take direction, the better.

I wrote the following lyrics in the spirit of their directions. Happily, they loved them and recorded them and the song was a hit:

SHAKEDOWN
Starting here
And starting now
(Do ya hear me)
I need a man
Who can show me how

Fit the bill
Or don't apply
(And I won't die)
And if your shoes
Point in my direction
Be sure they're dancing in time
I've seen the clues
The verdict is passion
Could you be guilty of the crime?

Chorus: *Watch out it's a Shakedown*
            Stand up to the takedown
            Hollywood's a fakedown
            Gimme a Break!

This is I, the showdown
Tell me, what's the lowdown?
Be there for the Shakedown, or beware!

Shut your eyes
And try to see
(Do you read me)
There's danger here
If you fool with me
Think it out
Before you start
Toward my heart

Don't get me wrong
Or Babe you won't get me
I hope I make myself clear
The heat is on
You'll lose if you bet me
That I believe you're sincere

(Repeat Chorus)

The gig is up
Now nothin' can help you
The truth is gonna come out
I interrupt
Your usual intro
There is fair play in turnabout

Stop the clock
There is no time
(Do you get me?)
I'm on your case
And you're on my mind

Make your move
And make it count
(Just make it count)
And if your shoes . . . (etc.)

(Repeat Chorus and Fade)

LYRICS/PAMELA PHILLIPS OLAND, MUSIC/FOSTER E. SYLVERS
AS RECORDED BY EVELYN "CHAMPAGNE" KING

Never Say "Never"

I'd be lying if I didn't tell you luck has a great deal to do with success. I'm referring to the old "being in the right place at the right time" sort of luck. Many years ago I was managing a fabulous singer named Robin Tapp who was supporting her career working in the mailroom at MGM Film Studios. She was a great fan of my songwriting and often walked around singing my songs during work. One day, Harry Lojewski, the long-time director of film music for the studio and a legend at MGM, stopped by to pick up his mail and said to Robin, "What's that song you're singing? I really like the lyrics!" She, being a devoted friend, said, "That's Pamela Phillips's lyrics! I have tons of them in the drawer. Do you want to see?" Then, raving on about how she felt about my work, she produced a stack of lyrics for Harry to read. "Have her call me tomorrow in my office!" Harry said enthusiastically. That resulted in my writing lyrics to themes for the film *International Velvet* and the TV shows *How the West Was Won* and *Logan's Run*.

If you think "Shakedown" was a difficult assignment, let me tell you about *Logan's Run*. What I was asked to write seemed impossible—I can't believe I got through it! I was still a novice in the music industry and had only dreamed of writing for film and TV at the time. Not only that, but—talk about starting at the top—I learned that the composer I would be collaborating with was the brilliant Lawrence Rosenthal. Frankly, just meeting him made me quake in my shoes! Harry Lojewski introduced me, and I felt so nervous and lightheaded I could hardly think. As I recall, the conversation ran something like this:

> *Lawrence:* I really don't think this melody is going to lend itself to a lyric. Do you really think you can write one?
> *Me:* Of course I can! I think it's a wonderful melody, and the words can be just beautiful.
> *Harry:* The thing is, *Logan's Run* is going to be about outer space, so the lyrics have to be about outer space.
> *Lawrence:* Except that I'd like them to be about right here on earth, too.
> *Harry:* You'll be dealing with universal love.
> *Lawrence:* But it should also be personal.
> *Harry:* It has to have a timeless, futuristic message.
> *Lawrence:* But it should also be about right now . . .

At that point they both sort of grinned at me and said, "That's really asking the impossible, isn't it? Are you sure you want to waste your time?"

Was I sure? Is grass green? Of course I was sure I wanted to waste my time. The unlikely lyric I concocted was as follows:

LOVE IS THE MAGIC (Theme from *Logan's Run*)
Someday . . . deep in the silence
Love will be music . . . to fill the heavenly skies
Like the stars fill our eyes
Our love and laughter will surely live on
Here in our love song
Touch me, I'm what you make me
Your kisses take me . . . to an incredible place
Out of time, out of space
Where there is no dream too crazy
To long for . . . and believe in
Wild impossible schemes may all come true
For love is the magic
And I've found its secret . . . in you

LYRICS/PAMELA PHILLIPS OLAND, MUSIC/LAWRENCE ROSENTHAL

I was incredibly anxious to please, and I crammed all of those contra-dictory ideas into those thirteen lines. Happily, they used my lyrics!

You have to have a pleasant and compliant attitude when asked to work on an assignment. Instead of thinking only in terms of how *you* see the song being written, it is important to stretch your brain out to encompass the direction envisioned by the producer or artist you are working with or for. This doesn't mean you should never offer suggestions. Sometimes your sug-gestions will be met with delight, even relief, if no clear direction has been decided on yet. But as in the case illustrated above, you must rise to the chal-lenge, and, unlike poets who write what is in their own hearts and reflect entirely their own opinions, you must try to read the minds and intentions of those who are entrusting you with the assignment. It's important not to act like a big-shot once you have the assignment. They don't really need to know how wonderful you are, only that you can come up with the lyrics. I once heard an ad for a bank that said, in effect, "We're the bank you never have to think about, because we're always taking good care of your money so you can think about everything else in your life." In the same way, as a lyricist, your team-player attitude should be something they don't even have to think about.

Writing on Assignment

Obviously, situations don't occur every day like the one that got me those three assignments at MGM. Assignment writing is something that you will grow into by virtue of the contacts you make and the quality of your work. For instance, when George Merrill and Shannon Rubicam were so successful with "How Will I Know?" for Whitney Houston's first album, they were assigned to write another song of similar caliber for her following album.

They wrote "I Wanna Dance With Somebody (Who Loves Me)," and thus had two No. 1 pop songs in a row! Diane Warren is a writer whose success has become the stuff of dreams. She is assigned to write songs for innumerable film and record projects. In fact, almost everything she writes gets recorded somewhere in the world. Her string of successes leads artists to ask for Diane Warren songs by name.

Getting in on assignment writing will come about if you continue to do your best work and stay in touch with all the contacts who like what you do. After you've had some measure of success as a lyricist, you will find producers and artists will increasingly phone you up and offer you the opportunity to work on their projects.

Before you write on assignment, however, you will have to be content with writing "on spec" in order to get your work known and recognized.

Writing on Spec

It's an age-old debate: If you refuse to write "on spec," how will anybody get to know what you can do; if you *do* write on spec, how will you ever get enough of a reputation so that you won't have to write on spec?

What's "on spec," anyway? It means on speculation, in hopes of, in competition for. And mostly it means at your own risk, and at your own expense, without a definite promise of compensation and definitely without any guarantee that your work will be used.

So why the big rush to work on "spec" projects? I mean, why, considering the writer's personal investment of time, money, energy, and considerable talent, do songwriters fall all over themselves and each other to compete for a chance at a spec assignment?

A typical spec assignment is a song in a film or TV show. The music coordinator of the show will receive a script from the production office, and the director will explain where he or she wants songs to go in the film. The music coordinator then calls up one to twenty music publishers and a few favored writers, announcing the opportunity to get a song in this film, and the pandemonium begins.

First comes the speculation, "What are they looking for? What does the director want to hear?" "He'll know it when he hears it" is one response, or more typically, "He's using James Brown's 'I Feel Good' in the temp track." (The *temp track* is the temporary music being used on the first cuts of the film when it's in its first showings to inside audiences.)

Twenty-five writers then scramble to write a song that sounds like "I Feel Good," which they slave over day and night for a week, writing, hiring musicians and singers, and demo-ing at their own expense. The publishers then call up the music supervisor and say, "I think I've got *the* song!" At this point, twenty-five "*the* songs" get messengered over to the music supervisor's office. It's a crap shoot as to which one will get chosen, as the producer's son-in-law might be a songwriter, and maybe he's written a Country crying-in-your-beer song that gets heard on the right day, and so much for the R & B feel of "I Feel Good!"—twenty-five writers and a host of publishers feel rotten.

Obviously, spec writing is a great gamble, and most of the time the songs written for such projects are very specific to the plot—especially when it comes to TV themes and movie theme songs incorporating the name of the movie. How many places, for instance, could you later shop a song called "Throw Momma From the Train"?

Yet, again and again, songwriters jump at the opportunity to invest time and money in the hope that they will win this musical lottery.

I have competed and lost, and competed and won, and even when I have won a "cattle call," the thrill is not as great as when I'm entrusted with an assignment. How much better I would have felt had I been contacted in the first place and allowed to meet with the director and study the script, and come up with exactly the song they were looking for, containing all of the substance and nuances they are hoping to get across. I'd have rewritten it ten times if need be (and I did just that for one movie—ten complete rewrites!).

The irony of "spec" pitching is that when those twenty-five songs are submitted in this competition, chances are none of them will actually nail the director's concept! Most songwriters, however gifted, are not mind readers, and they can only imagine an approach. In my humble opinion, producers and directors need to establish relationships with members of the songwriting community and hire these writers directly, giving them an opportunity to come up with exactly what is needed. A competent professional songwriter should be able to deliver the goods.

The list of writers who agree to cattle calls of spec writing for projects is stellar. Some of these songwriters have homes plastered in gold and platinum records, wallpapered in sheet music and BMI, ASCAP, and SESAC achievement awards. Yet they still continue to go to screenings and write spec songs—their presence, of course, making it doubly difficult for lesser-known writers to compete. (Though not impossible; nothing's impossible!)

What to do when a spec project appears on the horizon:

1. Study the project—Try to get hold of a copy of the latest draft of the script or, better still, try to get invited to a screening so you'll see how the song they've used on the temp track works.
2. Find out how many other writers are doing spec songs for this project, and if any have actually been paid to do so (sometimes big-name writers are paid to write spec songs; their agents won't let them do it any other way).
3. Check your catalogue to see if you already have a song that would be suitable for this project; if so, submit it.

(continued)

4. Decide whether it's worth your time and effort to compete for a spot on this project by writing and demo-ing a new song for it.
5. If you decide to write a song, you have three options:

   A. Try to make it as general as possible to justify spending the money and so that you can shop it elsewhere later if they don't choose it; or
   B. If you write a song that's spot-on for the project and cannot have any other earthly use, spend less money on the demo and hope they'll be able to hear the strengths of the song without your presenting them with a demo that sounds like a record; or
   C. Take your best shot, write a song made for the spot, demo it fabulously, and gamble that you'll win.

On the positive side, spec writing enables a songwriter to meet some wonderful people in the film and television industries that no other opportunity would afford. On the downside, it can be heartbreaking when you find you've done all that work for nothing. So if you get the idea that I don't think spec is entirely fair, you're right; and yet I, like everyone else, continue to do it, as it is a fact of our industry. Although we all mumble about how frustrating it is, until we can persuade the film industry to establish assignment relationships with specific songwriters, spec is here to stay.

When the Director Is in Love With the Temp Track

Peter Rodgers Melnick is the composer on a Showtime movie called *Mermaid,* which stars Ellen Burstyn. In one scene, the lonely young widow and her new friend/possible suitor are dancing to a Country band on a bandstand at a country fair. The song on the director's temp track was Patsy Cline singing Willie Nelson's matchless song, "Crazy." That's a hard act to follow, and the film's director, Pete Masterson, loved it for that spot, but rights were not negotiable.

Peter gave me a copy of the film to watch and asked me to write a lyric to underlie that moment. I didn't intend to try to write a clone of "Crazy," as it could never measure up. Instead, I wrote in the same bittersweet mood and flavor. Since the song was a "feature" performance, meaning it was the focal point of the scene, I wanted it to refer to the woman's story, yet point to a possible happy ending. On the other hand, I didn't want to hit the nail right on the head, so to speak, but rather to write something oblique to the storyline.

The title I came up with, which Peter also believed in and wrote a gorgeous melody to, is "Love Songs Make Me Cry." Evidently, it met with the director's approval, because it won the feature spot in the film. In this lyric I talk about loss of a relationship, and pining for it. My device for making this lyric oblique to the storyline is to talk about "the day we said goodbye" rather than being on point talking about the death of a lover. This is the lyric that appears in the film:

LOVE SONGS MAKE ME CRY

1.
Love songs—make me blue—
They make me—think of you
I thought that I would die
The day we said goodbye
The hardest thing—to do . . .

Is let go, and move on;
I don't know who I am now you're gone,
And love songs—
Lovely love songs—
Ma-ake me cry-y!

2.
Love songs—break my heart—
They tear it—all apart
The music plays and then
It all comes back again
Those crazy feelings start . . .

I'm with somebody new
And I'm thinkin' that I'm over you
And love songs—
Silly love songs—
Ma-ake me cry-y.

Bridge: *I'm a fool, holding on*
          To something that's gone
          And I need to be loved again
          And someday I know—I'll let you go—
          But darlin', until then . . .

Tag:
Love songs—make me blue
They make me—think of you
What I'd give for the chance
Just to hold you again when we dance

And love songs
Crazy love songs…
Ma-ake me cry… (Fade)

LYRICS/PAMELA PHILLIPS OLAND, MUSIC/PETER RODGERS MELNICK
© PAM-O-LAND MUSIC AND MELNICK MUSIC (ASCAP)

Simple is Good

Another assignment, this time for HBO's cult show *The Sopranos,* was to write a lyric that could pass for something thirteen-year-old Frankie Lymon & the Teenagers might have had as a hit record in 1955. The song in the temp track was Frankie's "Why Do Fools Fall In Love."

In this case, our song really had to duplicate the feel of that fifties' classic. Which meant it had to be very, very simple. I am known for writing complex ideas and wordplay. But this time, not only did the producers want something very specific, they also wanted something that would pass as authentic to a specific period.

Since we needed to write it literally overnight, the composer, Tom Harriman, worked up a melody that captured the essence of those times, then played his catchy, effervescent track and sang the melody into my answering machine. Not having the luxury of time, I wrote my lyrics in one sweep, after dinner! My title, "Fools Follow Angels," had the light, "bubble-gum" flavor of the period, and when we recorded it the next day with a great young singer, we were certain we'd captured the essence of a Frankie Lymon–style song.

When the song appeared in the show—which told the story of a fictitious young R & B group who were ripped off by one of the show's gangsters back in the fifties, who now was being asked to pay up back royalties—we were delighted. Many people watching told us later that they had thought this was an original Frankie Lymon song, which—since we fooled them completely—was a very high compliment indeed! The art of writing great lyrics in this case, was to simplify: get in, get on, get out.

FOOLS FOLLOW ANGELS

Foo-ools Follow Angels
Met a little girl who taught my heart to beat
Sure as I'm livin'
I'm 'a gonna get to hea-e-even

Fools fall for teasin' eyes
She's a walkin' talkin' heart-break
She tells such sweet lies
I'm su-u-uch a fool

Friends say I'm crazy
She's gonna make-a-me cry-iy
But none of them know the way we
Steal a little kiss and—Oh-My!

Fools Follow Angels
Wanna believe she's mine all mine alone
Why am I su-u-uch a fool

I'm such a fool
A fool in love
She's a angel . . .
Why am I such a fool?

LYRICS/PAMELA PHILLIPS OLAND, MUSIC/TOM HARRIMAN FOR *THE SOPRANOS*

Opening Title Songs vs. End-Title Songs

Approaching a title song for a film is a matter of common sense. If you have been invited to write an opening title, it should set up the film, but reveal nothing that will give the plot away. If you have been invited to write an end-title, it should reveal the message of the film, and tie it all up in a neat little bow.

If you can't find out where a title song would be used in a film, but want to take a stab at writing for it, I suggest that you write an end-title. Since many films begin with instrumental music only, often underscoring action, end-titles are used far more often than opening titles, and giving away key plot points with your lyrics isn't an issue. The point is, focus on one end of the film or the other, and be clear why you are writing this song.

A perfect example to illustrate this point is my song "Digga Digga Dog." It was to write an end-title song for the feature film "102 Dalmatians," that I got a call from Disney. While screening half an hour of the film, including the beginning and ending sequences, and while looking over a script, I took notes of images that came to mind that summed up what I'd seen. In the car, shortly after leaving the Walt Disney Studios, I found myself chanting "Digga Digga Dog, Digga Digga Dog." I had a hunch that I was on to something. Later, when I repeated it to the film's Music Supervisor, he agreed.

I invited my collaborator Mark Brymer to work on the project with me, and by the end of the weekend, we had finished a first draft of the end-title song called "Digga Digga Dog," which we demo'd immediately.

When I was told that the Director Kevin Lima liked the song I was very excited. But then I learned he had decided to use it for the opening title instead! I knew immediately that what I'd written was all wrong, and I'd have to re-write it.

So he showed me another screening, this time of the entire film, and then we discussed what I already knew, that my lyrics now didn't work! The reason? They summed up the film instead of setting it up.

I proceeded to write several pages of opening verse ideas—witty, serious, obscure, doggy—all sorts of approaches. Kevin ended up choosing the following opening title song, which gave away nothing but the attitude of the film as it related to the charm and resourcefulness of dogs:

DIGGA DIGGA DOG

Chorus: Digga Digga Dog, Digga Digga Dog
Digga Digga Dog, Digga Digga Dog
Digga Digga Dog, Digga Digga Dog
Dog—Dog—You Dawg, You!

Ain't that the man in the moon dancing over our heads
While all good dogs are asleep in their beds
Smilin' in their dreams at the crazy things people do
When you think you've fooled them, who'll make a fool out of who?
You Dawg, You!

Chorus: Digga Digga Dog, Digga Digga Dog
Digga Digga Dog, Digga Digga Dog
Digga Digga Dog, Digga Digga Dog
Dog—Dog—You Dawg, You!
Overlaid with:
Don't be believin'~~Looks are deceivin'~~

Ya think you're on top of the game—you've got a lot to learn
When life hangs tough, take a dog-leg turn
People, they think they're so cool if they throw you a bone
Wait till they discover—you've got some tricks of your own
You Dawg, You!

Chorus: Digga Digga Dog, Digga Digga Dog
Digga Digga Dog, Digga Digga Dog
Digga Digga Dog, Digga Digga Dog
Dog—Dog—You Dawg, You!
Overlaid with:
Don't be believin'~~Looks are deceivin'~~

Bridge: *Spotted Dog, Spotted Dog*
Where have you been?
I've been to London to look at the Queen

Can you tell a spotted story? Yes I can!
I saw a dog who was walkin' a man!
(You Dawg, You!)

Chorus: Digga Digga Dog, Digga Digga Dog
                 Digga Digga Dog, Digga Digga Dog
                 Digga Digga Dog, Digga Digga Dog
                 Dog – Dog – You Dawg, You!
Overlaid with:
                 Don't be believin'~~Looks are deceivin'~~
                 You Dawg, You!

The song evidently went over well in screenings, and we suddenly got word that Kevin had chosen to put the song in the end-title slot as well. So I was asked to once again look at the film and come up with end-title lyric ideas. Again, I wrote many many choices. Interestingly, the final lyric began with the very first end-title verse I had written after watching the initial screening! The final end title lyrics were very energetic and summed up these positive messages of the film: *go after what you want; sometimes you get a second chance;* and *don't miss an opportunity when it comes looking for you!*

Verse 1:   Can you keep that excitation down to a roar?
              When fate comes knocking—better open the door
              Rise to the occasion—answer the call
              If they're pitchin' second chances, don't you fumble the ball
              You Dawg You

Chorus: Digga Digga Dog, Digga Digga Dog
                 Digga Digga Dog, Digga Digga Dog
                 Digga Digga Dog, Digga Digga Dog
                 Dog—Dog—You Dawg, You!
Overlaid with:
                 Don't be believin'~~Looks are deceivin'~~

Verse 2:   Sometimes, well you gotta dream with eyes wide open
              Y'can't earn your spots just wishin' and hopin'
              Goin' out on a limb for a cause, the heart must be brave
              An' a miracle's a gift—for keeping the faith
              You Dawg, You!

(THE SONG "DIGGA DIGGA DOG" CONSISTS OF LYRICS AND MUSIC BY PAMELA PHILLIPS OLAND AND MARK BRYMER, AND SAMPLES FROM "ATOMIC DOG" BY GEORGE CLINTON, JR., GARRY M. SHIDER, AND DAVID L. SPRADLEY.)

Thus, even though the beginning and end title songs are the same song in terms of the hook and bridge, "Digga Digga Dog" accomplished the double feat of: (1) creating an opening title song that did not spoil the story for viewers by giving any story away; and (2) creating an end title song that viewers could relate to as they left the theater, summing up the impact of what they had just seen.

RELATIONSHIPS

There is an old maxim that runs, "You meet the same people going up as you do going down." It's true in every business, and the music business is no exception. It would not be an exaggeration to say that this entire industry runs on relationships.

Since becoming an "overnight success"—not just in the creative but also in the business side of the music business—often takes ten or twenty years, many of the familiar faces have been around forever and will continue to be around for the foreseeable future. People in the industry are each growing in their individual fields, occasionally crossing paths, and almost always aware of each other's lateral and vertical moves. Those who form and nurture lasting relationships early on eventually discover the joy of being able to help each other when they are in positions to do so. Those who have isolated themselves, jealously guarding their contacts and talents, find that the struggle for success and recognition virtually never ends, as they are not a part of that magical network of give-and-take and trust. Being a part of that network is no accident; it is the result of how you conduct yourself from the first day you enter this field as a professional.

While music publishers and record company A&R departments undeniably change their staff as often as Shaquille O'Neal changes his sweat socks, the same faces pop up again and again in different companies in new capacities. As the stakes, titles, and recognition factors increase, they play musical chairs with the jobs. Rarely do they leave the industry altogether. So you might have just gotten an "in" with a company and think it's easy street from here on, only to call one day and be told by a receptionist, "He's no longer with us." (That usually means he's changed jobs, not died!) But as one major music publishing executive once remarked to me when I went to see him at a new job and office, "You don't make relationships with the companies, you make relationships with the people, and you follow them wherever they go."

I have known various members of the music community who have gone from jobs in recording engineering into promotion; from artist management into production; from publishing into A&R. One respected vice-president of a major publisher began at the company years and years ago as a receptionist. The climb involves years of hard work and struggling to prove one's worth, and believe me, these people either fall by the wayside or grow to be strong and powerful—and you'd better believe that their opinions *count!*

You just never know where someone will turn up next. And almost always, it's in a greater capacity than previously. This is an industry that tends to promote from within. Rarely does an outsider come in and snatch a top job out of the path of an industry veteran. The only thing that changes for most of these industry pros is their job titles and the number of zeros in their paychecks!

Writers I have known as struggling amateurs with no money and no hope have emerged after a period of staunch stick-to-it-iveness as major forces in the creative community, not just writing songs, but arranging and producing hit records. Everyone has to start somewhere, usually at the bottom. But a combination of talent and tenacity will likely ensure you a climb to the top of the tree of ambition, where you can pluck the fruits of success.

There is a very tight-knit "family" sort of feeling among the working members of the creative community, other than when people are in direct competition for jobs. And even then, I have known songwriters who encourage their colleagues to try for the same spot in a film or on an album that they themselves are working on. Since the users of the music rarely know what they're looking for until they hear it, it's anybody's guess as to which approach to which song they'll find to their liking. So it comes down to, "May the best man/woman/combination thereof win." If it can't be you, maybe it can be someone you like and admire.

Ten listeners might each pick a different song out of the same field of ten. When a song is turned down, don't take it as a personal affront—it doesn't mean they don't ever want to hear your stuff again, that you have no talent, or that you should stay out of their face. *It just means it wasn't the right song.* Plain and simple. Just as when two beautiful women go after the same TV role and only one gets chosen as the "right face," it's crazy for the loser to rush out and get plastic surgery, as the next producer may just prefer her face. Many humongous hits have sat on the shelf in a publisher's office with no takers for several years before they click. Lois Blaiche, who wrote "Could've Been," a No. 1 pop song for Tiffany, relates that it was in the publisher/producer's hands for four years before he put it on that multiplatinum album. Richard Kerr tells of a six-year wait for the Dionne Warwick hit "I'll Never Love This Way Again." Both cuts were surely worth the wait! In the meantime, though, both writers continued to network and build reputations and relationships in the industry, so that when their songs took off, everybody was glad for them and wanted to have them work on other projects immediately.

Our industry encourages and looks kindly on referrals of talent: "Do you know a hot young female R & B singer?" someone might ask. Or "Hey, who played that great guitar part on that track?" Someone said to me once, "I asked three people for someone who writes killer lyrics and your name came up every time, so I figured I'd better call you!" Obviously, all of us thrive on that sort of recommendation and referral. It's a building, networking process that sets up a firm footing for anybody's career. It's one of the wonderful harmonious things that happen when you've finally earned a position of respect in the industry, and I'm proud to be a part of it.

Believe it or not, the pettiness and immature backbiting and jealousy you may have perceived at the early stages of your career among the other struggling members of the community will be replaced by great, respectful friendships and working relationships. You'll hook up to fun projects you've been referred to, and have endless chances to flex your creative muscles. Don't let the early frustrations get you down to the point that you take them out on the very people you're going to need in your corner.

What I'm saying here is this: Don't make enemies; the business is too small, and people have long memories. Someone you feel is of no account at this stage might be in a position to help or nurture you later on. What you perceive as an insult or slight now might later, in retrospect, turn out to be a helpful prod in the right direction, a motivating factor toward your improvement. A successful songwriter I know tells the story of how, in the early days, she kept going back again and again to a publisher with her songs, and he just kept rejecting them. Instead of telling him he was a fool or that he had no taste, which she most certainly thought, she became driven by the one burning desire to "blow him away" with one of her compositions, which she eventually did with a song that he subsequently published, got recorded, and earned a lot of money with.

The president of a major publishing company related to me how he had once spoken at a seminar and answered an attendee's question, "Can we send you tapes?" with a polite, "Of course, I'd be happy for you to send me tapes." Within the next month, more than 150 tapes came in the mail from the attendees at this seminar. He was overwhelmed, and he realized he didn't have the time to personally evaluate each and every aspiring writer's tape of several songs. So rather than be fair only to a random few, he decided to send all the tapes back with a polite letter saying that he just didn't have the time to evaluate the tape at this time. What followed, he remembers to his amazement, was a deluge of frustrated hate mail from songwriters who believed they had been spurned and insulted by him. Comments such as, "Who do you think you are?" and, "You have no right . . . " proliferated throughout the letters. He found them all very offensive, and couldn't figure out what prompted them to burn their bridges in this fashion.

As long as you're out there plugging away, writing songs and presenting them to artists/publishers/A&R representatives/music supervisors, and producers, you're opening yourself up to rejection.

So if you feel annoyed that you haven't gotten the respect or interest you thought you deserved from somebody in the industry, try to realize that you might have gotten to the person on a bad day— you're not the only one who has them!—and that, in any event, the next time you pitch a song, you might just strike oil with that person. It isn't always easy, but try to swallow your bile and hang in there! One day you'll be happy you behaved like a grown-up instead of throwing a temper tantrum like a spoiled brat!

Rejection

The music business is no place to be thin-skinned. Rejection is part of life; it occurs several times a month, even several times a week, depending on how active a person is in the industry. All I can say is, sure it's hard to turn the other cheek after you've been rejected, but you *must!*

I've received rejections from people at all levels of the industry, and have learned that I just can't please everyone all the time. In fact, there are days when I feel like I just can't please anyone, *any* of the time.

But, oh, those wonderful days when something goes right! Those days when I learn that a song has been put on hold for somebody magnificent! Those days when a producer I've been dying to work with calls me with a project out of the clear blue sky! Those days when I write something glorious!—that's all I need to keep me going.

Once upon a time, I made a vow to get over rejection quickly. I decided I'd allow myself to get depressed and upset over a rejection and experience the pain, but only on the day it occurs. Since then, I always let go of whatever hurts and move on. My theory is that the longer I hold onto something painful, the longer it will take for me to get back to being creative and trying to make something else happen.

It's only natural to be frustrated at dashed hopes. But, ultimately, rejection can make us stronger. Sure, it can also make us feel defeated and ready to give up, but defeat is a choice we each make. What I want you to do is get so galled by a rejection that, once you've dried your tears of frustration, you get your blood churning so all you can think about is the day you'll prove yourself to whoever did the rejecting. It works. It'll keep you sane and on track.

Sometimes a rejection can be a blessing in disguise. You can be praying for this certain cut to happen with this big, famous artist, and your song gets left off the project. You lose faith in the song, in your work, in life, and you contemplate joining a Tibetan monastery. Then, presto! A few months later, out of the blue, some unknown person cuts the song and you have a worldwide smash—and you note smugly that that big, famous person's album—which you cried yourself to sleep for a week over not getting a song on—bombed.

As long as you're out there plugging away, writing songs and presenting them to artists/publishers/A&R representatives/music supervisors, and producers, you're opening yourself up to rejection. If you hide away in your bedroom, no one will ever reject you, since they will never have the chance. But they will never praise or rejoice in you, either.

So you can avoid the heartache or meet it head-on. The choice is yours. Remember that those who reject you pull on their pants the same way you do. They're only people. And if life has given them an advantage that allows them to be the choosers, then allow them their own good karma. The thing is this: Don't go reading into it that you have *bad* karma! Just wait. Your day too shall come.

IT TAKES FOREVER FOR ANYTHING TO HAPPEN OVERNIGHT

They say a picture is worth a thousand words, so rather than plod along with some high and mighty advice about always keeping your goal in sight, I thought it might be more entertaining to share a couple of my experiences with you. I hope my personal stories will inspire your faith and hope, and give new strength to that aforementioned marvelous quality I know you've got inside you: *stick-to-it-iveness!*

After you've read my personal stories of tenacity, you will know why I say:

1. Never give up on a goal because, if you do, you might miss out on its real-ization and never know how close you came.

2. Sometimes the success you seek comes completely out of left field and bog-gles your mind by the quirky, unexpected course it has taken.

3. Don't get tangled up in what you think "ought" to happen to you. Instead, be open to the universe delivering surprise packages.

4. You can't force an issue, but you can keep it alive.

Writing for Old Blue Eyes
(How I Got My Sinatra Record)

By 1976, having written feverishly for a few years in L.A. and never having achieved the success I sought, I decided to visit England, my homeland, and see how I fared in the music industry. A friend of mine suggested that I visit a pal of his at Carlin Music, Mr. Paul Rich. So, during my round of appoint-ments, in due course I located Paul Rich's phone number, made a call, and set up a meeting. He liked my style of lyric writing, and after a few moments of reflection, came up with an idea. He said there wasn't much he could do for me there, since I was returning to the United States, but he had the British rights to a song called "Chanson D'Anna," a beautiful French composition by André Popp, that Don Costa had rights to in the United States. I knew Costa's name, as he was a famous record producer whose illustrious career had stretched from the beginning of the rock era and had included many projects with luminaries such as Paul Anka and Frank Sinatra. Paul Rich gave me Don Costa's phone number, wished me luck, bid me farewell, and went about his business.

When I returned to the States and my legal secretary temp work, I called Don Costa. In fact, I called his office for three years without getting a single returned call. At first I called about once a week, after that about once a month.

I always left a specific message, as I knew that if I just left my name and phone number he definitely wouldn't bother getting back to me.

One day my dancing teacher, Benn Howard, asked me if he could give a copy of my song "Valentino" to a torch singer friend of his to sing in the exclusive restaurant of a private Beverly Hills hotel. I went along one night to hear her perform. The flamboyant actor Oliver Reed happened to be in the restaurant that night, and drew everyone's attention by raving on loudly about how fantastic he thought this song was, and could he buy it! The boyfriend of an old friend of mine who also by sheer chance was dining there that night, asked if I indeed had written this song "Valentino," and said he was certain that his partner would want to manage me; could he arrange a meeting? Could he???!! So the next day I met him with his partner and their associate, Mark Lipsky, played my repertoire, and ended up with a manager.

Some days later, I was discussing with the manager all the myriad things I had tried to accomplish over the past seven or eight years, and in passing mentioned that I'd tried to make a contact with Don Costa for three years. The next morning I got a call from Lipsky, who said; "I understand you want to meet Don Costa?" To which I replied by starting to go into the whole story. He cut me off: "What time?" he asked. An hour later I was pulling up into the Trousdale Estates driveway of this great composer, arranger, and guitarist.

For three years after that initial meeting with Don, I submitted songs on a fairly regular basis, through his assistant Dave. I never heard another word from him personally until one night, at around 11:00 when I was just getting ready for bed, the phone rang. "Hi, this is Don Costa!" I couldn't believe it! "I've just cut a song of yours," he said, "called 'I've Never Loved Like This Before.'" Since I had written it three years earlier and forgotten it, I couldn't even remember how it went and started humming him my dummy melody that I'd written before the composer ever got it. He sounded perplexed. "That doesn't sound like it," he said. "Anyway, come over and listen. I've recorded it with an Australian artist."

When I got to the house, I asked a woman standing in the driveway for directions to the studio. She replied with an Aussie accent, and I realized she must be the artist. She was thrilled with the song, she said, and went inside with me. Don was very warm to me, and proceeded to tell me the most unlikely story.

Don's assistant Dave had been in the habit of rejecting most of the unsolicited tapes that came in, mine included. He routinely covered over the titles with plain white tape, then dumped all the cassettes in numerous huge cases and boxes, to be reused by Don for casual tape-copying purposes. Don had picked a song for the Aussie singer to record and had dug randomly into one of these overflowing cartons for a cassette to put it on. He pulled out a tape and put it in the cassette player, was about to press "record" and suddenly stopped and said, "Maybe I'd better listen and make sure there's nothing important on this tape." What was on the tape was my song. They heard it and, unbelievably, decided to use it instead of the one they had chosen to tape over it!

About six months later, I went to pick up the Aussie singer for dinner, and she asked if I minded if Don and his wife came with us. We met them and some other people at a restaurant, and during the course of dinner, Don suddenly inquired, "You got any songs for Sinatra??" I almost choked on my spaghetti. "If I don't, I'll write one!" I assured him. Half an hour later, we were discussing how capricious the music business can be, and I asked innocently, "How come everybody knows a hit record after it's been a hit record, even though they all turned it down before it was recorded??" Don grinned and replied, "That's because everybody's a Monday-morning quarterback!" My lyricist's mind immediately did a headstand. "That sounds like a title! What does it mean?" Don said it meant that they play football on Sunday and on Monday everyone sits around and says how they should have played. I immediately realized that's what we do in romance too: We mess it up on Sunday and realize what we *should* have done on Monday. I wrote the words and music in the car going home and called my Aussie friend at 3:00 A.M. to sing it to her. I went to see Don at 10:00 A.M., he loved the song and for the next two days I worked feverishly making corrections at his direction, writing in the car on the way to my legal secretary job, on my lunch breaks, and at my desk when nobody was looking. I wrote in shorthand, so they'd think it was their work! The next day Mr. Sinatra's long-time publisher Sarge Weiss met me at Don's house and I sang and played the song for him. He wanted to send it immediately to his boss, so he had Don demo it himself by singing and playing piano, while a limousine waited outside to rush it to the airport to airfreight it to Brazil, where Mr. S. was in concert. The next day, Don told me he got a phone call from Brazil: "Don, you can't sing! And Don, you're a lousy pianist. But even you can't ruin this song!" So the session was booked, and I was in an ecstasy the likes of which I'd never known. Then, the night before the session, Don called me from New York to say the recording was being postponed several months until after Mr. Sinatra's world tour because he wanted to "get his chops up" to sing it. I don't know how I got through that time!

But, eventually, Mr. Sinatra recorded "Monday Morning Quarterback" on his *She Shot Me Down* album. In the special way he has of applauding all his writers, he recognized me at all the famous theaters and halls in which he sang my song over the next few months. Truly, I can think of nothing more thrilling in my life than the first time I heard *that* voice singing *my* words and music!

And so, seven years after going to London and seeing Paul Rich to try and write a song for him, my efforts finally paid off, and handsomely, with My First Big Break.

One Thing Leads to Another
(How I Finally "Broke In")

But my real breakthrough in the industry did not take place for two more years after the Sinatra record. Even though it had opened many doors and provided my first visibility in the business, I had been able to create disappointingly few opportunities based on that success.

Life seemed to be one big round of submitting songs that got turned down. I kept trying to write better, be more original, injecting my lyrics with more insight and humor, and submitting, always submitting, always looking for leads. It didn't hurt that I lived in Los Angeles; that way, I was able to make personal appointments to play songs. Those of you who don't live in one of the major music centers, such as L.A., New York, or Nashville, ought to consider making regular trips to one of these cities to make some face-to-face contacts. You can be a successful writer no matter where you live, but it doesn't hurt to be a familiar face. That way, when your mailed submissions are received, they will be from a known entity, a person, not just a name on a cassette box.

Tenacity paid off, as it always does, and my next break began as one of many failed opportunities. I had presented a number of songs for a Maureen McGovern album to a producer named Ren Toppano, and he had turned them all down. I had gone home terribly disappointed and dispirited. I actually stopped writing, punishing myself for not having material that was good enough for the project. I wasn't suffering from burnout as much as emotional wipe-out. "When will something go right?" I asked my husband. "When you have the right song for the right project," he answered.

A month later, to my surprise, Ren Toppano called and asked if I remembered "an up-tempo song" that I'd played for him, the title of which he couldn't recall. I suggested, "Show Me Your Love and I'll Show You Mine"? Yes, that was the song. He asked me to send him a cassette to play for a Richard Aaron.

I sent it and forgot about it—it was just one more submission, and, anyway, it's pretty routine for people to ask for songs, get you all excited, and then never call you again. A week later Richard Aaron actually called, saying, "Where have you been? Who are you? How come I've never heard of you?" Ren had played him the song, and he wanted me to meet his associate Leon Sylvers III, who was looking for a lyricist. Leon was one of the most happening producers of R & B music of the day, whose distinctive early looped track, heavy bass, and drum-machine work earned the name of "The Leon Sylvers Sound," and actually forms the basis for much of what R & B sounds like today. Leon liked the tune and asked if I'd like to try to write a few lyrics for him on spec. He assigned me four melodies to start with, expecting not to see me for a while. But I was back four days later with all four songs completed. I had pushed myself very hard to impress him: I was incredibly anxious to find my niche in the industry after ten years of trying.

My efforts paid off. Finally! Leon recorded all four of these first songs, and this started one of the most dynamic and important collaborations of my career. It was a headfirst plunge into the world of Black music, of which I knew precious little. But my collaborators in Leon's organization were very supportive of the lyrics I was writing. There was a core group of us—composers, producers, and lyricists—who churned out songs twenty-four hours a day. It was kind of like being in a big musical family. We were always at the studio, and often I picked up idioms and phrases for lyric lines just from conversations I participated in or overheard. My lyrics began to reflect my collaborators' attitudes and humor. I think that after a while I was writing stories I picked up just by watching my colleagues' facial expressions and body language. I learned by doing, and anytime I wrote a lyric line that was inappropriate for R & B music, Leon was quick to point it out to me. By the time the company disbanded a year later, my collaborations with Leon and his Silverspoon writers had yielded 112 songs, 50 of which saw it to vinyl with major R & B artists on major labels!

To show you how one thing leads to another, one day shortly thereafter I got a call from Greg Philinganes, then an artist on Planet Records, who is a gifted keyboardist and has been a musical director and collaborator for such artists as Eric Clapton and Michael Jackson. He said he had heard some of my songs produced by Silverspoon, and that he liked my style, and would I collaborate on a song for his album? He had actually obtained my number by asking one of Leon's sisters to peek in his phone book!

It turned out that the melody for the song he wanted me to write was by Jackie Jackson, who was at the time away on the Jacksons Victory Tour and had no time to rewrite his lyrics for Greg's project. I was thrilled, and worked hard with Greg and his producer Richard Perry to come up with the exact lyric they wanted—which meant coming up with more than fifty titles and doing innumerable rewrites.

If you do your homework and learn your craft, injecting it with that unique perspective on life that is yours alone, you can find success and earn a living writing lyrics.

"Playin' with Fire," as it was called, got on the album, and Greg called me again a while later to co-write a song called "That's How You Play the Game," which, as is the way of the music industry, has been recorded gorgeously twice—once by Dionne Warwick and once by Roberta Flack—and never been released! But, they say, "Third time's the charm," and in this business, believe me, you just never give up!

Once people know and like your work, you'll find yourself sought after for project writing. Knowing my work on "Playin' with Fire," for instance, Jackie Jackson later called to ask me to collaborate on the theme for Whoopi Goldberg's film *Burglar* with him and his brothers Randy, Jermaine, and Tito, and producer Bernard Edwards.

But the most important event that came about as a result of my tenure with Silverspoon was that four of the company's producer/songwriters, with whom I still continued to write after the company's demise, became staff songwriter/producers for A&M Records' AlmoIrving Music (Rondor Music). So many of their songs had my name on them as lyricist that Brenda Andrews, vice-president of creative services, asked to meet me, already having decided I should be her staff writer!

TENACITY

There is no question in my mind that diligence and persistence pay off. If you do your homework and learn your craft, injecting it with that unique perspective on life that is yours alone, you *can* find success and earn a living writing lyrics. All the patient networking and getting to know people is eventually rewarded because, ultimately, the music industry is a very close-knit group of people, and the more involved you are, the more you find that it's actually quite a small community. If your work is excellent, you will be remembered.

The thing is, you must never get discouraged about any particular failed opportunity, as there is always some other chances around every corner. If you follow up every meeting and contact, and if you doggedly persist with writing better and better material and play it for enough listeners, sooner or later, it will be your turn to shine.

DON'T GIVE UP YOUR DAY JOB!

There's nothing worse than waiting to "make it." It's kind of like waiting for a kettle to boil: You can wait all you want to, but it won't start whistling until it's good and ready. The parallels to a career in the music business are obvious, of course. These are the danger signs:

• Are you spending hours sitting home waiting for the phone to ring because some writer/artist/publisher told you he or she was interested in working with you?

• Have you submitted a song somewhere and you're practically biting your fingernails waiting to hear what's happened, because you've already told your entire family, your grocer, your co-workers, and your exercise class that it's pending, so you can't possibly begin working on another project until you hear the results of this one?

- Are you working at a nowhere job that's beneath your talents and skills? Is your mother calling you every Sunday and asking you why you're "throwing your life away" on songwriting when you could be out being a *(fill in the blank)?*

- Are you living like a "struggling artiste" in a rundown, pokey little flat that no amount of happy posters and candles and incense can disguise?

- Have you got enough money to treat yourself to a nice evening of dinner and theater with friends? Can you afford to buy an attractive outfit to wear for it?

- Are you buying your food from a bin of dented and unmarked cans at the market?

- Do you want to be a Songwriter or do you want to be a Star?

- Do you understand that success as a songwriter is only achieved if you Do It for the Love of It? That doing it because of what you think you might earn or the attention and popularity you might achieve may only bring you heartbreak, since there are no guarantees as to how far down the road success might be?

A word on casting your own songs:
　　If you refuse to let an unknown artist record your song and save it for "something better" that you expect will come along later, this casting decision could result in one of the following scenarios:

- Nobody else will ever again ask to record it.
- The person you turned down as an unknown could be the next Whitney Houston.
- The song may become dated while it sits on the shelf.
- The demo production may become dated, requiring you to fork out money all over again for a new demo.
- You may later end up thinking the song is no good, based on your later level of expertise, and throw the song out of your catalogue altogether.
- *The Moral:* A song in the can is worth two on the shelf.

A very wise man I once met said to me, *"The Process is the Purpose."* I'm not sure whom he was quoting, but I thank that ancient for such wisdom. The point is that writing itself has to be enough of a reward for you. Every day you read stories in the paper about people who have "finally made it" after years and years of trying, because, first of all, they had tenacity and stayed with it, and second, because they loved what they were doing so much they couldn't *not* do it! We are all out here running around desperately trying to get to the end of the road. So it comes as rather a startling revelation that the end of the road is the road itself. The joy of simply sitting in a room, just you and your pen and paper, being intensely involved in the process of writing a song, must become an end in itself.

Thus, if you relate unhappily to any of the above questions, I think it's time you asked yourself if you're spending your life living in anticipation of a future event. Consider whether it's time to re-evaluate the sacrifices of today that you are making toward your eventual goal, and whether you aren't ready to settle in for a long winter and be comfortable for the process. I did. After a few years of "struggling," I decided to upgrade my lifestyle by working at a good-paying day job. Maybe everything I dreamed of didn't happen immediately—but aha! Now I could afford to wait, and in some style.

I hope for your sake that your climb to the success and recognition you deserve will be a very short one, and that you will achieve your goals and financial rewards without any heartache or struggle. This has happened to thousands of people, and I wish you their good fortune.

The point is this: I believe that you should set yourself up in a lifestyle that you can live with. When you think about it, what do you even have to offer the world as a lyricist if you're coming from a constant state of deprivation? If, after a while, all you can think of is depression and need, survival and longing, you will lose your focus. To write good, sane lyrics, you need to consider coming from a well-rounded point of view.

Moral: Your success as a lyricist is a brilliant light at the end of the tunnel, if you don't get lost in the dark!

A READING LIST OF BOOKS FOR SONGWRITERS

6 Steps to Songwriting Success: Comprehensive Guide to Writing and Marketing Hit Songs, by Jason Blume. New York: Watson-Guptill Publications, 1999.

88 Songwriting Wrongs & How to Right Them: Concrete Ways to Improve Your Songwriting and Make Your Songs More Marketable, by Pat Luboff, Pete Luboff (Contributor). Cincinnati: Writer's Digest Books, 1992.

Becoming Remarkable: For Songwriters and Those Who Love Song, by Harriet Schock. Nevada City: Blue Dolphin Publications, 1999.

Breakin' into Nashville: How to Write and Sell Country Music, by Jennifer Ember Pierce. Toronto: Madison Books, 1998.

The Complete Handbook of Songwriting: An Insider's Guide to Making It in the Music Industry, by Mark and Cathy Liggett. New York: Plume, 1993.

The Craft and Business of Songwriting, by John Braheny, co-founder/director of Los Angeles Songwriter's Showcase. Cincinnati: Writer's Digest Books, 1995.

How to Have Your Hit Song Published, by Jay Warner. Milwaukee: Hal Leonard Publications Corp., 1989.

How to Pitch and Promote Your Songs, by Fred Koller. New York: Allworth Press, 1996.

Making It in the Music Business: The Business and Legal Guide for Songwriters and Performers, by Lee Wilson. New York: Allworth Press, 1999.

Melody in Songwriting: Tools and Techniques for Writing Hit Songs, by Jack Perricone. Milwaukee: Hal Leonard Publications Corp., 2000.

Songwriters on Songwriting: The Expanded Version, by Paul Zollo. New York: Da Capo Press, 1997.

Songwriting: Essential Guide to Rhyming, by Pat Pattison. Milwaukee: Hal Leonard Publications Corp., 1992.

This Business of Music, by Sidney Shemel and M. William Krasilovsky. New York: Watson-Guptill Publications, 2000.

Tunesmith: Inside the Art of Songwriting, by Jimmy Webb. New York: Hyperion, 1998.

MAGAZINES FOR SONGWRITERS

Styles and interests vary among songwriters, and there are magazines to suit every taste. Pay a visit to your local newsstand to discover all the wonderful songwriter and artist-oriented magazines which are available to you. I believe it is helpful to keep your finger on the pulse of those aspects of the Music Industry which pertain to your career. Here are some of the more prominent magazines, many of which also have a Web presence on the Internet.

AP—ALTERNATIVE PRESS
6516 Detroit Avenue, Suite 5
Cleveland, Ohio 11102
Phone: 216-631-1510   Fax: 216-631-1016
Lots of current information for Alternative musicians and songwriters, includes interviews, reviews and commentary on bands and new albums, all with the Alternative slant.

AMERICAN SONGWRITER MAGAZINE
1009 17th Avenue South
Nashville, TN 37212-2201
Phone: 615-321-6096   Fax: 615-321-6097
Toll Free: 800-739-8712
Also on the Internet at *americansonwriter.com*
Has been serving songwriters' needs since 1984. One of the best resources songwriters have for staying in touch with the Industry.

BILLBOARD MAGAZINE
Billboard.com 770 Broadway New York, NY 10003-9595
Phone: 800-449-1402   Fax: 646-654-5584
Also on the Internet at *www.billboard.com*
If the Music Industry is a Wheel, this magazine is the hub! All the news about all the deals, legislative issues, artist tours, who's hot, new releases, album reviews, who's in power at the labels, which albums went gold and platinum, and of course the Billboard Charts, all updated weekly.

CMJ NEW MUSIC MONTHLY
P.O. Box 57414
Boulder, CO 80322-7414
On the Internet at: *http://cmj.com/*
An innovative magazine with a CD in every issue. It's all about the "hot sounds of tomorrow," bands that are on their way up, not typical top-40 "kiddie pop." Filled with current album reviews and commentary.

HITS
14958 Ventura Boulevard
Sherman Oaks, CA 91403
Also on the Internet at *http://www.hitsdailydouble.com/*
A magazine for lovers of all kinds of music. Includes a Breakout hits breakdown; keeps you in tune with what's hot and what's not.

KERRANG!
P. O. Box 2930
EMAP Performance
London W1A 60Z
e-mail: *kerrang@ecm.emap.com*
The best in England's Underground scene.

R&R (Radio and Records)
10100 Santa Monica Boulevard
Los Angeles, CA 90067
Also on the Internet at *www.rronline.com*
This is an established Music Industry magazine filled with topical information, charts, reviews, insider information.

RECORDING
5412 Idylwild Trail, Suite 100
Boulder, CO 80301
Phone: 303-516-9118   Fax: 303-516-9119
e-mail: *info@recordingmag.com*
"The Magazine for the Recording Musician." Filled with useful practical information for anyone seeking a career that involves recording music.

ROLLING STONE
1290 Avenue of the Americas
New York, N.Y. 10104-0298
Phone: 800-283-1549   Fax: 212-767-8214
Also on the Internet at *www.rollingstone.com*
An influential pop culture magazine with general interest articles, record and performance reviews that help to define the state of music, and interviews with performers whose music is of current relevance.

THE SOURCE
215 Park Avenue South, 11th Floor
New York, N.Y. 10003
Phone: 212-253-3700
Also on the Internet at *www.thesource.com*
A Magazine for Songwriters with an interest in Hip Hop and Rap. The Website deals with lifestyle and general news in addition to some music updates.

VIBE MAGAZINE
P.O. Box 59580
Boulder, CO 80322
e-mail at *info@vibe.com*
Also on the Internet at *http://vibe.com*
A magazine for musicians and followers of state-of-the art urban music, including hip hop and rap. Lots of album reviews and interviews of happening artists.

Songwriters' Resources

AACM
Association for the Advancement of Creative Music
P.O. Box 5757
Chicago, IL 60680 USA
Tel: 312-752-2212   Fax: 312-752-2226
On the Internet at *aacmchicago.org/mast2.html*
An organization providing leadership and vision for the development of Great Creative Black Music.

ALEXANDER UNIVERSITY
Online at *www.alexanderpublishing.com*
Phone: 310-559-3779
An online school which offers "the who, what, when, where and how of composing and producing music."

APPLAUSE MUSIC PRODUCTION AND PERFORMANCE CAREERS
Online at *www.cnvi.com/Applause/*
Applause offers "the tips, tricks, and secrets that will launch your show business career!"

ARTIST DIRECT
On the Internet at *http://artistdirect.com/*
A well-designed website chock-a-block with information about thousands of artists, music info, message boards and chat rooms, all with musicians, artists, songwriters and their fans in mind.

THE COMPLETE JINGLE COURSE
On the Internet at *www.jinglebiz.com*
Or Contact: RSM Direct
4542 E. Tropicana #211
Las Vegas, NV 89121
Tel: (702) 898-7070   Fax: (702) 395-6783
e-mail: *jingleman@lvcm.com*
LaDair Guzman instructs by showing musicians there are a lot more ways to make money than just playing in clubs; there are more venues for songwriters' talents than just writing for pop radio. Runs occasional hands-on clinics.

COUNTRY MUSIC ASSOCIATION, INC.
One Music Circle South
Nashville, Tennessee 37203
U.S.A.
Tel: (615) 244 2840
On the Internet at *www.CMAworld.com*
An organization dedicated to bringing the poetry and emotion of Country music
to the world, has trade publications, information, awards events.

DOGPILE, A SEARCH ENGINE
On the Internet at *www.dogpile.com*
Type in "songwriting" "country music association" "music business," etc.
This search engine will search a number of other search engines to bring you an
exceptionally thorough list of potential resources.

FEMMUSIC.COM
On the Internet at *www.femmusic.com*
Address: Attn: Alex Teitz
1470 S. Quebec Way # 175
Denver, CO 80231
303-521-3430
alex@femmusic.com
FEMMUSIC is a specialty international online monthly magazine devoted to
emerging Women In Music. Focuses on multiple genres, has interviews, CD and
show reviews, show previews, and resources to help the beginning artist.

FLYIN' SHOES
On the Internet at *www.flyinshoes.fsnet.co.uk/flyinshoes*
The Literary Songwriting Fine Arts Journal. Quarterly review (on the web only)
of all that's best in the field of literary songwriting. Edited by poet/artist/songster
Shaun Belcher in Oxford, England. Considers esoteric submissions from undis-
covered songwriters.

GOSPEL MUSIC ASSOCIATION
1205 Division Street
Nashville, TN 37203
Phone: (615) 242-0303
Online at *gospelmusic.org*
Offers educational seminars, creates a community for writers of Gospel and
Christian music, publishes newsletters.

(THE DICK) GROVE SCHOOL WITHOUT WALLS
Grove/Rasch Music
810 W. Peak Vista Place
Oro Valley, AZ 85737
1-800-994-7683   Fax 541-552-9610

On the Internet at *www.dickgrove.com*
An accredited, affordable on-line school offering programs in Guitar Technique and Improvisation, Musicianship, (Modern Harmony & Eartraining), Jazz Keyboard, Composing, Arranging, and Orchestration. Based on Dick Grove's lifetime method of teaching the musical arts.

GUIDE TO GRAMMAR AND WRITING
On the Internet at *webster.commnet.edu/HP/pages/darling/original.htm*
This is a fabulous site, a way to find out everything you need to learn about correct grammar, parts of speech, sentence structure, it's all here on line, broken down into easy and useful categories.

HARMONY CENTRAL
On the Internet at *www.harmony-central.com*
A plethora of current info about music, musicians, instruments, software programs, etc.

ITC'S ON-LINE MAGAZINE
On the Internet at *www.inthecrib.com*
A full service online magazine covering all aspects of the Music Industry. Watch this website evolve!

KARAOKEWOW.COM
Online at *www.karaokewow.com*
Or call (800) 293-sing
Where to go to purchase backing tracks of famous songs, karaoke music.

KEYBOARD MAGAZINE
On the Internet at *www.keyboardmag.com*
Vital Information on keyboards, concerts, seminars, etc.

THE MUSE'S MUSE
On the Internet at *www.musesmuse.com*
This site offers contacts, a magazine, writer connections, etc.

MUSIC BUSINESS REGISTRY
7510 Sunset Boulevard, #1041
Los Angeles, California 90046-3500 U.S.A.
Phone 800-377-7411   Fax 800-228-9411
On the Internet at *www.musicregistry.com*
Four Music business directories are published annually. The A&R Registry is published 6 times annually, Music Publisher Registry, Music Business Attorney, Legal & Business Affairs Registry, and Film & Television Music Guide are all twice annually. They are also available on Disks. If you want to know who does what in the music business, and how to contact them, these are excellent, if expensive, resources.

MUSICIAN'S INSTITUTE
1655 McCadden Place
Hollywood, CA 90028
(800)235-PLAY or (323) 462-1384 outside U.S.A.
A wonderful institution which offers a full hands-on curriculum for musicians and songwriters. A best bet for getting the grounding to be a professional in the music business.

NATIONAL ACADEMY OF RECORDING ARTS AND SCIENCES
4444 Riverside Drive, Suite 202
Burbank, CA 91505
On the Internet at *www.grammy.com*
Dedicated to improving the quality of life for music and its makers. An organization of more than 13,000 songwriters, musicians, producers and other recording professionals, has outreach, professional development, cultural enrichment, and education programs. Offers Member discount on records, tapes, publications. Professional members vote on the Grammy Awards.

NME.COM (NEW MUSICAL EXPRESS)
Kingsreach Tower, Stamford Street
London, England
e-mail: *mailsupport@nme.com*
The U.K.'s number 1 music site, *nme.com* has news on all the latest gigs and stories about the music world. The main sections of the site cover news, reviews, release dates, charts and chat. There's also an 'angst' section, where you can say what's on your mind.

PAMOLAND.COM
On the Internet at *www.pamoland.com/*
My personal website isn't just about me, it's about you also. I am providing you with a way of communicating with other songwriters, locating possible collaborators, and discussing the art of lyric writing with those who care to become excellent at it.

PERFORMING SONGWRITER.COM
On the Internet at *www.performingsongwriter.com*
"The Art of Songwriting and the Business of Making Music." Information about festivals, conferences, song competitions, schools, workshops and referrals to many songwriter organizations.

PROJECT ONE AUDIO-VIDEO
6613 Sunset Boulevard
Hollywood, California 90028
(323)464-2285
Many professional songwriters buy their discounted supplies such as cds, dats, cassette tapes and labels here. They also have a wide range of other music equipment such as cd burners, etc.

DANA RASCH'S BEYOND CHOPS GUITAR SCHOOL
Grove/Rasch Music
810 W. Peak Vista Place
Oro Valley, AZ 85737
1-800-994-7683   Fax 541-552-9610
Online at *www.beyondchops.com*
e-mail: *dana@beyondchops.com*
Offers "A revolutionary new approach to mastering the guitar." Locals can avail themselves of some live instruction.

READER'S DIGEST WORD POWER GAMES
On the Internet at *www.readersdigest.com*
Click on "word power" to play stimulating word comprehension games designed to increase and improve your vocabulary.

SONG LINK INTERNATIONAL
On the Internet at *http://songlink.com/*
23 Belsize Crescent
London NW3 5QY
United Kingdom
Tel: +44 (0)207 794 2540   Fax: +44 (0)207 794 7393
e-mail: *david@songlink.com*
This is a subscription service to a Song Plugger Magazine, which provides leads of inside information on who's recording, and what sort of songs they're looking for. This is a fee—not free—service, and now is available by e-mail subscription.

SONGWRITER'S GUILD OF AMERICA
6430 Sunset Boulevard, Suite 317
Hollywood, CA 90028
(213) 462-1108
This venerable songwriter organization recently merged with National Academy of Songwriters/Los Angeles Songwriters' Showcase. Offers songwriter protection, education, publications, general writer assistance.

SONGWRITERS' RESOURCE NETWORK
On the Internet at *www.songpro.com*
Provides many useful resources to help smooth a songwriter's path; lots of links to publications and organizations for songwriters.

TONOS.COM
On the Internet at *www.tonos.com*
A wonderful new website whose purpose is to not only seek out and develop undiscovered talent through innovative online Challenges contests, but also to inspire, enlighten and educate musicians and artists around the world.

UCLA EXTENSION
Department of Performing and Integrated Arts
10995 Le Conte Avenue
Los Angeles, CA 90024
(213) 825-9064
UCLA Extension pioneered professional training for the music industry in 1977 with the country's first certified program in the music business. Offers certified programs in songwriting, recording engineering, and film scoring; all such courses conducted exclusively by top professionals.

WHO DAT MUSIC PRODUCTIONS
On the Internet at *www.whodat.com*
Streaming Media Solutions for the Internet. Cool links to music related download sites such as "Shockwave" and free "Real Player."

United States Performing Rights Societies

ASCAP
American Society of Composers, Authors and Publishers
In New York:
1, Lincoln Plaza
New York, New York 10023
Phone: 800-952-7227

In Los Angeles:
7920 Sunset Boulevard
Los Angeles, CA 90046
Phone: 323-883-1000

Online at *www.ascap.com*
A performing rights society wholly owned and run by writers and publishers, vigilantly fighting songwriters' battles, has the largest repertory to collect income from, has been around since 1909.

BMI
Broadcast Music, Inc.

New York:
320 West 57th Street
New York, NY 10019-3790
(212) 586-2000

Los Angeles:
8730 Sunset Boulevard, 3rd Floor West
Los Angeles, CA 90069
Phone: 310-659-9109
Online at *www.bmi.com*
A performing rights society operated by broadcasters of music, represents a diverse group of writers, was first to represent styles outside mainstream pop, has been operating since 1940.

SESAC

New York:
421 West 54th Street
New York, N.Y. 10019
Phone: 212-957-7945   Fax 212-489-5699

Los Angeles:
501 Santa Monica Boulevard
Suite 450
Santa Monica, CA 90401-2430
Phone: 310-393-9671   Fax 310-393-6497

Online at *www.sesac.com*
A privately held performing rights society, has been in business since 1930.
Represents smaller repertory, is big on technology, utilizes the state-of-the-art
BDS and MusiCode systems for performance detection.

PERMISSIONS

"After the Dance is Through"
Lyrics by Pamela Phillips Oland, William Zimmerman, and Wilmer Raglan, Jr.
© 1985 Chappell & Co., Unichappell Music, Inc., Mr. Dapper Music & Richer Music
All rights on behalf of Mr. Dapper Music administered by Unichappell Music, Inc.
All rights on behalf of Richer Music administered by Chappell & Co.
All rights reserved. Used by permission.

"All We Have Is Now"
Lyrics by Pamela Phillips Oland. Music by Anthony Marinelli.
© 1999 Cherry Lane Music
All rights reserved. Used by Permission.

"At Long Last Love"
by Cole Porter. © 1937 Chappell & Co. (renewed)
All rights reserved. Used by permission.

"Child of Two Worlds"
Lyrics by Pamela Phillips Oland. Music by Jeff Silverman.
© 1986 Irving Music, Inc., Pamalybo Music, Palette Music (BMI),
   and Stone Diamond Music Corporation
All rights reserved. Used by permission.

"Cover to Cover"
Lyrics by Pamela Phillips Oland. Music by Joey Gallo and Wardell Potts, Jr.
© 1986 Almo Music Corp., Don't You Know Music, He Gave Me Music (ASCAP),
   Irving Music, Inc., and Pamalybo Music (BMI)
All rights reserved. Used by permission.

"Dancing All Over the World"
Lyrics by Pamela Phillips Oland. Music by Johnny Warman.
© 1989 Irving Music, Inc., War-cops Music (PRS), and Pamalybo Music (BMI)
All rights for War-cops Music for the Western Hemisphere administered by
   Chappell & Co. (ASCAP)
All rights reserved. Used by permission.

All rights on behalf of Mr. Dapper Music administered by Unichappell Music, Inc.
All rights on behalf of Richer Music administered by Chappell & Co.
All rights reserved. Used by permission.

"Show Me the Way to Your Heart"
Lyrics by Pamela Phillips Oland. Music by Ryo Azuka.
© 1989 Irving Music, Inc., Pamalybo Music (BMI), Fuji Pacific Music Inc.,
   (JAFRA), Johnny Company (JASRAC)
All rights reserved. Used by permission.

"Show Me What You've Got for Me"
Lyrics by Pamela Phillips Oland. Music by Rick Neigher.
© 1986 Songs of Polygram International, Inc., Irving Music, Inc.,
   Pamalybo Music, and Vogue Music (BMI)
International Copyright Secured. All rights reserved. Used by permission.

"Starting Over"
Lyrics by Pamela Phillips Oland. Music by Wayne Tester.
© 2000 Pam-O-Land Music (ASCAP) Wonderland Music (ASCAP)
All rights reserved. Used by permission.

"Starting Tonight"
Lyrics and Music by Pamela Phillips Oland and Paul Chiten.
© 1989 Irving Music, Inc., Pamalybo Music, and Ensign Music Corporation (BMI)
All rights reserved. Used by permission.

"Step Right Up"
Lyrics by Pamela Phillips Oland. Music by Dana Meyers & William Zimmerman.
© 1985 Almo Music Corp., Suit Music, Zimdog Music (ASCAP),
   Irving Music, Inc., and Pamalybo Music (BMI)
All rights reserved. Used by permission.

"Until You"
Lyrics by Pamela Phillips Oland. Music by Joe Curiale.
© 1984 Gold Horizon Music Corp.
c/o Filmtrax Copyright Holdings, Inc.
International Copyright Secured. Made in U.S.A. All rights reserved.

"Wars of the Heart"
Lyrics by Pamela Phillips Oland. Music by Barry Bergman.
© 1989 Irving Music, Inc., Pamalybo Music, and Justrossi Music (BMI)
All rights reserved. Used by permission.

"What Do You Dream About?"
Lyrics and Music by Pamela Phillips Oland.
© 1989 Irving Music, Inc., and Pamalybo Music (BMI)
All rights reserved. Used by permission.

INDEX

BOOKS FROM ALLWORTH PRESS

Moving Up in the Music Business by Jodi Summers (softcover, 6 × 9, 224 pages, $18.95)

The Songwriter's and Musician's Guide to Nashville, Revised Edition by Sherry Bond (softcover, 6 × 9, 256 pages, $18.95)

How to Pitch and Promote Your Songs, Third Edition by Fred Koller (softcover, 6 × 9, 208 pages, $19.95)

Profiting from Your Music and Sound Project Studio by Jeffrey P. Fisher (softcover, 6 × 9, 224 pages, $18.95)

Creative Careers in Music by Josquin des Pres and Mark Landsman (softcover, 6 × 9, 224 pages, $18.95)

Making It in the Music Business: The Business and Legal Guide for Songwriters and Performers, Revised Edition by Lee Wilson (softcover, 6 × 9, 288 pages, $18.95)

Making and Marketing Music: The Musician's Guide to Financing, Distributing, and Promoting Albums by Jodi Summers (softcover, 6 × 9, 240 pages, $18.95)

Booking and Tour Management for the Performing Arts, Revised Edition by Rena Shagan (softcover, 6 × 9, 272 pages, $19.95)

The Copyright Guide: A Friendly Guide to Protecting and Profiting from Copyrights, Revised Edition by Lee Wilson (softcover, 6 × 9, 208 pages, $19.95)

The Trademark Guide: A Friendly Guide to Protecting and Profiting from Trademarks by Lee Wilson (softcover, 6 × 9, 208 pages, $18.95)

Artists Communities: A Directory of Residencies in the United States That Offer Time and Space for Creativity, Second Edition by the Alliance of Artists' Communities (softcover, 6¾ × 10, 256 pages, $18.95)

The Artist's Quest for Inspiration by Peggy Hadden (softcover, 6 × 9, 272 pages, $15.95)

Please write to request our free catalog. To order by credit card, call 1-800-491-2808 or send a check or money order to Allworth Press, 10 East 23rd Street, Suite 510, New York, NY 10010. Include $5 for shipping and handling for the first book ordered and $1 for each additional book. Ten dollars plus $1 for each additional book if ordering from Canada. New York State residents must add sales tax.

To see our complete catalog on the World Wide Web, or to order online, you can find us at *www.allworth.com*.